Computer Accounting
Essentials
with
QuickBooks® 2014

Computer Accounting Essentials
with
QuickBooks® 2014
Versions Pro, Premier & Accountant

Seventh Edition

Carol Yacht, MA
Software Consultant

Susan V. Crosson, MS, CPA
Emory University

Mc
Graw
Hill
Education

Mc
Graw
Hill
Education

COMPUTER ACCOUNTING ESSENTIALS WITH QUICKBOOKS® 2014,
SEVENTH EDITION
Carol Yacht and Susan Crosson

Published by McGraw-Hill Education, 2 Penn Plaza, New York, NY 10121. Copyright © 2015 by McGraw-Hill Education. All rights reserved. Printed in the United States of America. Previous editions © 2013, 2011, and 2009.

1 2 3 4 5 6 7 8 9 0 RMN/RMN 1 0 9 8 7 6 5 4
ISBN   978-0-07-802573-0
MHID   0-07-802573-7

Senior Vice President, Products & Markets: *Kurt L. Strand*
Vice President, Content Production & Technology Services: *Kimberly Meriwether David*
Managing Director: *Tim Vertovec*
Executive Brand Manager: *Steve Schuetz*
Executive Director of Development: *Ann Torbert*
Product Developer: *Jonathan Thornton*
Director of Digital Content: *Patricia Plumb*
Digital Development Editor: *Julie Hankins*
Digital Product Analyst: *Xin Lin*
Senior Marketing Manager: *Michelle Nolte*
Director, Content Production: *Terri Schiesl*
Content Project Manager: *Emily Kline*
Content Project Manager: *Susan Lombardi*
Senior Buyer: *Michael R. McCormick*
Design: *Jana Singer*

www.mhhe.com

About the Authors

Carol Yacht is an accounting educator and textbook author. Carol is the author of McGraw-Hill's QuickBooks, Sage 50 (formerly Peachtree), and Microsoft Dynamics-GP textbooks. She also prepares the QuickBooks and Sage 50 *Student Guides* for use with McGraw-Hill's accounting textbooks (www.mhhe.com/yacht).

Carol taught on the faculties of California State University-Los Angeles, West Los Angeles College, Yavapai College, and Beverly Hills High School. To help students master accounting principles, procedures, and business processes, Carol includes accounting software in her classes.

An early user of accounting software, Carol Yacht started teaching computerized accounting in 1980. Yacht's teaching career includes first and second year accounting courses, accounting information systems, and computer accounting. Since 1989, Yacht's textbooks have been published by McGraw-Hill.

Carol contributes regularly to professional journals and is the Accounting Section Editor for *Business Education Forum*, a publication of the National Business Education Association. She is also the Editor of the American Accounting Association's Teaching, Learning, and Curriculum section's *The Accounting Educator*.

Carol Yacht was an officer of AAA's Two-Year College section and recipient of its Lifetime Achievement Award. She is an emeritus board member of the Microsoft Dynamics Academic Alliance, worked for IBM Corporation as an education instruction specialist, served on the AAA Commons Editorial Board, NBEA's Computer Education Task Force, and works for Intuit and Sage as an education consultant. She is a frequent speaker at state, regional, and national conventions.

Carol earned her MA degree from California State University-Los Angeles, BS degree from the University of New Mexico, and AS degree from Temple University

Susan V. Crosson is a Senior Lecturer at Emory University. Previously she was a Professor and Coordinator of Accounting at Santa Fe College in Gainesville, FL. She has also taught on the faculties of University of Florida, Washington University in St. Louis, University of Oklahoma, Johnson County Community College, and Kansas City Kansas Community College. Susan is known for her innovative application of pedagogical strategies online and in the classroom. She likes to speak and write on the effective use of technology throughout the accounting curriculum. Susan is co-author of several accounting textbooks including the *Computer Accounting Essentials* series.

Susan is the 2012-2014 President of the Teaching Learning and Curriculum Section of the American Accounting Association (AAA) and AAA's Southeast Regional Meeting Co-Program Chair for 2014. Previously she served AAA as Chair of the Conference on Teaching and Learning in Accounting, Chair of the Membership Committee, Council Member, and Chair of the Two-Year Accounting Section. For the American Institute of Certified Public Accountants (AICPA), she has served on the Pre-certification Education Executive Committee. Susan also continues to be involved with AAA and the AICPA-sponsored *Pathways Commission: Charting a National Strategy for the Next Generation of Accountants*.

Susan earned her Master of Science in Accounting from Texas Tech University and her undergraduate degree in accounting and economics from Southern Methodist University. She is a CPA.

Preface

Computer Accounting Essentials with QuickBooks 2014, 7th Edition, teaches you how to use QuickBooks (QB) 2014 software. QuickBooks 2014 is a financial management program created for small businesses.

QuickBooks 2014 is a comprehensive accounting program that includes customer and vendor processing, banking, inventory management, and payroll. You can also share information with Office programs, such as Word, Excel, and Outlook.

Read me: Student software CD included with textbook *and* classroom site licenses.

For Students:

The single user software included with the textbook is accessible for 140 days. Students can work both at school and on their personal computers using external media, such as a **USB drive**, to backup and transport their files between locations.

For Classrooms:

For software installation in the school's computer lab or classroom, please refer to the Intuit Education Program at http://accountants.intuit.com/intuit-education-program or email education@intuit.com.

As of this writing, the cost for QuickBooks 2014 Accountant for Windows classroom site licenses is:

o   10 user license $300.00*
o   25 user license $460.00
o   50 user license $690.00
*Pricing is subject to change.

QuickBooks Accountant 2014 includes access to other QB versions with the toggle feature.

Additional resources are available on the Online Learning Center (OLC) at www.mhhe.com/QBessentials2014. The OLC includes chapter resources, including troubleshooting tips, narrated PowerPoints, online quizzes, and QA templates with multiple-choice and true/false questions.

QUICKBOOKS 2014

Each textbook includes a 140 day copy of QuickBooks Accountant 2014 software.

Computer Accounting Essentials with QuickBooks 2014, 7e, shows how to set up and operate a merchandising business. After completing the textbook, you will have a working familiarity with QuickBooks software.

TEXTBOOK ORGANIZATION BY CHAPTER

1: Software Installation and Creating a New Company

After verifying your computer meets or exceeds the system requirements, install QB 2014. Following the Express Start Interview, you create a new company and then back up. Using the Learning Center Tutorials, videos provide instruction about QuickBooks tasks and workflows.

2: Exploring QuickBooks

There are numerous sample companies included with the software. To learn about QB 2014's user interface, internal controls, and help resources, you explore a sample product company and a sample service company. In addition, you review user roles, customize the privileges of a user, and e-mail a company backup to your professor.

3: New Company Setup for a Merchandising Business

In Chapter 3, you begin operating a retail business called Your Name Retailers Inc. You enter beginning balances for October 1 of the current year, edit the chart of accounts, record and post bank transactions, complete bank reconciliation, and print reports. Detailed steps and numerous screen images help you learn how to use QB 2014.

4: Working with Inventory, Vendors, and Customers

In Chapter 4, to learn basic business processes you complete two months of transactions. You set up vendor preferences, defaults and inventory items, record vendor transactions, make vendor payments, record sales transactions, and collect customer payments. You also complete bank reconciliation, display various reports, and prepare financial statements.

5: Accounting Cycle and Year End

In Chapter 5, you review the accounting cycle and complete end-of-year adjusting entries, print financial statements, and close the fiscal year.

6: First Month of the New Year

In Chapter 6, you begin the new fiscal year, record one month of transactions for your business, make adjusting entries, and print reports.

Project 1: Your Name Hardware Store is a comprehensive project that incorporates what you have learned in Chapters 1-6. In Project 1, you analyze typical source documents used by a merchandising business and complete the accounting cycle.

Project 2: Student-Designed Merchandising Business asks you to create a merchandising business from scratch.

Appendix A: Review of Accounting Principles. Appendix A is a review of basic accounting principles and procedures.

Appendix B: Troubleshooting and QuickBooks Tips. Refer to this window for additional troubleshooting tips.

Appendix C: Glossary. Appendix C is a glossary of terms.

Index: The textbook ends with an index.

Online Learning Center: www.mhhe.com/QBessentials2014. Each chapter includes additional resources online.

Practice Sets: The Online Learning Center at www.mhhe.com/QBessentials2014 includes two additional projects: Practice Set 1, Your Name Accountant; and Practice Set 2, Your Name Sports.

SAVING (BACKING UP) QUICKBOOKS 2014 FILES

QuickBooks can store your data several different ways. In this text, you save or backup work using either QuickBooks backup files (.QBB extensions) or QuickBooks portable company files (.QBM extensions).

Local backup: .QBB

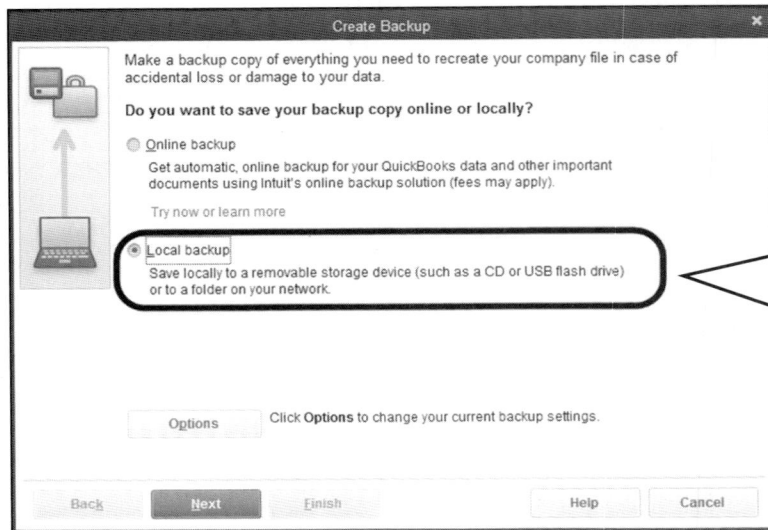

From the menu bar, select File; Backup Company, Create Local backup. Local backups have a .QBB extension.

Portable company file: .QBM

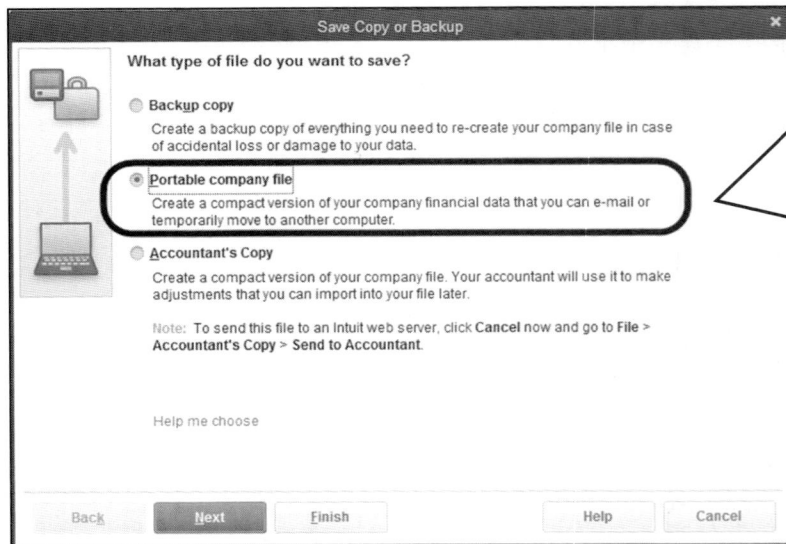

From the menu bar, select File; Create Copy, Portable company file. The backup file extension is .QBM.

(*Hint:* If you select Backup copy, a .QBB extension is created. This is the same file type as the Local backup above.)

CONVENTIONS USED IN TEXTBOOK

As you work through the chapters, read and follow the step-by-step instructions. Numerous screen illustrations help you check work.

1. Information that you type appears in **boldface**; for example, Type **Melody Harmony** in the Customer name field.
2. Keys on the keyboard that are pressed appear like this: <Tab>; <Enter>.
3. Buttons and icons are shown as they appear on QuickBooks' interface; for example, , , etc.
4. Read Me boxes go into more detail about a QB feature. Whenever you see a Read Me box, read this information.
5. Dates are shown with Xs; for example, 10/1/20XX. For the Xs, substitute the current year.
6. Footnotes provide information about the task you are completing.

Refer to the chart on the next page for chapter, backup file names, file sizes and page numbers where files were backed up.

Read Me: Backup Preference

Check with your instructor for the backup file preference.

Backups can be made a couple of ways.

1. Portable Company Files (.QBM extension): From the *menu bar*, select File; Create Copy, Portable company file.
2. Backup Copy (.QBM extension): From the menu bar, *either* File; Back Up Company, Create Local Backup; or File; Create Copy, Backup Copy.

Both backup files types are shown in the text.

The chart on the next page shows the backups made in Chapters 1 through 6 and Project 1. The chart includes the page number where the backup is made and the file size. The authors recommend that you back up to a USB flash drive. Backups can also be made to the desktop, network drive, or hard drive location.

Chapter, Project, PS	Backups (.QBB and .QBM extensions)	File Size*	Page No.
1	Your Name Retailers Inc.QBB	6,548 KB	15-18
	Your Name Hardware Store.QBB	6,488 KB	24
2	sample_product-based business.QBM	2,029 KB	28-31
	Your Name Chapter 2 End.QBM	2,034 KB	60-62
	Your Name sample_service-based business.QBM	1,356 KB	69
3	Your Name Chapter 3 October 1.QBB	6,644 KB	85-86
	Your Name Chapter 3 October Check Register.QBB	6,752 KB	95-96
	Your Name Chapter 3 October End.QBB	6,864 KB	104-105
4	Your Name Chapter 4 Vendors and Inventory.QBB	7,484 KB	125
	Your Name Chapter 4 Vendors.QBB	7,483 KB	139
	Your Name Chapter 4 November.QBB	7,488 KB	159
	Your Name Chapter 4 End.QBB	7,496 KB	167
	Your Name Exercise 4-2 December.QBB	7,508 KB	174
5	Your Name Chapter 5 December UTB.QBB	7,528 KB	183
	Your Name Chapter 5 December Financial Statements.QBB	7,524 KB	191
	Your Name Chapter 5 EOY (Portable).QBM	680 KB	196
6	Your Name Chapter 6 January Check Register.QBB	7,568 KB	210
	Your Name Chapter 6 UTB.QBB	7,632 KB	214
	Your Name Chapter 6 January Financial Statements.QBB	7,664 KB	217
	Your Name Exercise 6-1 (Portable).QBM	779 KB	221
Project 1	Your Name Hardware Store Chart of Accounts (Portable).QBM	373 KB	227
	Your Name Hardware Store Beginning Balances (Portable).QBM	373 KB	228
	Your Name Hardware Store Vendors Inventory Customers (Portable).QBM	382 KB	233
	Your Name Hardware Store January (Portable).QBM	437 KB	244
	Your Name Hardware Store Complete (Portable).QBM	490 KB	246
Practice Set 1**	Your Name Accounting	OLC**	OLC
Practice Set 2	Your Name Sports	OLC	OLC

*File sizes may differ.

**There are two practice sets on the Online Learning Center at www.mhhe.com/QBessentials2014. They include additional practice with a service business, Your Name Accounting, and a merchandising business, Your Name Sports. Both practice sets include reminders to back up portable company files.

Table of Contents

Online Learning Center: www.mhhe.com/QBessentials2014

Comment:
The Timetable for Completion is meant as a guideline for hands-on work. Work can be completed in class or as an outside-of-class project. Work not completed in class is homework. In most Accounting classes, students can expect to spend approximately two hours outside of class for every hour in class.

TIMETABLE FOR COMPLETION		Hours
Chapter 1	Software Installation and Creating a New Company	1.0
Chapter 2	Exploring QuickBooks	2.0
Chapter 3	New Company Setup for a Merchandising Business	2.0
Chapter 4	Working With Inventory, Vendors, and Customers	4.0
Chapter 5	Accounting Cycle and Year End	2.0
Chapter 6	First Month of the New Year	1.0
Project 1*	Your Name Hardware Store	3.0
Project 2	Student-Designed Merchandising Business	2.0
Practice Set 1	Service Business (Online Learning Center)	4.0
Practice Set 2	Merchandising Business (OLC)	4.0
TOTAL HOURS:		**25.0**

*In Project 1, typical source documents are used for transaction analysis, including accounts payable, inventory, accounts receivable, cash, and bank reconciliation. The accounting cycle is completed for one month. An audit trail report is also completed.

Chapter 1

Software Installation and Creating a New Company

OBJECTIVES

1. System Requirements.
2. Download QuickBooks 2014.
3. Install Software from CD.
4. Starting QuickBooks.
5. Creating a New Company.
6. Registering QuickBooks.
7. Backing up Company Data.
8. QuickBooks Learning Center.

IMPORTANT MESSAGE: QuickBooks 2014 Student Trial Edition

QuickBooks 2014 Student Trial Edition will operate for 140 days **after** registering the software on a single computer. After installation, you have <u>30 days</u> to register. **If you fail to register, after 30 days your software will stop working.** Registering QuickBooks is shown on pages 12-15.

The Student Trial Edition has limited use and cannot be networked in computer labs. Schools must purchase and install QuickBooks 2014 licenses for their classrooms or computer labs. (Refer to the Preface, page vii, For Students and For Classrooms sections.)

SYSTEM REQUIREMENTS

The following systems requirements are online at http://accountants.intuit.com/accounting/quickbooks/accountant/. Select

Tech Specs

.

- Windows 8 (including 64-bit), 7 (including 64-bit), Vista (SP1 including 64-bit
- 2.0 GHz processor, 2.4 GHz recommended
- 1GB of RAM for a single user, 2 GB of RAM recommended for multiple users

---

- 2.5 GB available disk space (additional space required for data files)
- 60 MB disk space for Microsoft .NET 4.0 Runtime (provided on the QuickBooks CD)
- Minimum 1024x768 screen resolution. 16-bit or higher color
- 4x CD-ROM
- Product registration required
- 2GB or higher USB drive for backups.

Integration with Other Software

- Microsoft Word and Excel integration requires 2003, 2007, or 2010 (including 64-bit)
- Synchronization with Outlook requires QuickBooks Contact Sync for Outlook 2003, 2007, and 2010 (including 64-bit; downloadable for free at: www.quickbooks.com/contact_sync)
- Email estimates, invoices and other forms with Gmail, Yahoo! Mail, windows Mail
- Compatible with QuickBooks Point of Sale version 10 and later

DOWNLOAD QUICKBOOKS 2014

Go online to http://support.quickbooks.intuit.com/support/ProductUpdates.aspx to download QuickBooks Accountant 2014.

1. To read installation steps, link to Visit the Install Center .

2. If Your product is **QuickBooks Accountant 2014** is shown, select
   Download . (If 2014 is not shown, select Choose a different product. Refer to a. and b. on page 3)

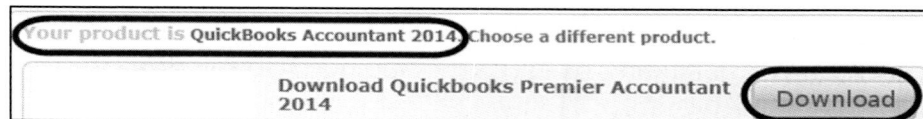

Your product is **QuickBooks Accountant 2014** Choose a different product.

Download Quickbooks Premier Accountant 2014   Download

If a screen prompt appears asking "Do you want to run or save Setup_QuickBooksPremier 2014.exe (525 KB) from http-download.intuit.com?," click Run. When the User Account Control window appears, click <Yes>. The Download Manager begins showing the progress of your download.

OR, on the Download window, select Choose a different product.

a.   In the Select your product list, select QuickBooks Premier.

b.   In the Select your version list, select Accountant 2014.

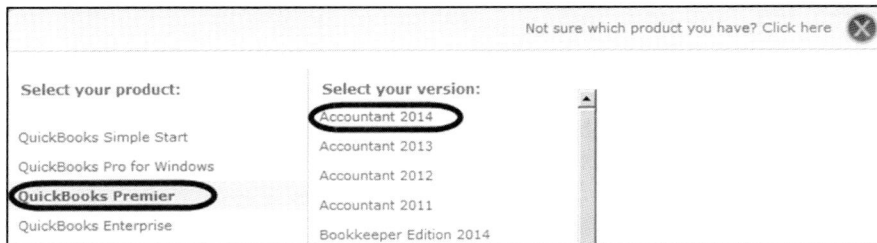

	Not sure which product you have? Click here ⊗
Select your product:	**Select your version:**
	(Accountant 2014)
QuickBooks Simple Start	Accountant 2013
QuickBooks Pro for Windows	Accountant 2012
(QuickBooks Premier)	Accountant 2011
QuickBooks Enterprise	Bookkeeper Edition 2014

3.   When the Welcome to the InstallShield Wizard for QuickBooks Financial Software 2014 window appears, follow the screen prompts to complete the download. For detailed steps with screen images, refer to Steps 4 through 12, pages 4-6.

IMPORTANT: Use the License and Product Numbers included with *Computer Accounting Essentials with QuickBooks 2014, 7e.* (Refer to the CD label on the inside front cover.) The License and Product numbers can be used one time.

INSTALL SOFTWARE FROM CD

This section gives you instructions for installing QuickBooks 2014 software on a single computer. (Instructions for uninstalling QuickBooks are included in Appendix B, page 269.)

If your computer does <u>not</u> have CD or DVD drive, refer to Download QuickBooks 2014, pages 2-3.

Step 1:   Turn on your computer. Close all programs and sign off the Internet. *QuickBooks works best if you are not connected to the Internet.* Microsoft Outlook should *not* be open. If Microsoft Outlook or any Virus protection programs are open, close them, along with other programs that may be open.

Step 2:   Insert the QuickBooks 2014 Student Trial Edition Limited Use Only CD into the CD drive.

Step 3:   Click Run setup.exe. When the User Account Control window appears, click <Yes>. (If Setup does *not* start, open Windows Explorer and double-click the QuickBooks icon.) Be patient, it will take a few minutes for the installer to start.

Step 4:   The Welcome to QuickBooks! window appears. Click `Next >`.

Step 5:   The License Agreement window appears. After reading the terms of the License Agreement, read or print it for your files. Select I accept the terms in the license agreement. Click `Next >`.

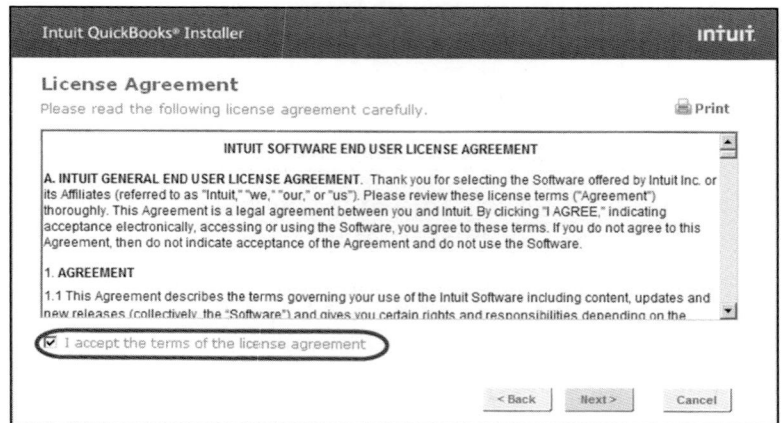

Step 6:   For Installation type, select Express (recommended). Click `Next >`.

Step 7:   When the License Number and Product Number window appears, enter your license number and product number. These can be found on the Intuit label attached to the CD envelope which is included with the text. (Keep your installation

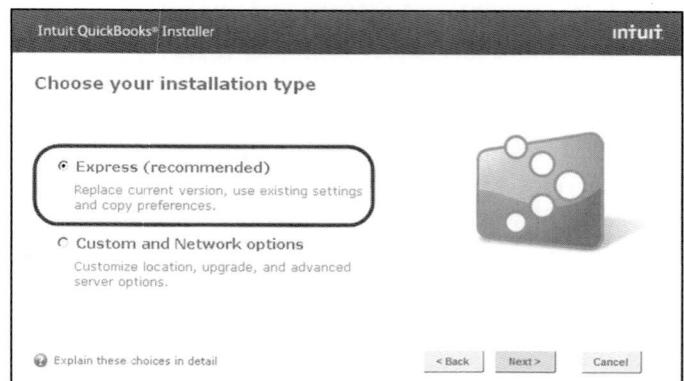

numbers in a safe place. You will need them if you reinstall your QuickBooks software.)

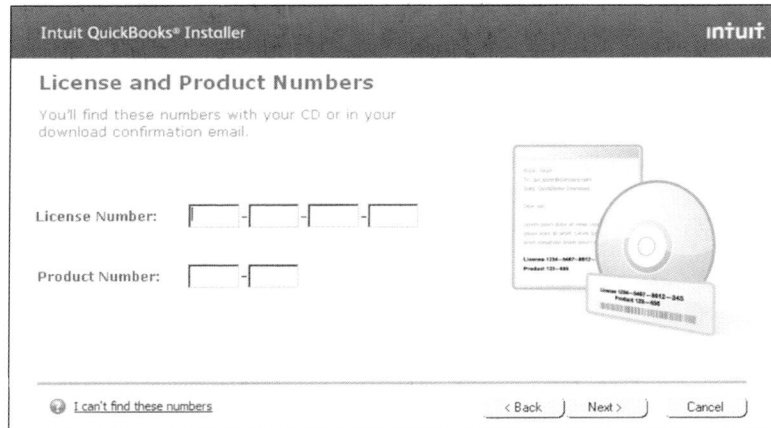

Step 8:   Proofread your License and Product numbers, then click Next >.

Step 9:   The Ready to install window appears. Review the information on this window. Click Install .

Step 10:   If a While QuickBooks is installing, let's take care of your registration window appears, click Skip this. After installation, steps for Registering QuickBooks are on pages 12-15. The Installing QuickBooks 2014 scale shows the progress of installation. This process may take some time. Read the information while QuickBooks installs. Note: If any Firewall or Security pop-up windows occur during setup, select Always Allow.

Step 11:   The Congratulations! window appears. Select Open QuickBooks.

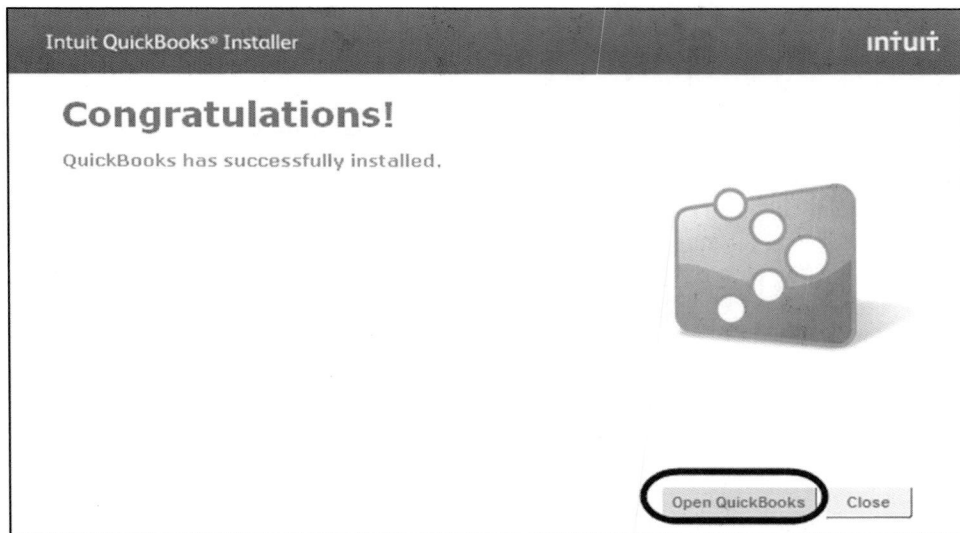

Step 12:　The Let's get your business set up quickly! window appears.
Click Express Start.

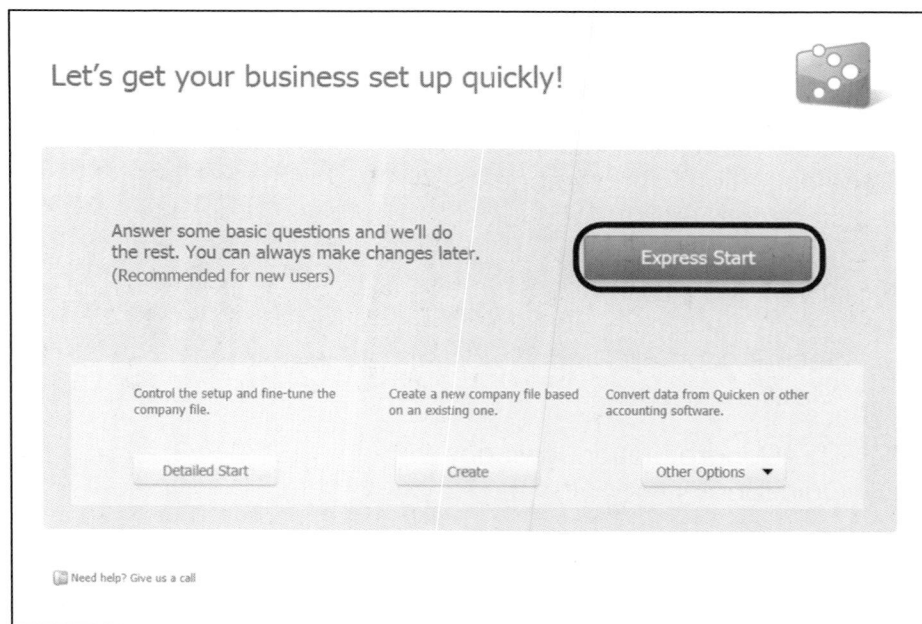

(*Hint:* If QuickBooks is open, you can go to the Express Start
window from the menu bar by selecting File; New Company.)

Step 13:　Remove the QuickBooks 2014 CD.

CREATING A NEW COMPANY

Follow these steps to create a new company in QuickBooks 2014.

1. When you selected [Express Start], the Tell us about your business window displayed.

2. Complete the Company Name field, **Your Name Retailers Inc. (use your first and last name)**, for example, Carol Yacht Retailers Inc.

Tell us about your business
Enter the essentials so we can create a company file that's just right for your business.

* Company Name   Your Name Retailers Inc.
We'll use this on your invoices and reports, and to name your company file.

3. For Industry, link to Help me choose. The Select Your Industry window appears. Scroll down the list and highlight Retail Shop or Online Commerce. Click <OK>.

Select Your Industry

Search for the industry that matches your company.

[Enter your industry]

Or select an industry and view accounts we recommend for it.
(You can add or delete accounts later.)

Industry	Accounts
Manufacturer Representative or Agent	Income Accounts
Manufacturing	Merchandise Sales
Medical, Dental, or Health Service	Sales Discounts
Non-Profit	Cost of Goods Sold Accounts
Professional Consulting	Merchant Account Fees
Property Management or Home Association	Expense Accounts
Real Estate Brokerage or Developer	Advertising and Promotion
Rental	Automobile Expense
Repair and Maintenance	Bank Service Charges
Restaurant, Caterer, or Bar	Computer and Internet Expenses
Retail Shop or Online Commerce	Depreciation Expense
Sales: Independent Agent	Insurance Expense
Transportation, Trucking, or Delivery	Interest Expense
Wholesale Distribution and Sales	Janitorial Expense

Can't find your industry? Select General Product or General Service instead.

OK   Cancel

4. For Company Type, click on down arrow, then select Corporation.

5. Leave Tax ID # Blank. For Employees, select No, but I might in the future.

6. Compare your entries to the window shown here, when satisfied, select Continue. (*Hint:* The Company Name field shows your first and last name should be used.)

7.   The Enter your business contact information window appears. Complete it using your contact information.

Legal name: **Your Name Retailers Inc.** (Use your first and last name.)
Street: **Your address**
City: **Reno**
State: **Nevada**
Zip: **89557**
Country: U.S.
Phone: **Your phone number** (Asterisk indicates required field.)
E-Mail: **Your e-mail**
Web site: leave blank

Enter your business contact information
Once you enter your contact information, you're ready to create your company file.

❶ ──── ❷ ──── ❸ ──→
Tell   Contact   Add
us   info   info

Legal Name	Your Name Retailers Inc.
Address	
City	Reno
State	NV
* ZIP	89557
Country	U.S.
* Phone	555-555-5555
Email	
Website	

Enter basic contact information so you can instantly print and email invoices and other forms.

We value your privacy and security. This information is stored safely on Intuit servers.

* Required

Back   Preview Your Settings   Create Company File

Your address, phone (required), and email should be completed.

When satisfied, click Create Company File .

8.   Wait while QuickBooks creates the new company file.

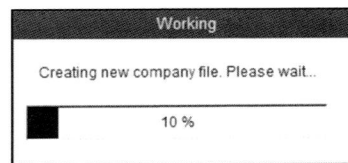

Working

Creating new company file. Please wait...

10 %

9. When the You've got a company file! Now add your info. window appears, select Add your bank accounts by clicking on [Add].

10. On the Add your bank accounts window, type **Home State Bank** for the account name. Then click [Continue].

11. Select No Thanks to ordering checks from Intuit. Click [Continue].

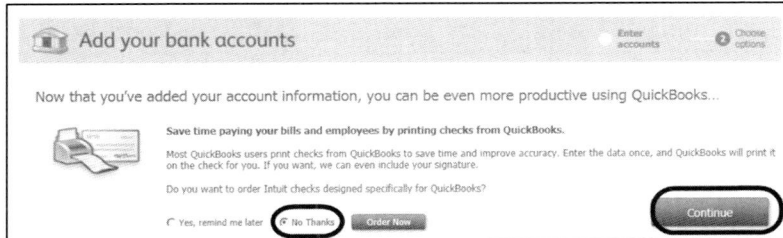

12. The You've got a company file! Now add your info. window reappears. Since you will add the people you do business with and the products and services you sell later, select [Start Working].

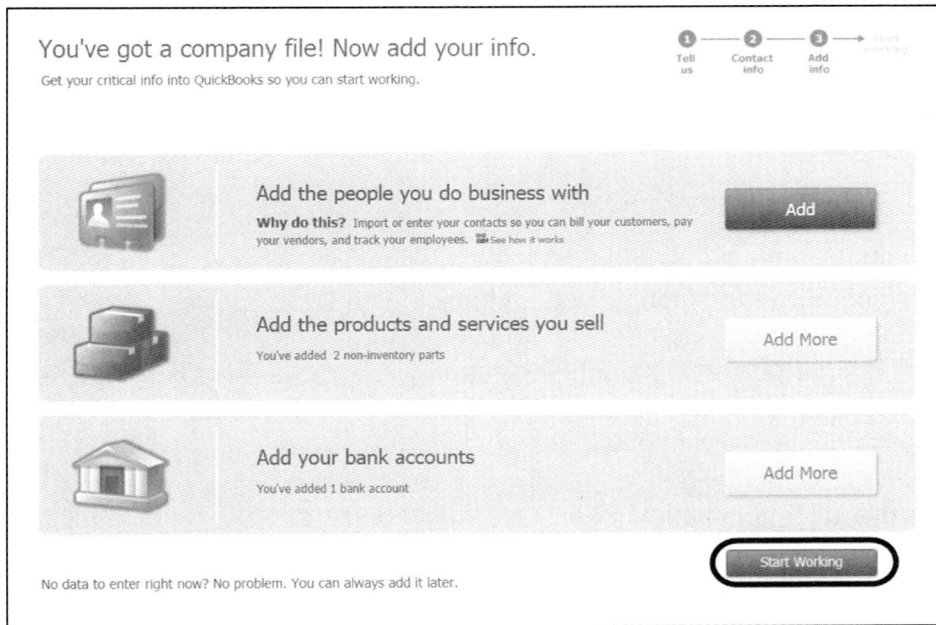

13. If the Accountant Center window window appears, close it by clicking <X> on its title bar. When the Close Accountant Center window appear, click <OK>. Close the Quick Start Center window too.

14. The Your Name Retailers Inc. desktop appears which includes the *Icon Bar* on the left side of the screen and the Home page in the middle. If any other pop-up windows appear, return to your desktop.

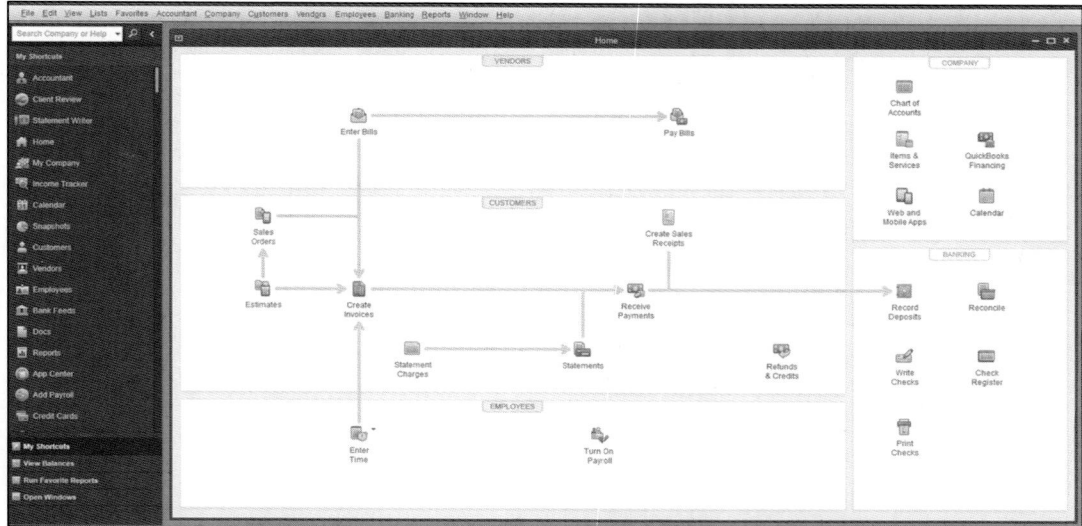

REGISTERING QUICKBOOKS

To use QuickBooks more than 30 days, you must register with Intuit. Follow these steps to register your account with QuickBooks.

1. From the Help menu, select Register QuickBooks. The Register QuickBooks Now window appears saying "You have 30 days remaining."

   Comment: If you have already exited and started QB, your days remaining will be less than 30 days.

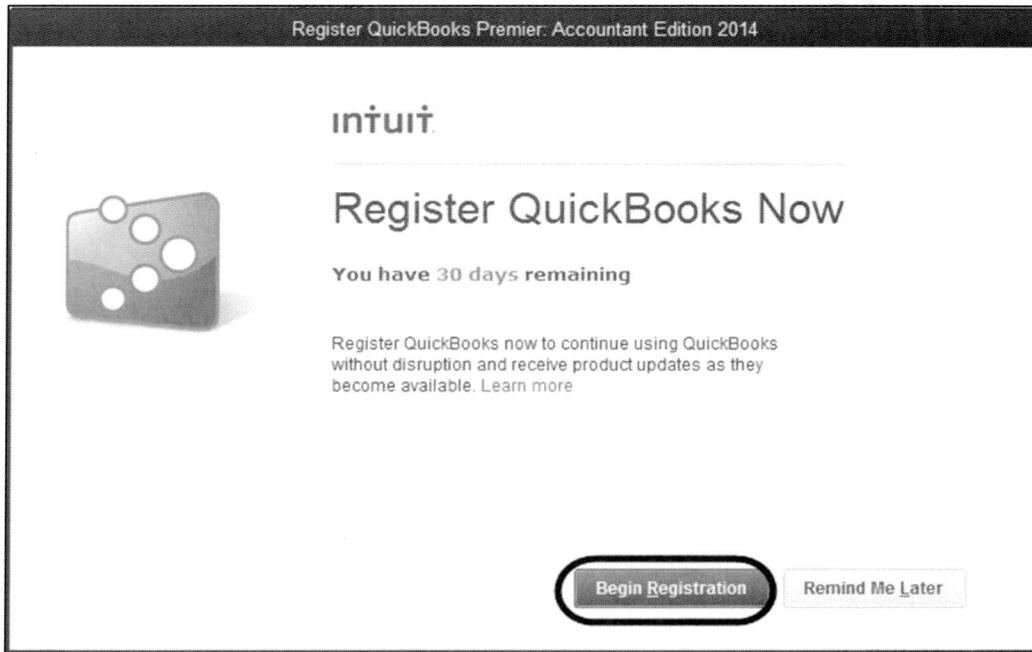

Register QuickBooks Premier: Accountant Edition 2014

ıntuıt

Register QuickBooks Now

You have 30 days **remaining**

Register QuickBooks now to continue using QuickBooks without disruption and receive product updates as they become available. Learn more

[Begin Registration]   [Remind Me Later]

2. Select Begin Registration. If you are asked to obtain a Validation code, call the phone number shown.

    If you are asked to create an Intuit account, do that by providing an email address and password.

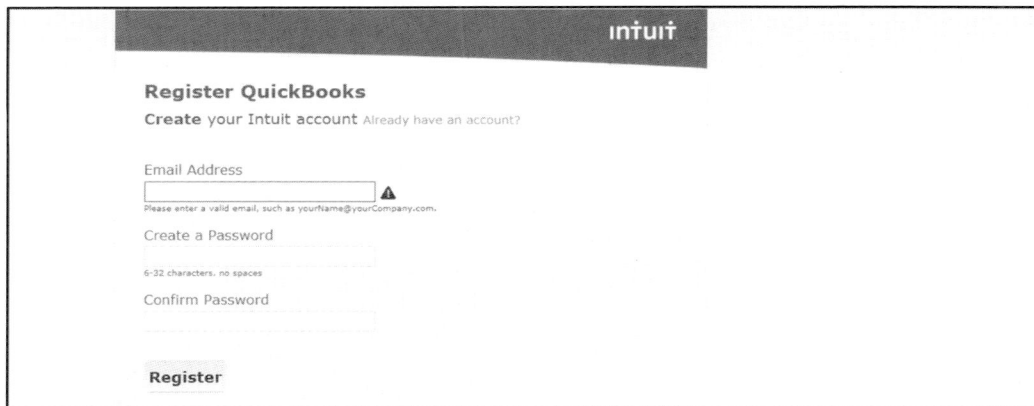

ıntuıt

Register QuickBooks

Create your Intuit account Already have an account?

Email Address

[   ] ⚠

Please enter a valid email, such as yourName@yourCompany.com.

Create a Password

6-32 characters. no spaces

Confirm Password

Register

3. If necessary, from the Icon Bar, select [🏠 Home]. The Home page appears.

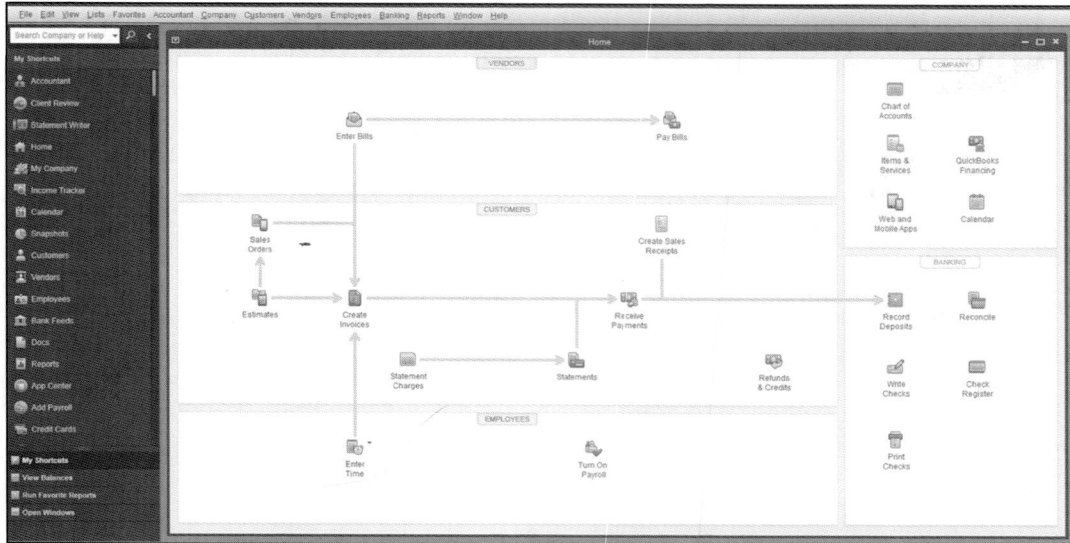

Failure to complete registration within 30 days will result in being locked out of the program with no recourse.

Software Registration

If Register QuickBooks is available on the Help menu, you have not registered your copy of QuickBooks. You can verify that your copy of QuickBooks is registered by pressing the [F2] function key when QuickBooks is open. The Product Information window appears and displays either REGISTERED or UNREGISTERED based on the registration status.

You can register QB by calling 800-316-1068 or 888-246-8848; or outside US, 520-901-3220. Once the software included with the textbook is registered, you have access for 140 days.

---

4. To view your completed registration information, press the [F2] function key. **You have 140 days of use. After that time, the software is not accessible**.

The Product Information window shows REGISTERED. Your Release number may differ. Your license and product numbers are shown and the date QB was installed.

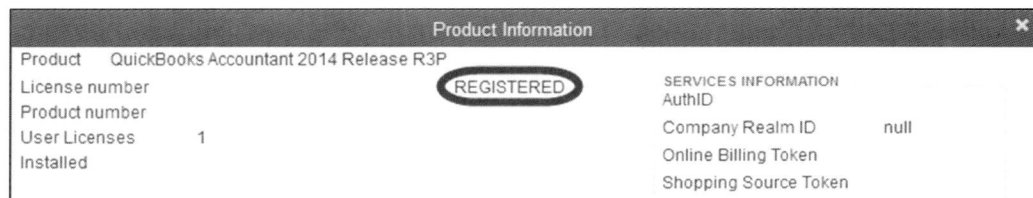

Product Information		
Product QuickBooks Accountant 2014 Release R3P		
License number	REGISTERED	SERVICES INFORMATION AuthID
Product number		
User Licenses 1		Company Realm ID null
Installed		Online Billing Token
		Shopping Source Token

5. To close the Product Information window, click <OK>.

BACKING UP COMPANY DATA

Frequent saving or *backing up* of company data is a good business practice. In this textbook, you are shown how to backup to the desktop or external media location. Backing up to a drive other than the computer's hard drive or network drive is called backing up to *external media*. (Words that are boldfaced and italicized are defined in Appendix C, Glossary.) Authors suggest you backup to an USB flash drive.

When you back up, you are saving to the current point in QuickBooks. Each time you save or make a backup, the date and time of the backup will distinguish between them. In this way, if you need to *restore* an earlier backup (for example, you make a mistake), you have the data for that purpose. See Preface, page xii, for a list of backups that are made in this text and their file size.

In the business world, backups are unique for each business day. Daily backups are necessary. If you are working in a computer lab, *never leave the computer lab without first backing up your data to external media, for example, your USB flash drive.*

Saving to the Desktop or External Media
As a part of QuickBooks' attention to internal control and risk avoidance, the program will ask if you are certain that you want to back up company data to your desktop since the backup will reside in the same place as the actual data. Saving or backing up to external media such as a USB drive minimizes risk!

Follow these steps to save Your Name Retailers Inc. company data.

1. From the QuickBooks Desktop, click File; Back Up Company, Create Local Backup.

2. The Create Backup window appears. Local backup is selected. Insert a USB flash drive. If an AutoPlay window appears, close it. On the Create Backup window, click [Next >].

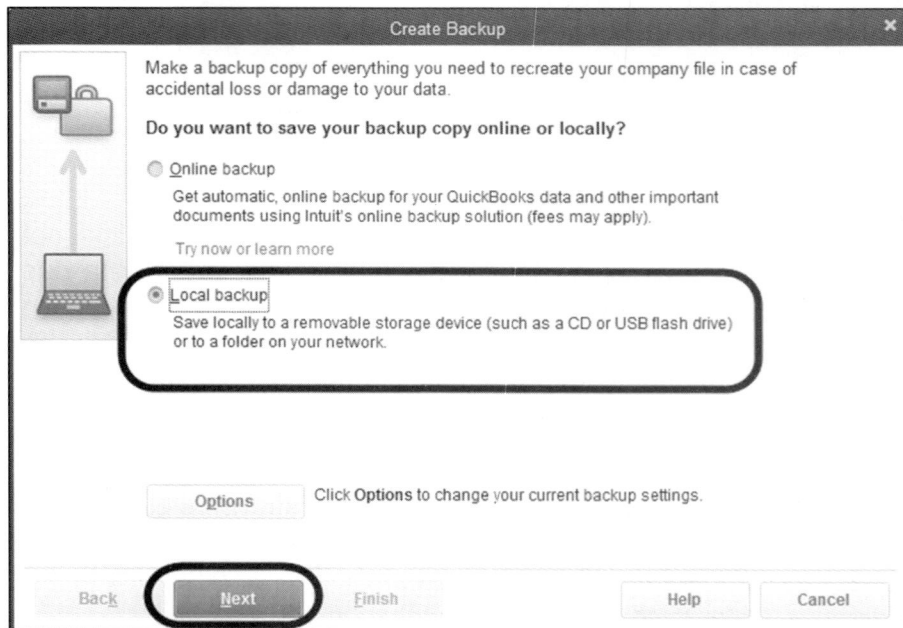

3. The Backup Options window appears. Click [Browse...], then select your USB drive. Click [OK]. In the illustration, drive H:\ is shown. (Your drive letter may differ.) You can backup to a USB drive, other external media, or the desktop.

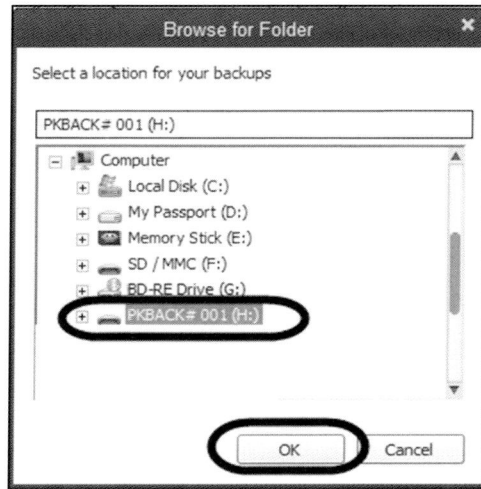

4. Type **1** in the Remind me to back up when I close my company file. Click [OK].

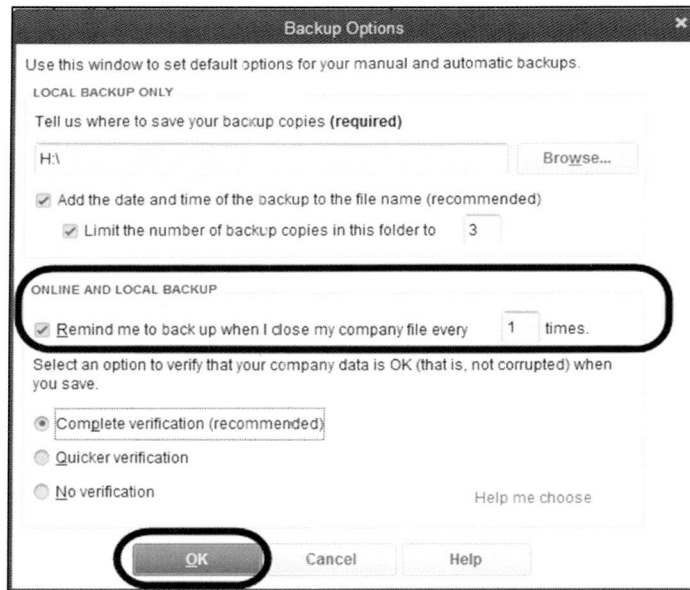

5. The When do you want to save your backup copy? window appears, select Save it now. Click [Finish].

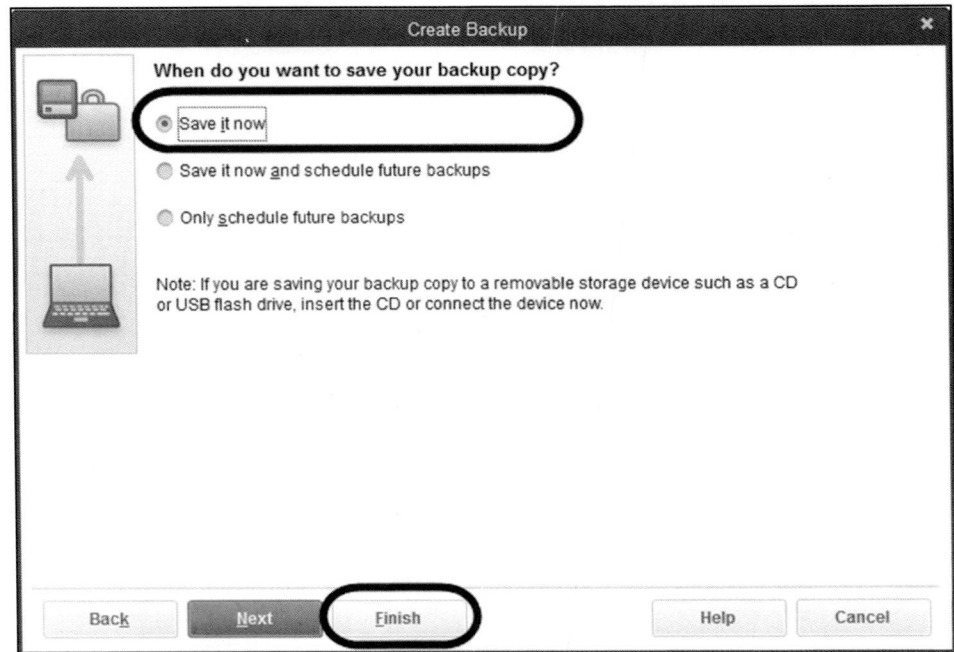

6. The Working window appears while your file is being backed up. When the backup is complete, a window like the one shown below appears to confirm the date, time, and location of the saved company data. Click [OK].

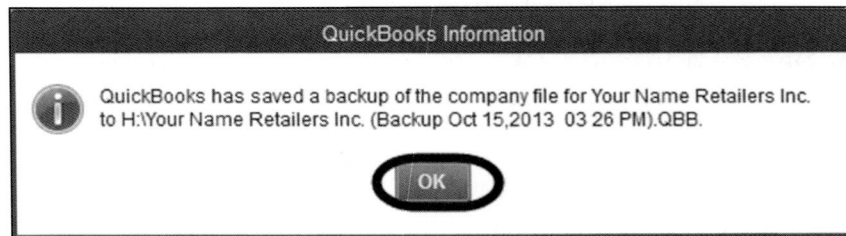

7. You are returned to the QuickBooks desktop.

8. Exit program or continue working on the next section. If you exit QB, an Automatic Backup window may appear. Read it, then click [No].

QUICKBOOKS LEARNING CENTER

QuickBooks includes extensive learning resources, videos, and guides available as you learn the program. Let's take a look at how QuickBooks coaches you.

1. From the menu bar, select Help; Quick Start Center. The Ready to start working window appears. Review the information on this window.

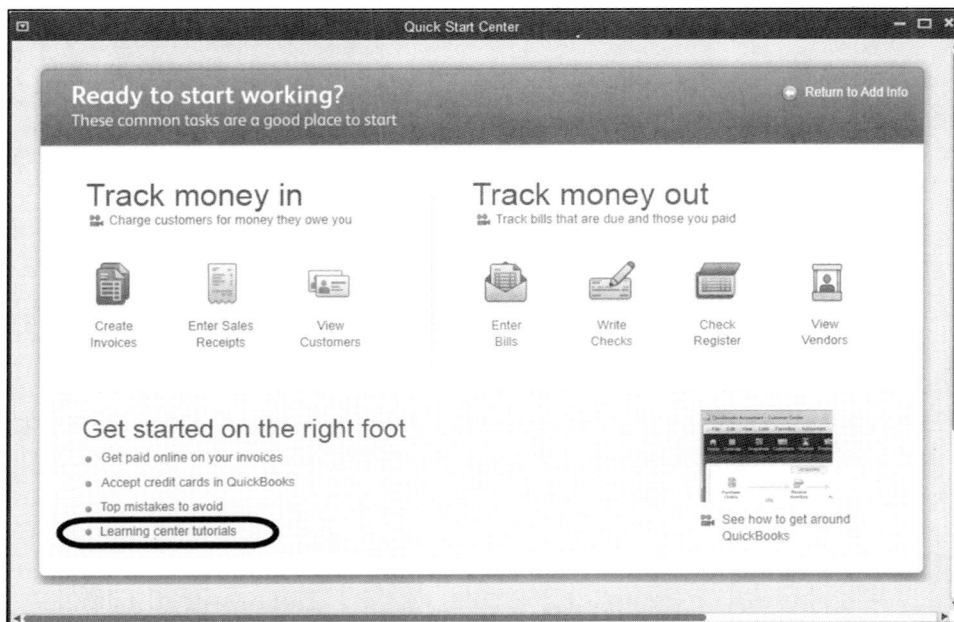

2. To learn more about QB, select the Learning center tutorials.

3. In the Setting up QuickBooks section, select a video to learn how to set up the basics, for example, Setting up QuickBooks.

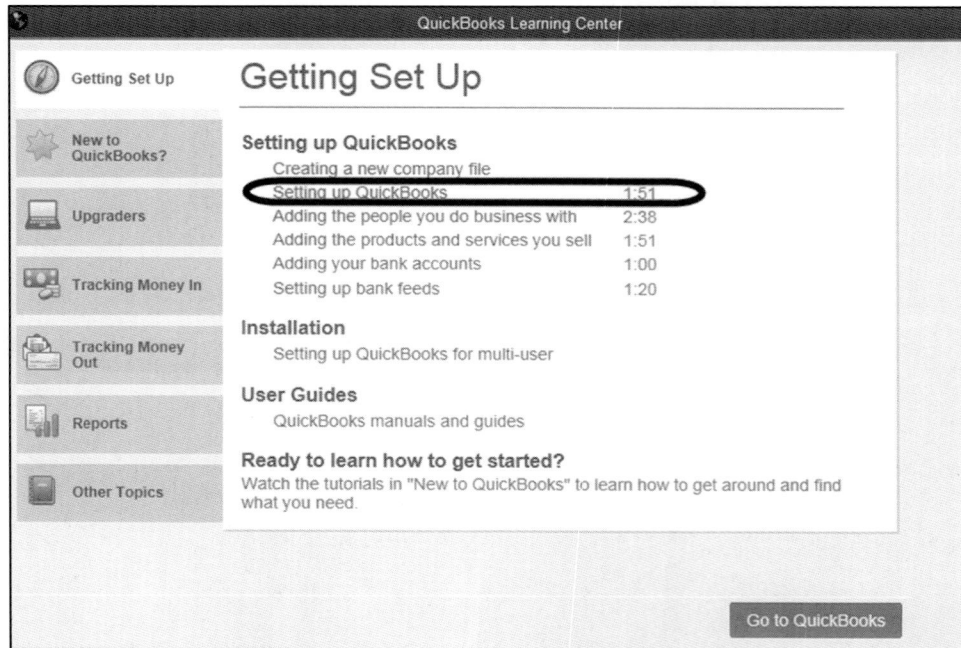

4. Watch the videos. Close windows to return to the Quick Start Center. Explore the Track money in and Tracking money out links. You may also want to link to See how to get around QuickBooks. When you are through, close the Quick Start Center window.

SUMMARY AND REVIEW

OBJECTIVES:

1. System Requirements.
2. Download QuickBooks 2014.
3. Install Software from CD.
4. Starting QuickBooks.
5. Creating a New Company.
6. Registering QuickBooks.
7. Backing up Company Data.
8. QuickBooks Learning Center.

Additional resources are on the textbook website at www.mhhe.com/QBessentials2014. They include chapter resources, online quizzes, narrated PowerPoints, QA Templates, etc.

RESOURCEFUL QUICKBOOKS

Go to the QuickBooks website http://quickbooks.intuit.com/. Explore the website, then answer the following questions.

1. Why will you love QuickBooks?

2. List the devices that work with QuickBooks.

3. Why is QuickBooks what you need to run your business?

4. Click on the Support tab and then select Intuit New User Resource Center (within Intuit QuickBooks Support) and list two of the Top Mistakes to Avoid. (*Hint:* Link to Top Mistakes to Avoid.)

5. From the New User Resource Center, select Tips for a Smooth Start. List the first five tips for getting off to a smooth start with QuickBooks.

Multiple Choice Questions: The Online Learning Center includes the multiple-choice questions at www.mhhe.com/QBessentials2014, select Student Edition, Chapter 1, Multiple Choice.

_____1. QuickBooks Student Trial Edition will operate for how many days after registration?

    a. 30 days.
    b. 60 days.
    c. 120 days.
    d. 140 days.

_____2. Once QuickBooks Student Trial Edition is installed, which of the following icons appear on the desktop:

    a. Support for QuickBooks.
    b. QuickBooks Library.
    c. QuickBooks 2014.
    d. Payroll for QuickBooks.

_____3. The Welcome to QuickBooks window allows users to:

    a. Explore QuickBooks.
    b. Open an existing company file.
    c. Create a new company.
    d. All of the above.

_____4. The name of the company created in Chapter 1 is:

    a. Your Name Retailers Inc.
    b. Your Name Merchandisers.
    c. Sample product-based business.
    d. Sample service-based business.

_____5. The type of business created in Chapter 1 is:

    a. Nonprofit.
    b. Repair and maintenance.
    c. Retail shop or online commerce.
    d. Sales-independent contractor.

_____6. The business created in Chapter 1 will operate as a:

    a. Sole proprietorship.
    b. Corporation.
    c. LLP.
    d. LLC.

_____7. The business created in Chapter 1 does:

    a. Accept credit cards.
    b. Print checks.
    c. Employ many employees.
    d. Accept cash and checks.

_____8. Software registration with Intuit must be completed within how many days of installation?

    a. 30 days.
    b. 60 days.
    c. 120 days.
    d. 140 days.

_____9. Account registration information can be viewed from the QuickBooks desktop by selecting which function key?

    a. <F1>.
    b. <F2>.
    c. <F3>.
    d. <F4>.

_____10. The cash balance at Home State Bank is:

    a. $0.
    b. $50,000.
    c. $80,000.
    d. $100,000.

True/Make True: To answer these questions, go online to www.mhhe.com/QBessentials2014 , link to Student Edition, Chapter 1, QA Templates. The analysis question on the next page is also included.

1. QuickBooks Pro 2014 Student Trial Edition can only run on personal computers with the Windows Vista operating system.

2. QuickBooks 2014 Student Trial Edition can be installed on both individual and computer lab computers.

3. If QuickBooks is registered, the Help menu shows Register QuickBooks.

4. Creating a new company in QuickBooks is easy with the Express Start Interview.

5. You can close the application you are working with if you single click with your mouse on the close button ().

6. It is a good idea to regularly back up or save to the hard drive instead of external media such as a USB drive.

7. The new company that you created is a sole proprietorship.

8. The new company that you created accepts credit cards.

9. The new company that you created prints checks.

10. The software included with the book does not have a time limit.

Exercise 1-1: Follow the instructions below to complete Exercise 1-1:

1. Start QuickBooks. If an Update Company window appears, refer to Appendix B, pages 271-272. The authors recommend installing the update.

2. From the menu bar, select File; New Company.

File	Edit	View	Lists	Favorites	Accountant
New Company...

    .

3. Use Express Start to create a corporation named **Your Name Hardware Store.** This is the business you will use to complete Project 1. *HINT:* Use the Creating a New Company information on pages 7-12, steps 1-14, to set up Your Name Hardware Store.

4. Continue with Exercise 1-2.

Exercise 1-2

1. Back up. The suggested file name is **Your Name Hardware Store.QBB**. Detailed steps for backing up data are shown on pages 16-18, steps 1-8.

2. Exit QuickBooks 2014.

Analysis Questions:

1. How do you locate information about whether or not your software is registered?

2. How long do you have to register the software?

3. After registering the software, what is the time period for accessing the QuickBooks Accountant 2014 student trial edition software included with the textbook?

Chapter 2

Exploring QuickBooks

OBJECTIVES:

1. Start QuickBooks 2014 (QB).
2. Open the sample product-based business.
3. Backup and restore the sample business.
4. Graphical User Interface.
5. Icon Bar and menu bar.
6. Help, Preferences, and Product Information.
7. Internal Control features.
8. Using Windows Explorer.

Additional resources are on the textbook website at www.mhhe.com/QBessentials2014. They include chapter resources, online quizzes, narrated PowerPoints, QA Templates, etc.

In Chapter 2, you become familiar with some of the QB features. There are two sample businesses included with the software: a product company and a service company. You explore the sample product business to learn about the QB user interface, internal controls, and help resources. In addition, you review procedures to backup and restore company data, use Windows Explorer, and e-mail a company backup to your professor.

GETTING STARTED

1. Start QuickBooks 2014 by double clicking on the QuickBooks icon on the computer desktop.

2. If a Register QuickBooks Now window appears, you have not registered. You have 30 days from the installation date to register.

   Connect to the Internet, then click **Begin Registration**. Refer to the Registering QuickBooks section in Chapter 1.

OPEN SAMPLE COMPANY

Sample company data files for a sample product-based business and a sample service-based business are included with the software. Follow the steps below to open starting data for the sample product-based company, Sample Rock Castle Construction. Similar steps can be followed to open data from the sample service-based company, Sample Larry's Landscaping and Garden Supply.

1. From the QuickBooks 2014 desktop, select File; Close Company.

2. A No Company Open window appears. Select the down arrow next to Open a sample file. Then select Sample product-based business.

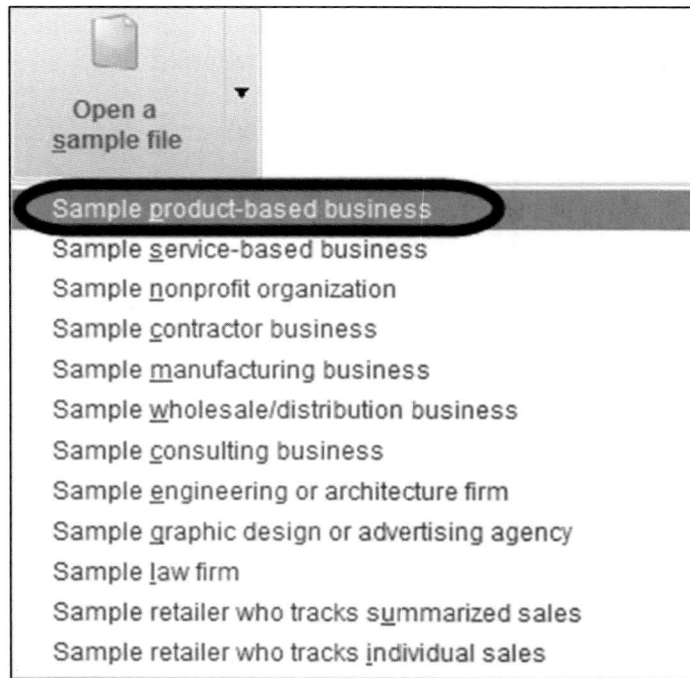

Open a
sample file

Sample product-based business
Sample service-based business
Sample nonprofit organization
Sample contractor business
Sample manufacturing business
Sample wholesale/distribution business
Sample consulting business
Sample engineering or architecture firm
Sample graphic design or advertising agency
Sample law firm
Sample retailer who tracks summarized sales
Sample retailer who tracks individual sales

3. When the QuickBooks Information window prompts "This is the QuickBooks sample file," read the information, then click OK.

A product based company purchases merchandise from vendors,

and then sells that merchandise to customers. Products fall into two categories: inventory and non-inventory items. Another way to describe a product-based company is to call it a merchandising or retail business. The sample company that you are going to use, Sample Rock Castle Construction, is a product based business.

4. The Sample Rock Castle Construction – QuickBooks 2014 Home page appears. Compare yours with the one shown. The various parts of the QB Home page are explained later in the chapter.

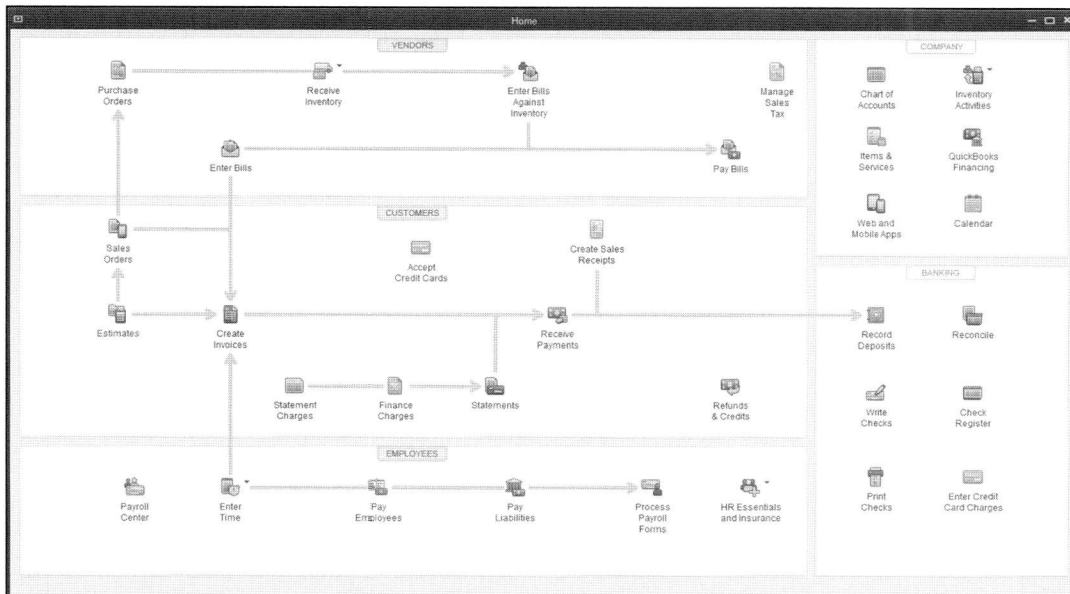

BACK UP AND RESTORE SAMPLE COMPANY

When using QB, information is automatically saved to the hard drive of the computer. In a classroom setting, a number of students may be using the same computer. This means that when you return to the computer lab or classroom, your data is gone. **Backing up** your data means saving it to a hard drive, network drive, or external media. Backing up ensures that you can start where you left off the last time you used QuickBooks 2014.

Back Up Sample Company

In this section you will create a backup of the original starting data for the sample product-based business and then restore the backup. This backup is made *before* any data is added to the sample company so if you want to start with fresh, beginning data again, you can restore from this backup of the original data.

Comment

In this textbook, you are shown how to backup to external media, i.e., an USB drive location. Backing up to a drive other than the hard drive or network drive is called backing up to external media. The instructions that follow assume you are backing up to external media. Authors recommend backing up to at least a **2 GB USB flash drive *OR* if you are working on your own computer, your desktop.**

When you back up, you are saving to the current point in QB. Each time you make a backup, you should type a different backup name (file name) to distinguish between them. In this way, if you need to restore an earlier backup, you have the data for that purpose. See Preface for the list of backups made in this text and their file size.

In the business world, backups are unique for each business day. Daily backups are necessary. If you are working in a computer lab, *never leave the computer lab without first backing up your data to external media, for example, your USB flash drive.*

The text directions assume that you are backing up to *an external media* location. Follow these steps to back up QuickBooks 2014.

1. From the menu bar, select File; Create Copy.

2. The Save Copy or Backup window appears. Select Portable company file for the type of file you want to save.

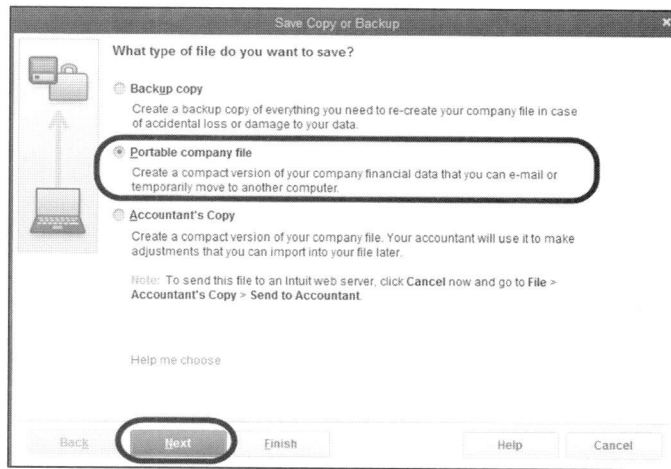

3. Click [Next]. When the Save Portable Company window appears, go to your USB drive location and create a new folder titled, Your Name (your first and last name) QB Backups.

4. Click on Your Name QB Backups folder to open it. Notice the File name is sample_product-based business (Portable). The Save as type is QuickBooks Portable Company Files (*.QB). .

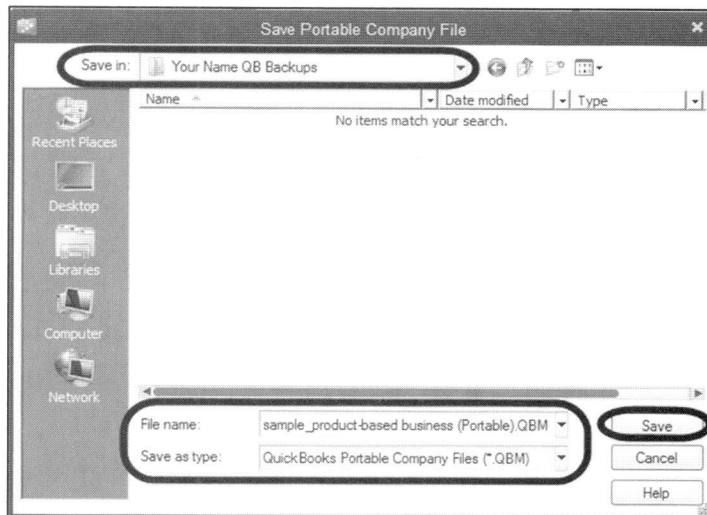

5. Click [Save]. The Close and reopen window appears.

> **Close and reopen**
>
> ⚠ QuickBooks must close and reopen your company file before creating a portable company file.
>
> **OK**   Cancel

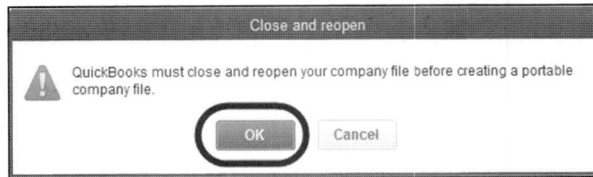

6. Click [OK]. The QuickBooks Information window appears. Read the information.

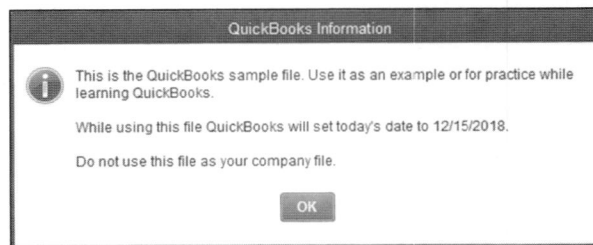

> **QuickBooks Information**
>
> ℹ This is the QuickBooks sample file. Use it as an example or for practice while learning QuickBooks.
>
> While using this file QuickBooks will set today's date to 12/15/2018.
>
> Do not use this file as your company file.
>
> **OK**

7. Click [OK]. While your file is being backed up, the Creating Portable Company File window appears.

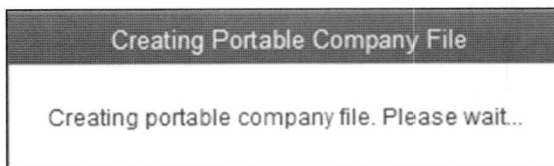

> **Creating Portable Company File**
>
> Creating portable company file. Please wait...

8. When your file is backed up, the QuickBooks information window appears read the information.

> **QuickBooks Information**
>
> ℹ QuickBooks has saved a portable file version for Rock Castle Construction to H:\Your Name QB Backups\sample_product-based business (Portable).QBM.
>
> **OK**

9. Click [OK]. A window appears that says "This is the QuickBooks sample file. Use it as an example or for practice while learning QuickBooks. While using this file QuickBooks will set today's date to 12/15/2018. Do not use this file as your company file."

QuickBooks Information

This is the QuickBooks sample file. Use it as an example or for practice while learning QuickBooks.

While using this file QuickBooks will set today's date to 12/15/2018.

Do not use this file as your company file.

OK

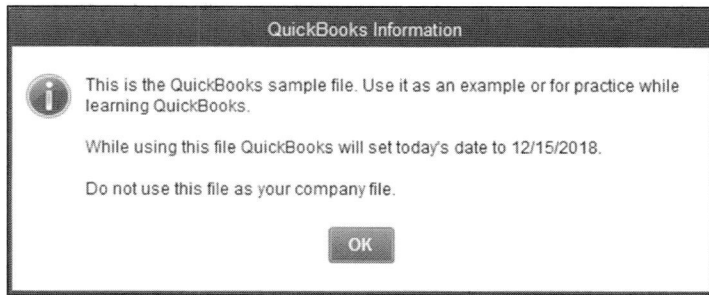

10.   Click [OK]. The Sample Rock Castle Corporation - QuickBooks Accounting 2014 desktop appears.

11.   Click [x] on the title bar to exit Sample Rock Castle Construction or File; Exit and return to the windows desktop. (**Or,** continue with the next section without exiting.)

Read me: Data Files

Refer to the Preface, to review information about the several types of QB files. The Preface also lists the names of all the backups you will make in this text.

Locate the Backup File

The steps that follow assume that the backup was saved to external media. Follow these steps to locate the backup file.

1.   To locate your backup file, open Windows Explorer.

2.   Select your USB drive. In this example PKBACK# 001 (H:) identifies the USB drive. Click on the drive letter.

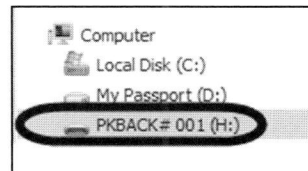

Computer
Local Disk (C:)
My Passport (D:)
PKBACK# 001 (H:)

3.   Open the Your Name QB Backups folder
Your Name QB Backups .

4.   Observe the Name, Type and Size of your backup file. Your file size may differ.

□ Name ▲	Type	Size	
🗂 sample_product-based business (Portable).QBM	QuickBooks Portable Company File	2,029 KB	

Portable files automatically add a .QBM extension to the file name. If your file extension does <u>not</u> appear, do this:

a. From the Windows Explorer menu bar, select Organize, Folder and search options.

b. The Folder Options window appears. Click the View tab. Hide extensions for known file types should be *unchecked*.

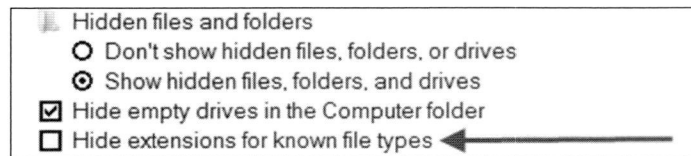

> 📁 Hidden files and folders
> ○ Don't show hidden files, folders, or drives
> ◉ Show hidden files, folders, and drives
> ☑ Hide empty drives in the Computer folder
> ☐ Hide extensions for known file types ⟵

c. On the Folder Options window, click <OK>. Close Windows Explorer.

5. Exit QuickBooks. (*Hint:* Click on the ❌ on the title bar, *or* select File; Exit.)

Restore Sample Company

1. Start QuickBooks 2014. If an Update Company window appears, refer to pages 271-272. The authors recommend installing the update.

2. The QuickBooks 2014 desktop appears. If a company opens, from the menu bar, select File; Close Company. If an Automatic Backup window appears, read the information. Then, click [No].

3. The No Company Open window appears. Click [Open or restore an existing company].

4. The Open or Restore Company window appears. Select Restore a portable file.

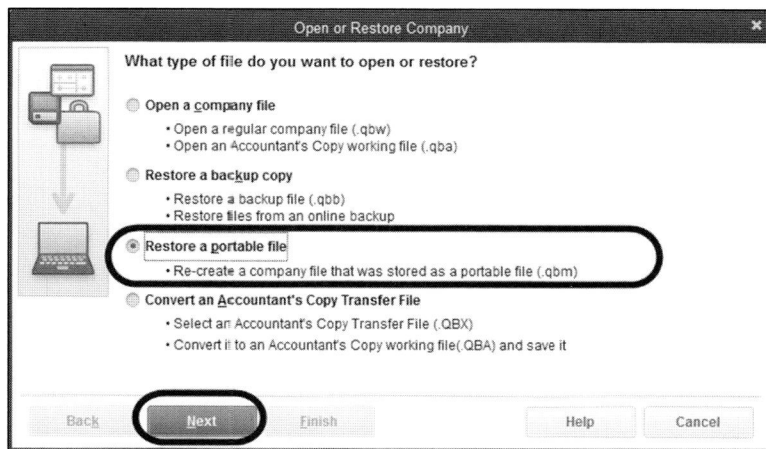

5. Click [Next]. The Open Portable Company File window appears. Go to the location of your USB drive and open the Your Name QB Backups folder. Select the sample_product-based business (portable).QBM file.

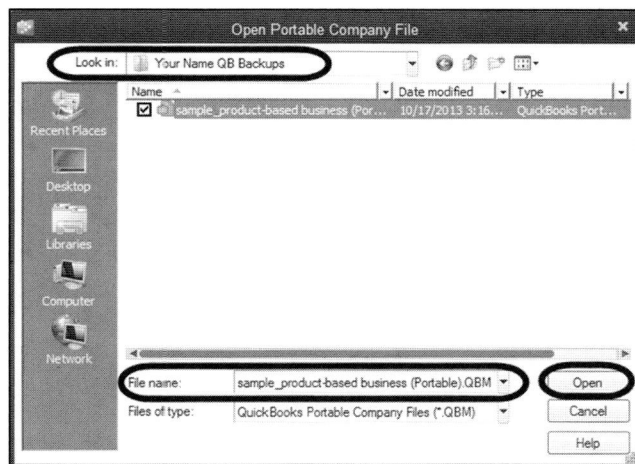

6. Click [Open] (*or,* you can double-click on the file name).

7. Read the information on the Where do you want to restore the file window.

8. Click .

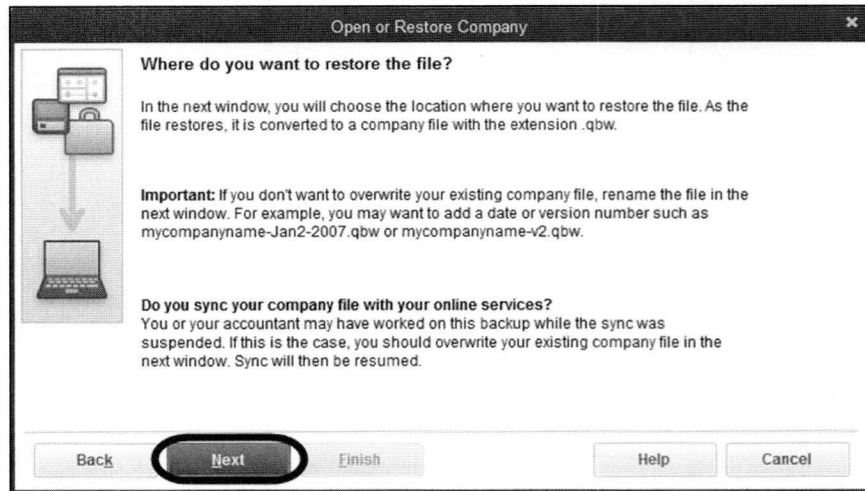

9. Type Your first and last name in front of File name.

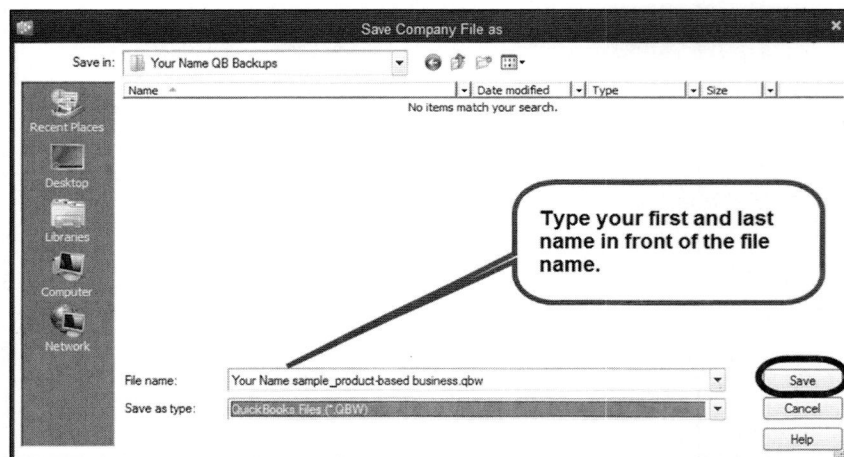

10. Click . The Working window appears. Be patient. Opening a portable company file takes several minutes.

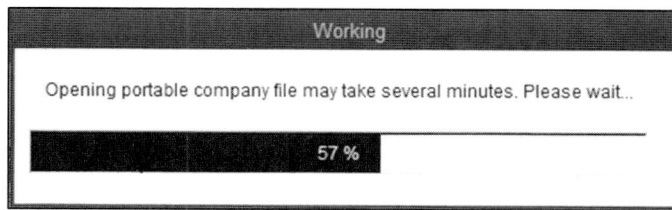

Working

Opening portable company file may take several minutes. Please wait...

57 %

11. When the QuickBooks Information window appears, read the information.

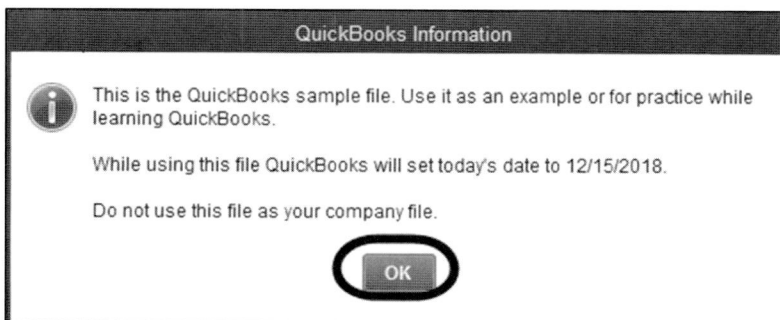

QuickBooks Information

This is the QuickBooks sample file. Use it as an example or for practice while learning QuickBooks.

While using this file QuickBooks will set today's date to 12/15/2018.

Do not use this file as your company file.

OK

12. Click OK. When the window prompts "The QuickBooks portable company file has been opened successfully," your file is restored.

QuickBooks Information

The QuickBooks portable company file has been opened successfully.

OK

13. Click OK. You are restored to the Sample Rock Castle Construction – QuickBooks Accountant 2014 desktop.

14. Exit QB or continue.

GRAPHICAL USER INTERFACE (GUI)

If you exited QuickBooks, follow these steps to open Sample Rock Castle Construction.

1. Start QuickBooks. If an Update Company window appears, refer to pages 271-272. The authors recommend installing the update.

2. From the menu bar, select File; Open Previous Company, C:\Users\....\.....\Your Name sample_product-based business.qbw. (*Hint:* Your file location will differ.) Observe that the file extension is .QBW which indicates the company file.

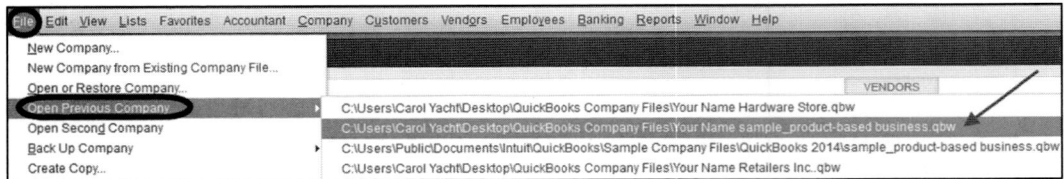

3. When the QuickBooks Information window appears, click [OK].

> **Read me: Open a Previous Company or Restore a Back up File?**
>
> Opening a previous company (.QBW extension) is an alternative to restoring a file. This works well on your own individual computer. If you are working in the computer lab, restoring the portable company backup file (.QBM extension) is best.

The general look of a program is called its graphical user interface. As you know, most programs include the mouse pointer, icons, toolbars, menus, and an Icon Bar. QuickBooks' GUI is shown on the next page.

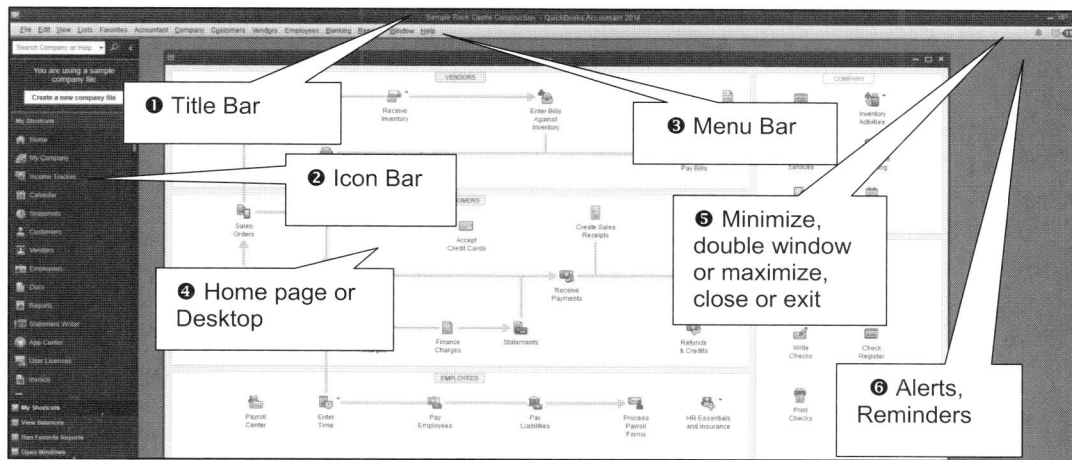

In this textbook, you will use Icon Bar, menu bar, and Home page selections.

For now, let's study the parts of the window. Some features are common to all software programs using Windows. For example, in the upper right corner is the Minimize ▬ button, Double Window ⧉ button, and the Close ☒ button. The title bar, window border, and mouse pointer are also common to Windows programs. Other features are specific to QB: Icon Bar, menu bar, and Home page selections. The contents of these menus differ depending on the application.

❶ *Title Bar:* Contains the company name and the software version.

> Sample Rock Castle Construction - QuickBooks Accountant 2014

❷ *Icon Bar:* The Icon Bar contains shortcuts to the tasks and reports you use most. You can place the Icon Bar to the left of the QB desktop, above it, or hide it.

❸ *Menu Bar:* Contains the menus for File, Edit, View, Lists, Favorites, Accountant, Company, Customers, Vendors, Employees, Banking, Reports, Window and Help. You can click with your left-mouse button on the menu bar headings to see the selections.

> File   Edit   View   Lists   Favorites   Accountant   Company   Customers   Vendors   Employees   Banking   Reports   Window   Help

❹ *Home Page or Desktop:* Displays information about the company. The following content appears when the Company opens: Vendors, Customers, Employees, Company, and Banking. Each section of the Home page shows workflow diagrams or processes.

❺ Minimize ▭, Double Window ▭, or Maximize ▭, and Close or Exit ✕ buttons: Clicking once on Minimize ▭ reduces the window to a button on the *taskbar*. In Windows, the ▭ start (Windows 7) button and taskbar are located at the bottom of your window. Clicking once on Double Window ▭ returns the window to its previous size. This button appears when you maximize the window. After clicking on the Double Window ▭ button, the symbol changes to the Maximize ▭ button. Click once on the Maximize ▭ button to enlarge the window. Click once on the Exit or Close ✕ button to close the window, or exit the program.

❻ Alerts and Reminders: In the upper right corner of the window, QB gives you instant access to important alerts and reminders.

Typical QuickBooks 2014 Windows

The Icon Bar contains shortcuts to quickly access information about the company; for example, Home, My Company, Income Tracker, Calendar, Snapshots, Customers, Vendors, Employees, etc.

When one of the Icon Bar's buttons are selected, an information rich page appears. For example, click ▭ Customers , and the Customer Center window is shown. Compare your Customer Center window to the one shown on the next page.

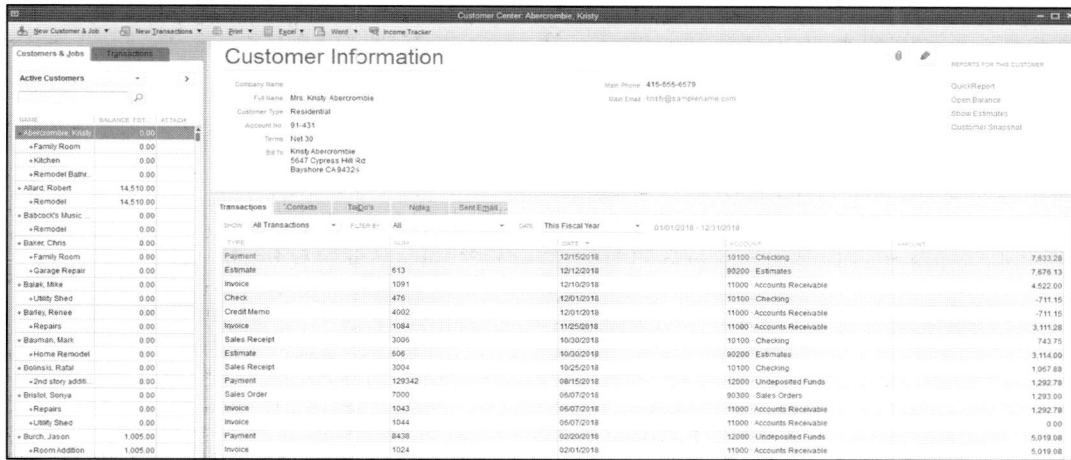

Click on the down-arrow next to Active Customers. A list populates that includes All Customers, Active Customers, Customers with Open Balances, Customers with Overdue Invoices, Customers with Almost Due Invoices, Custom Filter. Active Customers is the default. (*Hint:* The checkmark indicates the default.)

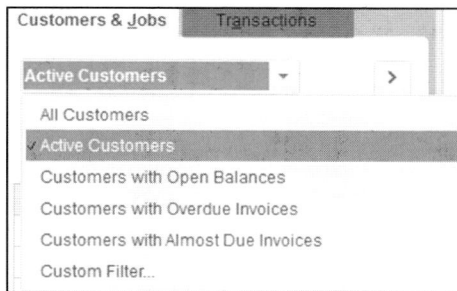

The Customer & Jobs tab and the Transactions tab both show customer data. To see the same customer data presented in different ways, select a customer, then select the Customers & Jobs tab. After looking at the Customers & Job tab information, select the Transactions tab.

From the Customers & Job tab, the following selections appear: New Customers & Job, New Transactions, Print, Excel, Word, and Income Tracker. Explore these selections. Observe that both Excel and Word are included, along with an Income Tracker, entering new transactions or new customers.

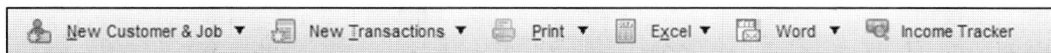

Select the Transactions tab—[Transactions]. It includes selections for New Customer, New Transactions, Print, Customer & Job Info, and Export.

Explore these selections; for example, click [⊞ Export...].

To close the Customer Center, click <X> on its title bar.

ICON BAR AND MENU BAR

To access tasks, use the Icon Bar or menu bar. The Icon
Bar contains shortcuts to the tasks and reports used the
most. Using the Icon Bar on the left side offers the
quickest access but it can also be placed on the top or
hidden. Some of the most frequently used Icon Bar
selections are Home, Accountant, Customers, Vendors,
Reports.

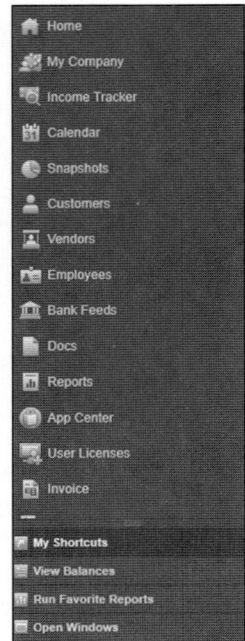

Icon Bar

1. The Icon Bar is usually on the left side of your
    desktop. (Refer to Icon Bar Location, page 269.)

2. Select [👤 Accountant]. (*Hint:* If the Icon Bar does not
    include Accountant, from the menu bar select View; Customize Icon

    Bar, [Add...], Accountant, [OK]. To select [👤 Accountant],
    scroll down the Icon Bar.) The Accountant Center includes access to
    the QuickBooks features that accountants use most; for example,
    Make General Journal Entries and the General Ledger.

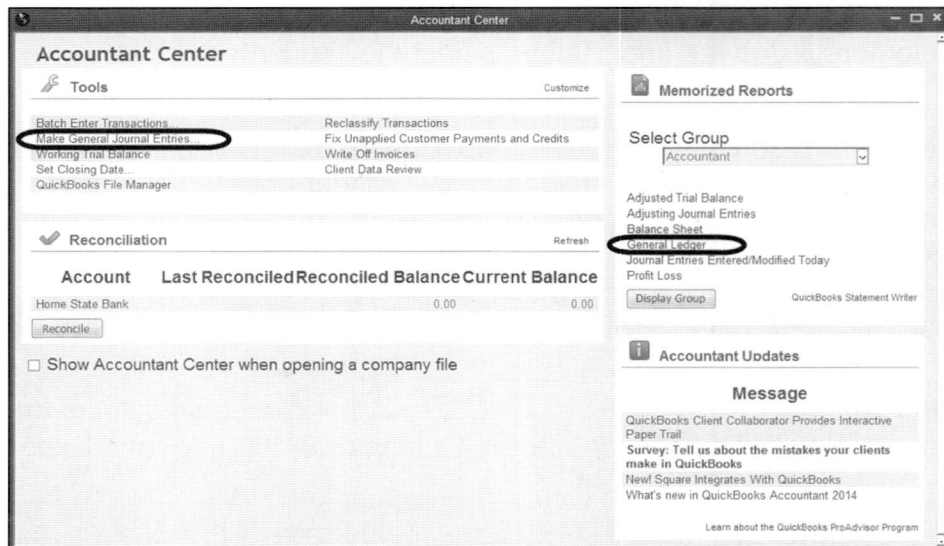

| 🏠 Home |
| 🖥 My Company |
| 📊 Income Tracker |
| 📅 Calendar |
| 🌐 Snapshots |
| 👤 Customers |
| 👤 Vendors |
| 👥 Employees |
| 🏛 Bank Feeds |
| 📄 Docs |
| 📊 Reports |
| 🔵 App Center |
| 💳 User Licenses |
| 📋 Invoice |
| ◾ My Shortcuts |
| ◾ View Balances |
| ◾ Run Favorite Reports |
| ◾ Open Windows |

Accountant Center

🔧 Tools   Customize   📘 Memorized Reports

Batch Enter Transactions   Reclassify Transactions   Select Group
Make General Journal Entries   Fix Unapplied Customer Payments and Credits   [Accountant   ▼]
Working Trial Balance   Write Off Invoices
Set Closing Date...   Client Data Review   Adjusted Trial Balance
QuickBooks File Manager   Adjusting Journal Entries
                                                                             Balance Sheet
✔ Reconciliation   Refresh   General Ledger
                                                                             Journal Entries Entered/Modified Today
Account   Last Reconciled Reconciled Balance Current Balance   Profit Loss

Home State Bank   0.00   0.00   [Display Group]   QuickBooks Statement Writer
[Reconcile]
                                                                             ℹ Accountant Updates
☐ Show Accountant Center when opening a company file
                                                                                      Message

                                                                             QuickBooks Client Collaborator Provides Interactive
                                                                             Paper Trail
                                                                             **Survey: Tell us about the mistakes your clients
                                                                             make in QuickBooks**
                                                                             New! Square Integrates With QuickBooks
                                                                             What's new in QuickBooks Accountant 2014

                                                                                        Learn about the QuickBooks ProAdvisor Program

3. Select [Customers]. The Customer Center's Customer Information window appears. The Customers & Jobs list shows information about the people and companies to whom you sell products and services. If you set up jobs for a customer, they appear indented under the customer's name. The screen image shows the customer, Babcock's Music Shop.

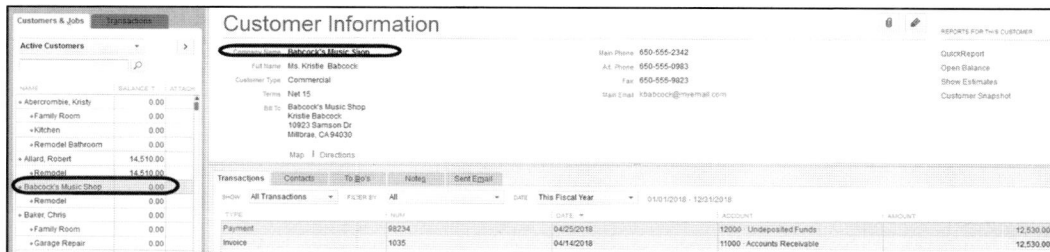

The Customer Center can be accessed from the Home page's [CUSTOMERS] button or the menu bar's Customers selection.

4. Select [Vendors]. The Vendor Center appears. QuickBooks uses the Vendors list to hold information about the people and companies they do business with. For example, the list includes the company name, balance total, phone numbers, email, reports, a list of transactions, etc. The Vendor center can be access from the Home page's [VENDORS] button or the menu bar's Vendors selection.

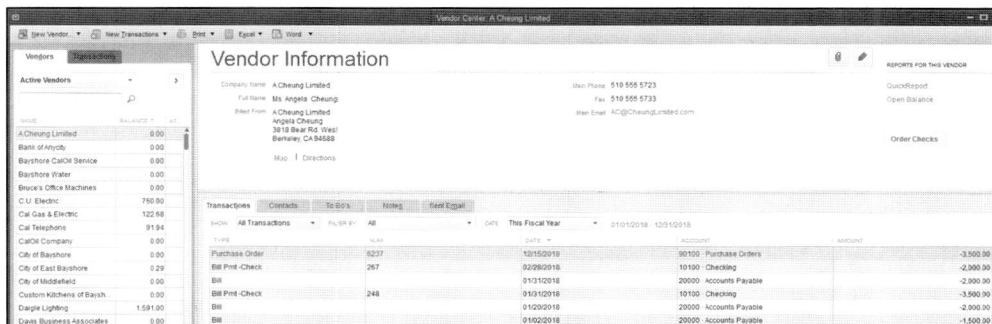

5. Click [Reports]. Run detailed reports from the Report Center. Observe that numerous types of reports are listed: Company & Financial, Customers & Receivable, Sals, Jobs, Time & Mileage,

Purchases, Inventory, etc. The default window is Company & Financial. Reports can all be accessed from the menu bar.

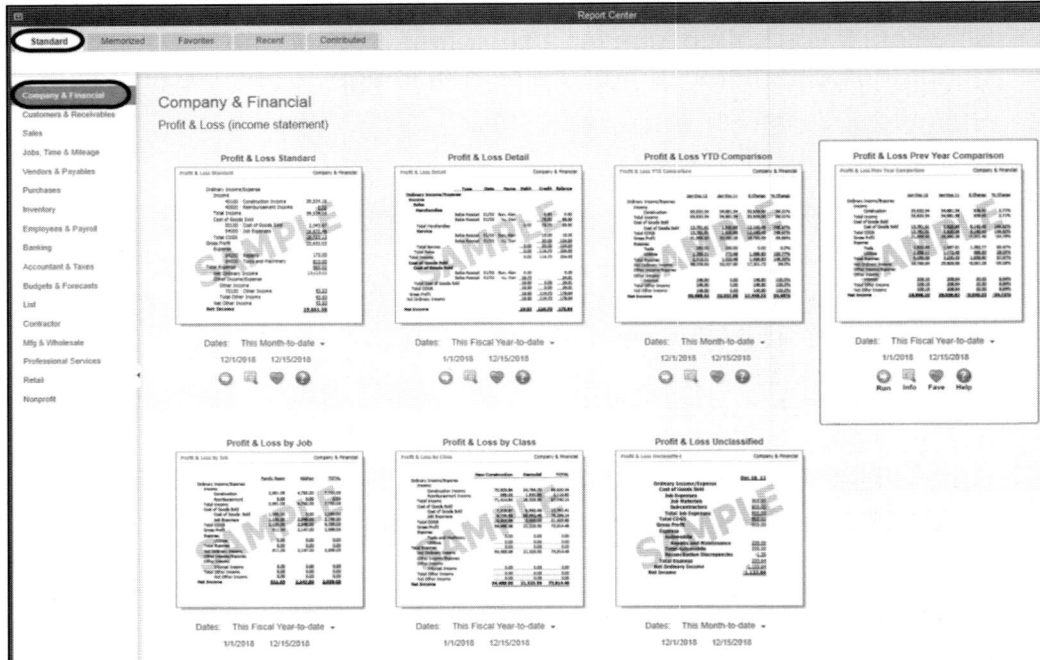

6. Close open windows. (*Hint:* From the menu bar, Window, Close All.

   To see the Home page, click **🏠 Home** .

Menu Bar

Now that you've looked at the Icon Bar, let's explore some menu bar selections. When you want to go to tasks or reports, you can use either the Icon Bar or menu bar. The menu bar selections shown are from Sample Rock Castle Construction.

The horizontal menu bar is another way to access tasks and reports. The Sample Rock Castle Construction menu bar has 14 selections: File, Edit, View, Lists, Favorites, Accountant, Company, Customers, Vendors, Employees, Banking, Reports, Window, and Help.

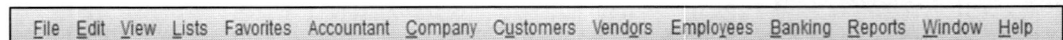

1. From the menu bar, click File to see the file menu options. The file menu includes selections for New Company, New Company from Existing Company File, Open or Restore Company, Open Previous Company, Open Second Company, Back Up Company, Create Copy, Close Company, Switch to Multi-user Mode, Utilities, Set Up Intuit Sync Manager, Accountant's Copy, Print (since a report is open, Print is active), Save as PDF, Print Forms, Printer Setup, Send Forms, Shipping, Update Web Services, Toggle to Another Edition, and Exit. If any of the items are gray, they are inactive. An arrow (▶) next to a menu item (for example, Utilities) indicates that there are additional selections. Ctrl+P or Alt+F4 means you can use press those keys together for the same result.

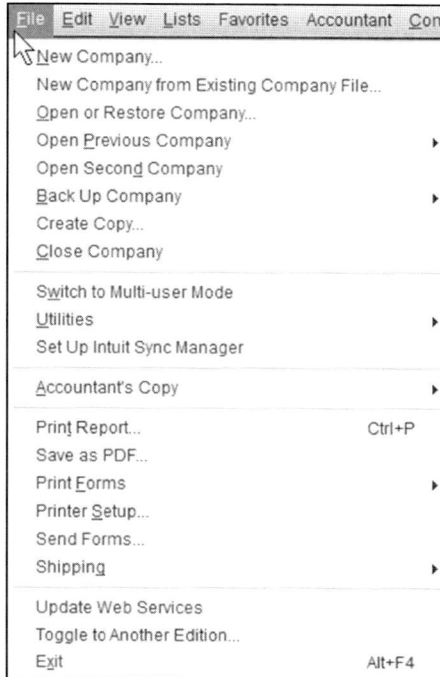

2. To see the Edit menu, make a selection from the Home page; for example, click [Chart of Accounts]. From the menu bar, select Edit. The edit menu includes selections for Nothing to Undo (inactive), Revert (inactive), Cut (inactive), Copy Account, Paste (inactive), Copy Line (inactive), Paste Line (inactive), Edit Account, New Account, Delete Account, Make Account Inactive, Show Inactive Accounts, Customize Columns, Use Register, Use Calculator, Find Search Preferences. Edit menu choices vary depending on what window is selected. The edit menu illustrated shows Chart of Accounts selections.

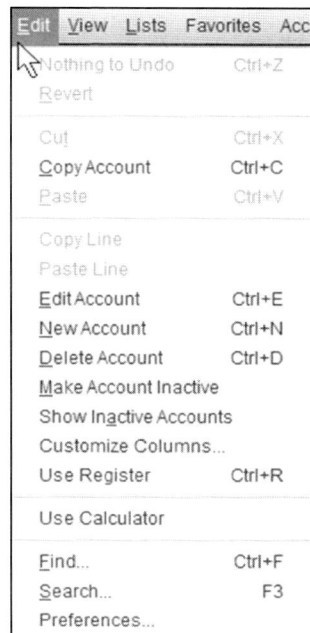

3. From the menu bar, click View. The View menu allows you to Open Window List; place the Icon Bar on the top, left or hide it; Search Box (inactive); Customer Icon Bar; Add Home to Icon Bar; Favorites Menu; One Window; and Multiple Windows. Observe that a checkmark next to Left Icon Bar, Favorites Menu, and Multiple Windows.

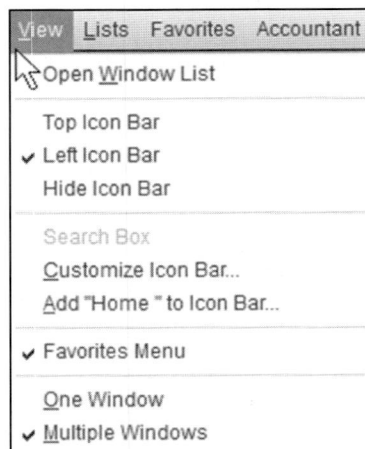

4. From the menu bar, click Lists. The Lists menu includes selections for Chart of Accounts, Item List, Fixed Asset Item List, U/M Set List, Price Level List, Billing Rate Level List, Sales Tax Code List, Payroll Item List, Class List, Workers Comp List, Other Names List, Customer & Vendor Profile Lists, Templates, Memorized Transaction List, and Add/Edit Multiple List Entries.

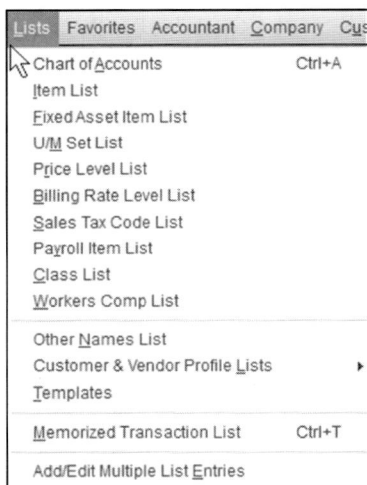

5. From the menu bar, click Favorites. The Favorites menu allows you to customize menus.

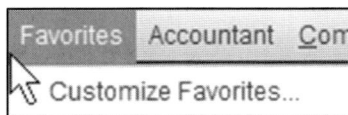

6. From the menu bar, select Accountant. The selections include Accountant Center, Chart of Accounts, Fixed Asset Item List, Batch Enter Transactions, Client Data Review, Make General Journal Entries, Send General Journal Entries, Reconcile, Working Trial Balance, Set Closing Date, Condense Data, Remote Access, Manage Fixed Assets, QuickBooks File Manager, QuickBooks Statement Writer, ProAdvisor Program, and Online Accountant Resources.

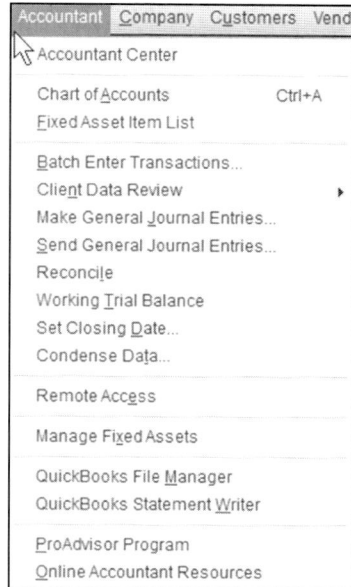

Accountant	Company	Customers	Vend

Accountant Center

Chart of Accounts	Ctrl+A
Fixed Asset Item List	

Batch Enter Transactions...
Client Data Review   ▶
Make General Journal Entries...
Send General Journal Entries...
Reconcile
Working Trial Balance
Set Closing Date...
Condense Data...

Remote Access

Manage Fixed Assets

QuickBooks File Manager
QuickBooks Statement Writer

ProAdvisor Program
Online Accountant Resources

7. From the menu bar, click Company. Selections include Home page, Company Snapshot, Calendar, Documents, Lead Center, My Company, Advanced Service Administration, Set Up Users and Passwords, Customer Credit Card Protection, Set Closing Date, Planning & Budgeting, To Do List, Alerts Manager, Maintenance Alerts, Chart of Accounts, Make General Journal Entries, Manage Currency, Enter Vehicle Mileage, and Prepare Letters with Envelopes.

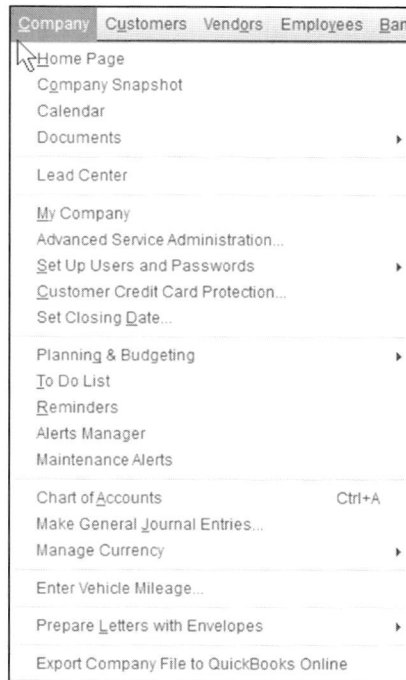

Company	Customers	Vendors	Employees	Bank

Home Page
Company Snapshot
Calendar

Documents	▶

Lead Center

My Company
Advanced Service Administration...

Set Up Users and Passwords	▶

Customer Credit Card Protection...
Set Closing Date...

Planning & Budgeting	▶

To Do List
Reminders
Alerts Manager
Maintenance Alerts

Chart of Accounts	Ctrl+A

Make General Journal Entries...

Manage Currency	▶

Enter Vehicle Mileage...

Prepare Letters with Envelopes	▶

Export Company File to QuickBooks Online

8. Click on Customers to see its menu. This selection includes Customer Center, Create Estimates, Create Sales Orders, Sales Order Fulfillment Worksheet, Create Invoices, Create Batch Invoices, Enter Sales Receipts, Enter Statement Charges, Create Statements, Assess Finance Charges, Receive Payments, Create Credit Memos/Refunds, Income Tracker, Lead Center, Add Credit Card Processing, Add Electronic Check Processing, Link Payment Service to Company File, Intuit PaymentNetwork, Enter Time, Item List, and Change Item Prices.

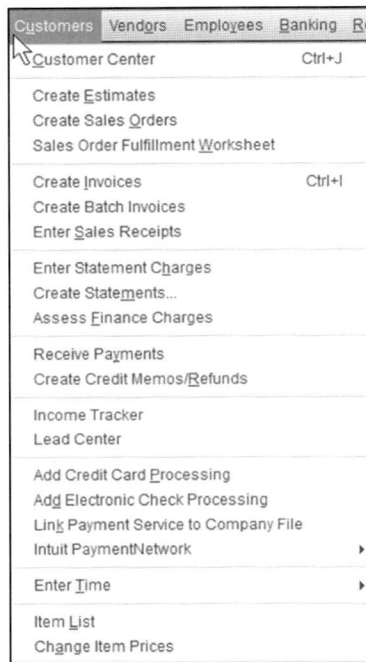

9. Click on Vendors to see its menu. This selection includes Vendor Center, Enter Bills, Pay Bills, Sales Tax, Create Purchase Orders, Receive Items and Enter Bill, Receive Items, Enter Bill for Received Items, Inventory Activities, Print/E-file 1099s, and Item List.

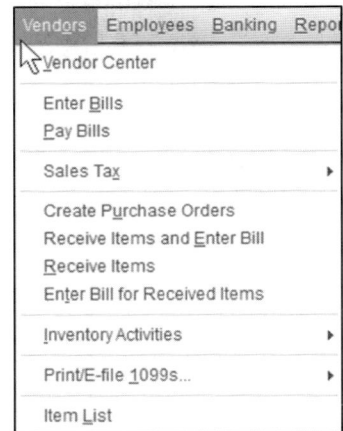

10. Click Employees. This selection includes Employee Center, Payroll Center, Enter Time, Pay Employees, After-the-Fact Payroll, Add or Edit Payroll Schedules, Edit/Void Paychecks, Payroll Taxes and Liabilities, Payroll Tax Forms & W-2s, Labor Law Posters, Workers Compensation, Intuit Health Benefits, My Payroll Service, Guide to Hiring Employees, HR Essentials and Insurance, Payroll Setup, Manage Payroll Items, Get Payroll Updates, and Billing Rate Level List.

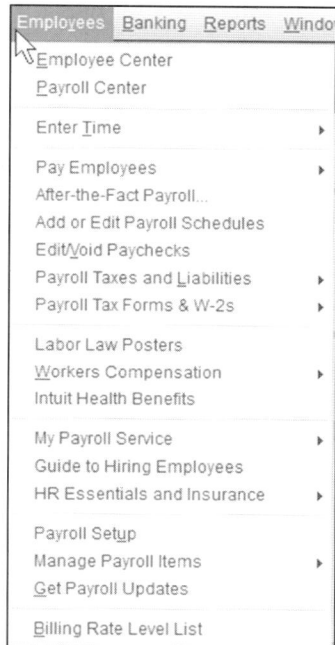

Employees	Banking	Reports	Windo
Employee Center			
Payroll Center			
Enter Time			▸
Pay Employees			▸
After-the-Fact Payroll...			
Add or Edit Payroll Schedules			
Edit/Void Paychecks			
Payroll Taxes and Liabilities			▸
Payroll Tax Forms & W-2s			▸
Labor Law Posters			
Workers Compensation			▸
Intuit Health Benefits			
My Payroll Service			▸
Guide to Hiring Employees			
HR Essentials and Insurance			▸
Payroll Setup			
Manage Payroll Items			▸
Get Payroll Updates			
Billing Rate Level List			

11. Click Banking. This selection includes Write Checks, Order Checks & Envelopes, Enter Credit Card Charges, Use Register, Make Deposits, Transfer Funds, Reconcile, Bank Feeds, Loan Manager, and Other Names List.

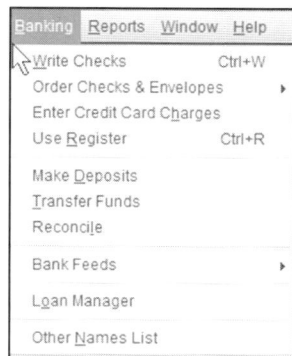

Banking	Reports	Window	Help
Write Checks			Ctrl+W
Order Checks & Envelopes			▸
Enter Credit Card Charges			
Use Register			Ctrl+R
Make Deposits			
Transfer Funds			
Reconcile			
Bank Feeds			▸
Loan Manager			
Other Names List			

12. Click Reports. This selection includes Report Center; Memorized Reports; Company Snapshot; Process Multiple Reports; QuickBooks Statement Writer; Company & Financial; Customers & Receivables; Sales, Jobs, Time & Mileage; Vendors & Payables; Purchases; Inventory; Employees & Payroll; Banking; Accountant & Taxes; Budgets & Forecasts; List; Industry Specific; Contributed Reports; Custom Reports; Quick Report (inactive if Chart of Accounts window is closed); Transaction History; and Transaction Journal.

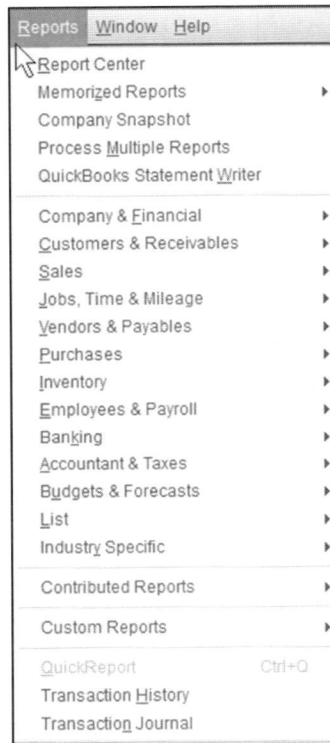

13. Click Window. This selection includes Arrange Icons, Close All, Tile Vertically, Tile Horizontally, Cascade, and 1 Home. (*Hint:* If other windows are open, they are listed after 1 Home.)

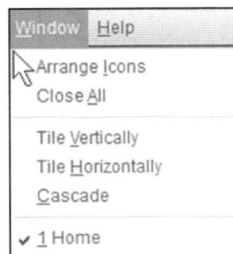

14. Click Help. This selection includes QuickBooks Help, Ask Intuit, What's New, Quick Start Center, Find Training, Learning Center Tutorials, Support, Find A Local QuickBooks Expert, Send Feedback Online, Internet Connection Setup, Year-End Guide, Add QuickBooks Services, App Center:Find More Business Solutions, Update QuickBooks, Manage My License, Manage Data Sync, QuickBooks Privacy Statement, About Automatic Update, and About QuickBooks Accountant 2014.

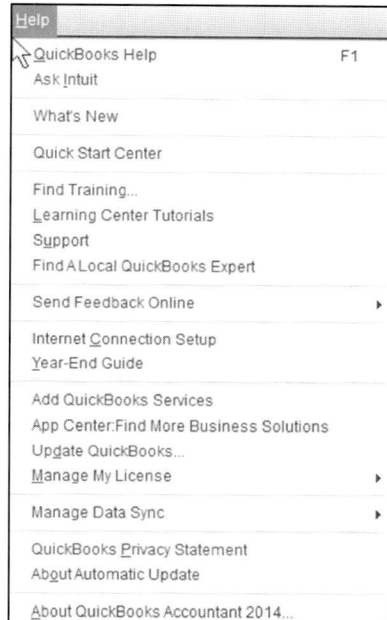

Help
QuickBooks Help   F1
Ask Intuit
What's New
Quick Start Center
Find Training...
Learning Center Tutorials
Support
Find A Local QuickBooks Expert
Send Feedback Online   ▸
Internet Connection Setup
Year-End Guide
Add QuickBooks Services
App Center:Find More Business Solutions
Update QuickBooks...
Manage My License   ▸
Manage Data Sync   ▸
QuickBooks Privacy Statement
About Automatic Update
About QuickBooks Accountant 2014...

HELP, PREFERENCES, AND PRODUCT INFORMATION

QuickBooks 2014 includes user support or help. The instructions that follow demonstrate Help files.

1. From the menu bar, click Help; QuickBooks Help.

2. The Have a Question? window appears. Notice you can type in a question, then click the Search icon [icon] to learn more. Also, notice that a question mark icon appears at the bottom of your screen on the taskbar - [icon]

3. From the Have a Question? window you have choices, you can type a question, or link to various parts of the screen.

4. For example, type **How to get help** in the Search field, then click

   . Two windows appear: Help article and Have a Question.

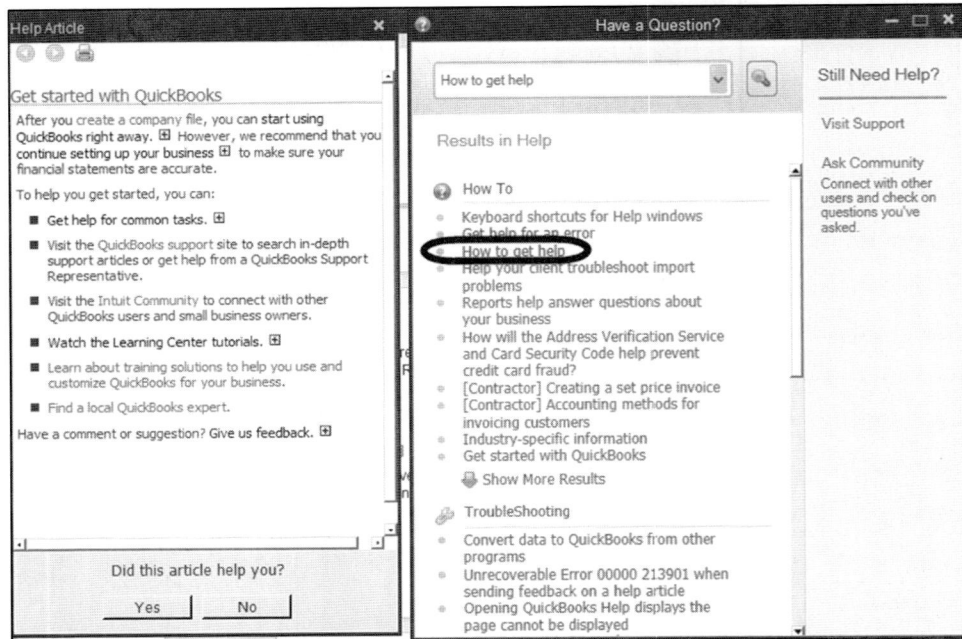

5. From the Have a Question? window, select How to get help. Read the information on the Help Article window. In response to the information provided, you can also select <Yes> or <No>, and provide feedback. When finished, close the Help Article and Have a Question? windows.

Company Preferences

Follow these steps to look at the User and Company Preferences for Sample Rock Castle Construction.

1. From the menu bar, select Edit; Preferences. The Preferences window appears. If necessary, click on the Company Preferences tab. Select a variety of topics on the left side of the screen to view or change preferences. For example, view General preferences. Read

the information on the Company Preferences window. Observe where the checkmarks are placed.

2. Click on My Preferences tab to see user preferences. Select a variety of topics on the left side of the screen to view or change preferences. For example, view General preferences. Read the information on the Company Preferences window. Observe where the checkmarks are placed.

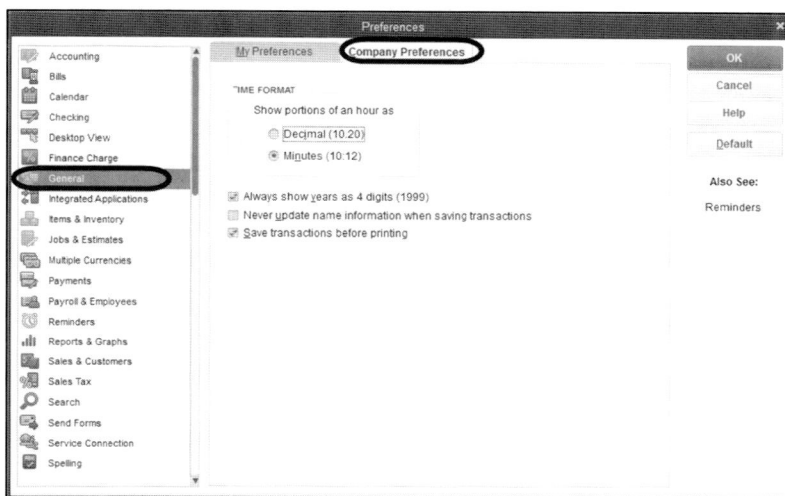

As you complete work in this book, you will learn more about setting QB Preferences.

3. To close the window, click <X> on the Preferences title bar.

Displaying Product Information

1. From the menu bar, click on Help; About QuickBooks Accountant 2014. The About QuickBooks 2014 window appears. (Your License Number, Product Number, and User Licenses are completed.)

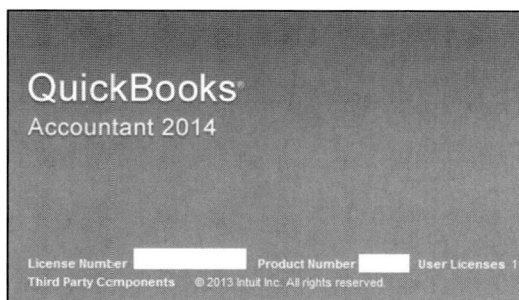

2. After reviewing the window, press <Esc> to close.

INTERNAL CONTROL FEATURES

Security Roles and Permissions

Having user roles with defined permissions allows QB to keep sensitive financial data secure and maintain good company internal controls. Good internal controls reduce a business' risk for wrongdoing and fraud by limiting what users can do or view. Users with administrative rights have full access to all aspects of the software including setting up what other users can view or do in QB. Each user can be permitted different authorized access to QB by the administrator. In this text, since you are the administrator, you can set up users and grant them permissions.

The QB Administrator can give a user access to any or all of these areas when a user's password is set up: sales and accounts receivable, purchases and accounts payable, checking and credit cards, inventory, time tracking, payroll, sensitive accounting activities, and sensitive financial reports. (*Hint:* Using QB Help, type **roles** in the search field. Then, link to Access permissions in QuickBooks.)

Add User Roles

To add a role, follow these steps.
1. From the Sample Rock Castle Construction menu bar, select Company; Set Up Users and Passwords, Set Up Users.

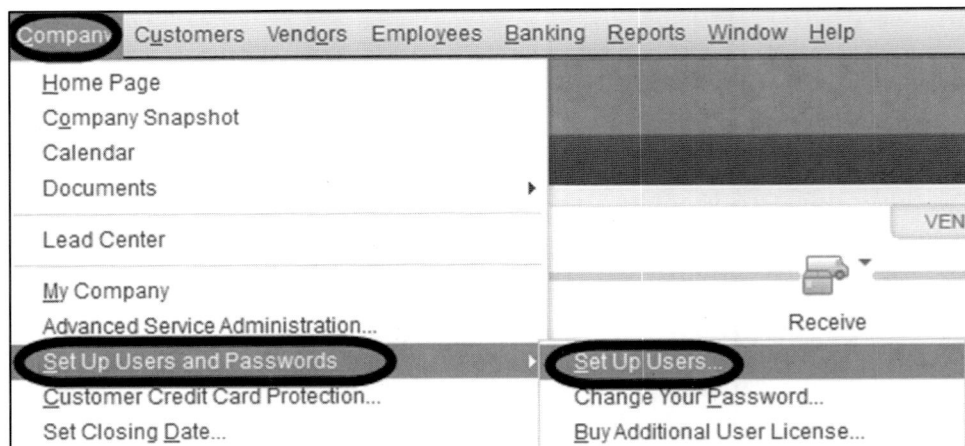

2. The User List window appears.

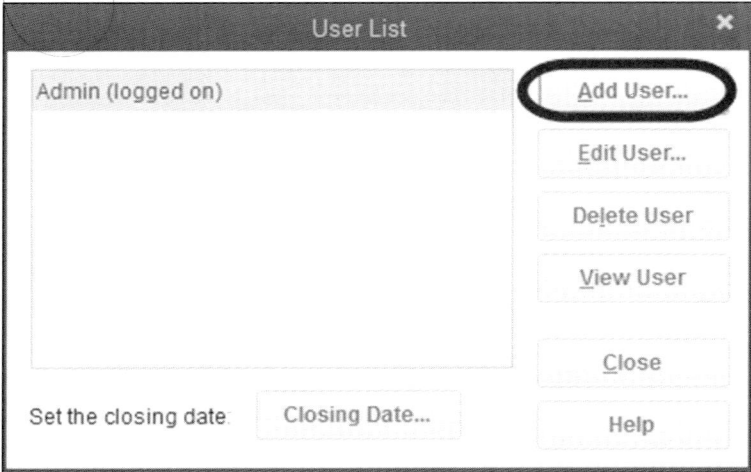

3. Click on Add User. The Set up password and access window appears for adding a User Name and Password. You are going to add the Cashier role. A cashier enters customer purchases and collects cash payments or credit card payments from customers. For example, a grocery store cashier, store sales clerk, or restaurant wait staff. In the User field type **Cashier**.

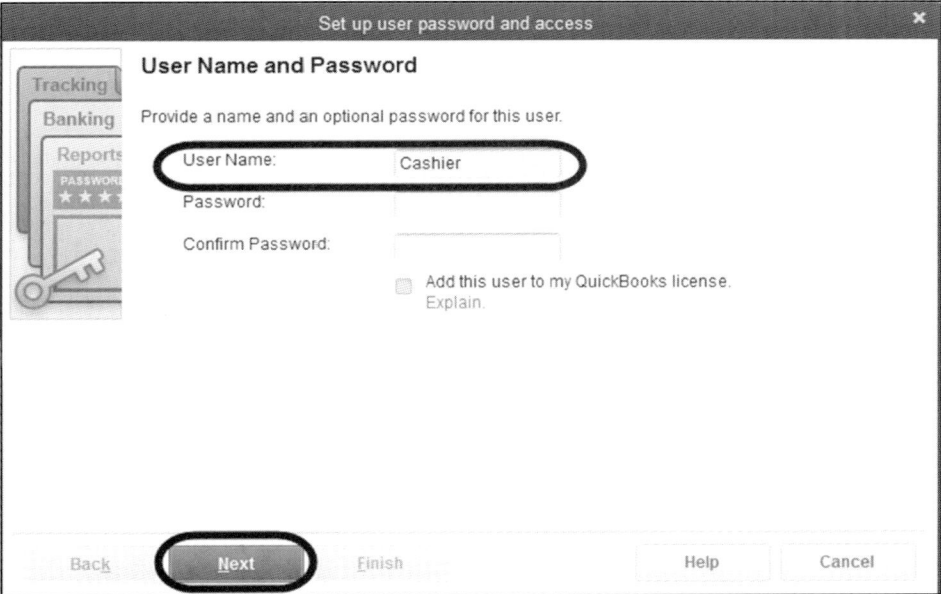

4.   Click [Next >]. The No Password Entered window appears. Read the information. (*Hint:* If you type a password, you will need to enter it every time you restore a backup file. Do *not* type a password.)

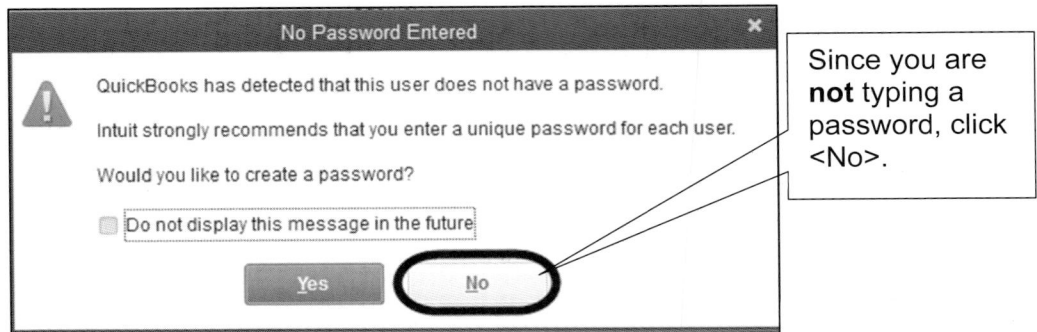

Since you are **not** typing a password, click <No>.

5.   Click [No]. The Access for user: Cashier information appears. If needed, choose Selected areas of QuickBooks (You will make the selections in the screens that follow).

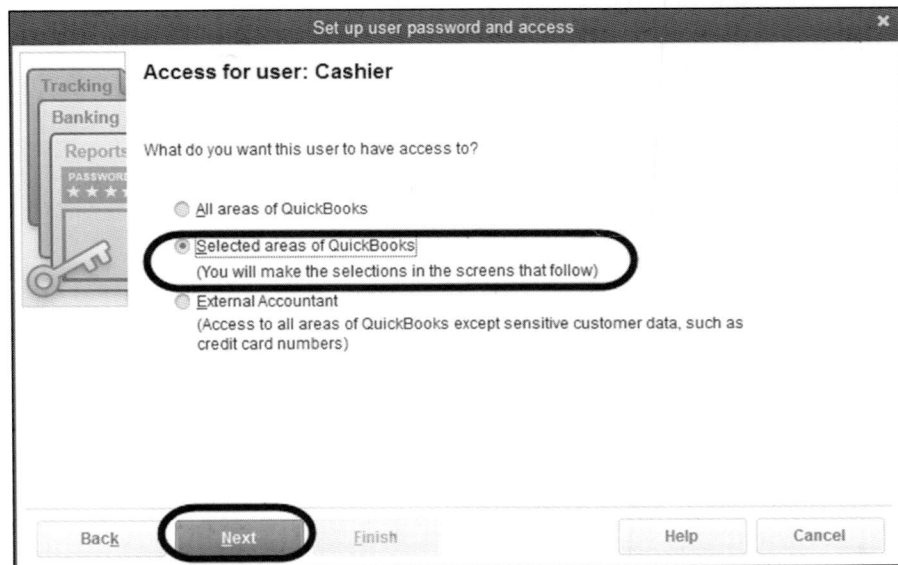

6.   Click [Next >]. The Sales and Accounts Receivable information appears. Since cashiers process customer payments and give customers receipts, the cashier must have selective access to create and print transactions. Choose Selective Access, Create and print transactions.

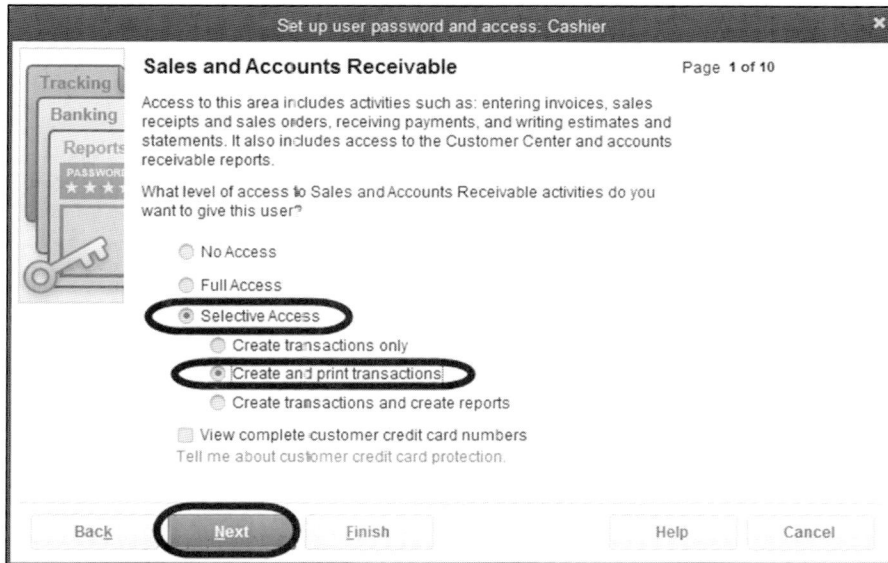

7. Click [Next >]. The Purchases and Accounts Payable information appears. Select No Access. Good internal control separates the duties of cash collection from cash payments.

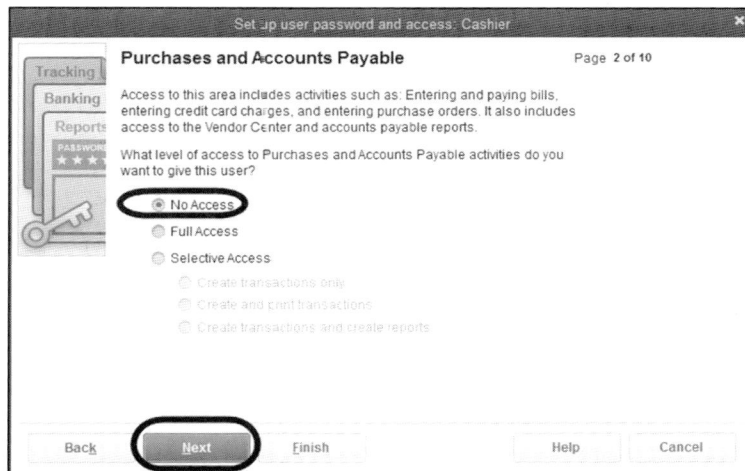

8. Click [Next >].

9. The Checking and Credit Cards information appears. Select No Access. Good internal control assigns different employees the task of making bank deposits versus processing customer payments.

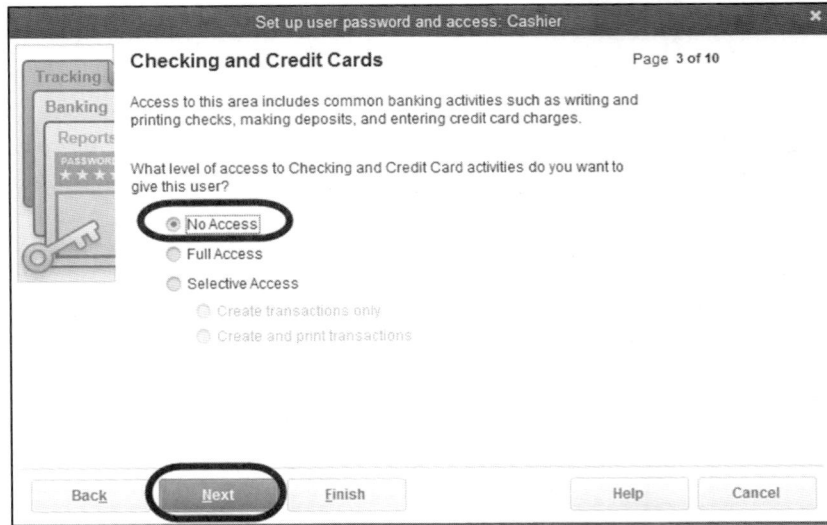

10. Click [Next >]. In Inventory, select No Access. Continue selecting No Access for Time Tracking, Payroll and Employees, Sensitive Accounting Activities, and Sensitive Financial Reporting. Click [Next >] between each window.

11. For Changing or Deleting Transactions, select <No> for both questions since good internal control generally requires supervisor authorization of any changes.

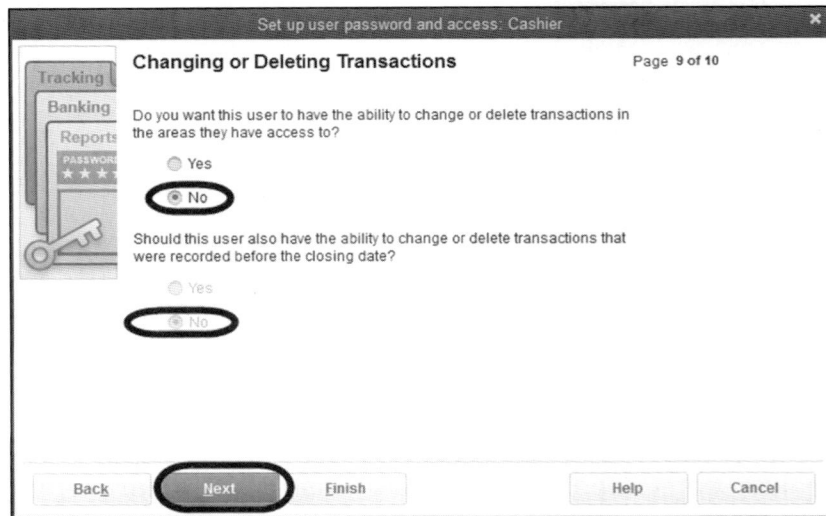

12.   Click [Next >]. Review access for user: Cashier. Make any changes by clicking <Back>if necessary. Observe that you are on Page 10 of 10.

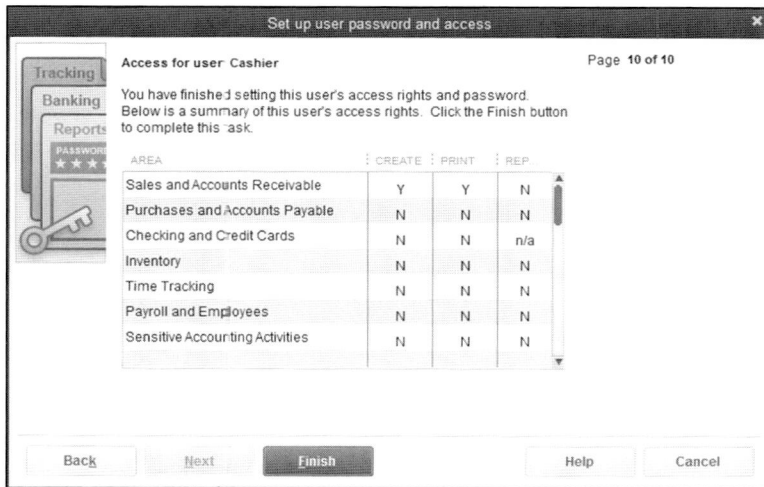

Scroll down to see all the selections.

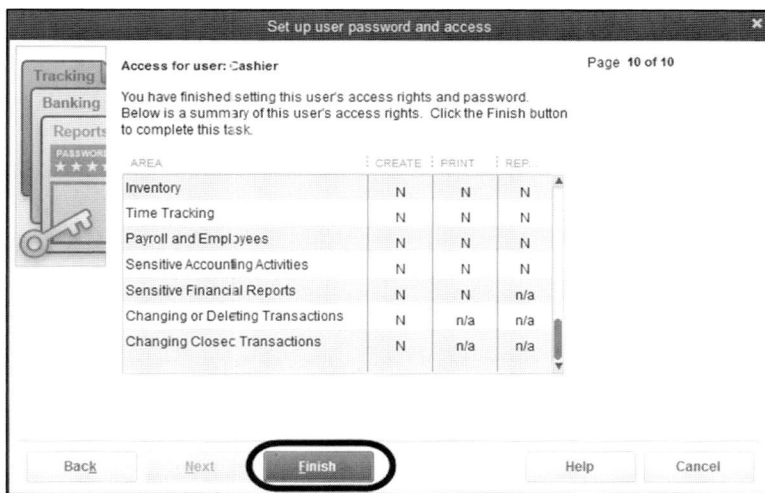

13.   Click [Finish].

14.   When the Warning window appears, read the information,

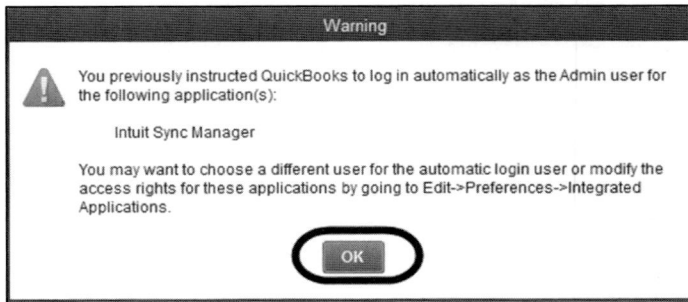

15. Click **OK**. Notice the User List now contains two user roles, Admin and Cashier.

16. Click **Close** to return to the QuickBooks desktop.

EXTERNAL ACCOUNTANT REVIEWS

When a company wants their external accountant to review accounting records, the accountant generally must physically visit the business. With QB Accountant features, a physical visit is no longer necessary and both the company and the accountant can continue to work simultaneously with the data. Company data can be shared with the accountant various ways. It can be shared using a CD or USB flash drive, or sent via e-mail as an attachment, or uploaded to a shared secure website. In this text, your Accountant is your professor. Periodically throughout the text, you will be sending your company files via e-mail to your professor. In other words, you will be submitting your work for grading purposes. For example, in Exercise 2-1 you will send an e-mail attachment to your professor.

AUDIT TRAIL

Software programs generally have an audit trail feature to keep track of users accessing the software, when they are using it, and what they are doing in the software. An audit trail is another internal control feature of QuickBooks which documents all business activities to keep company data safe. Periodically in this text, you will be printing your audit trail and submitting it to your professor to document your work. To create and view the audit trail of the sample product company, follow these steps.

1. From the Icon Bar, select ; Accountant & Taxes. Scroll down the Accountant & Taxes window. In the Account Activity area, select Audit Trail.

2. Click . If the Date Entered/Last Modified field shows Today, press on the keyboard to see all of the information on the report . A Building Report window appears, and the Audit Trial is shown. A partial Audit Trail is shown on the next page. Your Date column may differ. Review the

type of information the audit trail provides and how the report can be customized.

The Audit Trail report lists each accounting transaction and any additions, deletions, or modifications that affect that transaction. Any information about the transactions that has been changed is highlighted in *Bold Italic type* in the report. If there are multiple versions of a transaction, the earliest version will have no highlighting, but subsequent versions will highlight each value that differs from the previous version's value in that field by displaying the value in bold italics. If a line item was added to the transaction, that entire line of the report is highlighted.

3. To close the Audit Trail, click <X> on its title bar. Close the Report Center.

CHAPTER 2 DATA BACK UP

At the end of each chapter, the authors recommend that you backup. Backing up insures that you have data to restore if you make a mistake or are transporting your work between computer labs. For example, let's say you would like to start Sample Rock Castle Construction from the beginning. The backup made early this chapter, sample_product-based business (Portable).QBM, contains fresh, starting data. If you back up your work now and restore the backup file made below (Your Name Chapter 2 End (Portable).QBM), you can start the sample company from the end of this chapter.

1. From the menu bar, select File; Create Copy.

2. When the Save Copy or Backup window appears, select Portable company file.

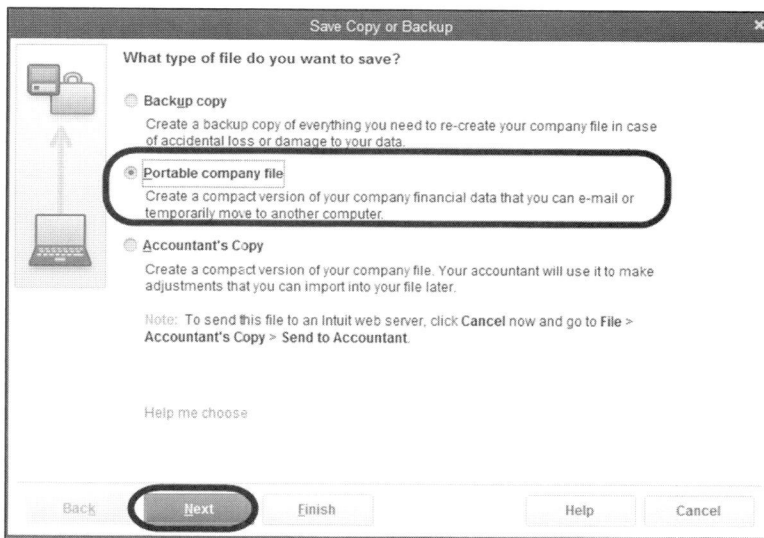

3. Click [Next]. Go to the location of your USB drive's Your Name QB Backups folder. Type **Your Name Chapter 2 End (Portable)** in the File name field, for example, your First and Last Name Chapter 2 End. The Save Portable Company File window is shown on the next page.

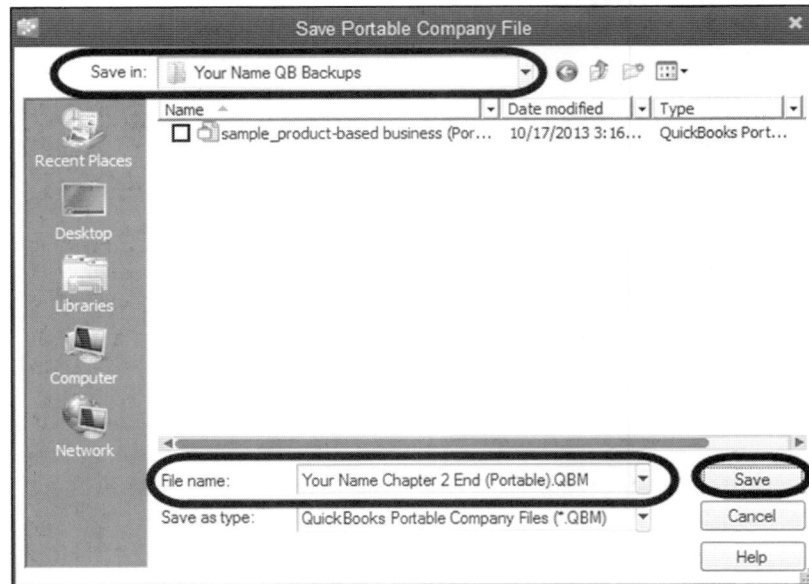

4. Click [Save]. Follow the screen prompts to back up. To return to Rock Castle's desktop, click [Home].

USING WINDOWS EXPLORER

The instructions that follow show you how to identify the QB program path, directories, and subdirectories on the hard drive of your computer. You also see the size of QB and its associated files and folders.

Follow these steps to use Windows Explorer to identify the QB location on your computer system.

1. If necessary, minimize QuickBooks 2014. Your Windows desktop should be displayed.

2. There are a different ways to go to Windows Explorer. If your desktop has a Windows Explorer folder [icon], click on it. *Or*, right click on the <Start> button, left-click Open Windows Explorer. Another way to launch Wndows Explorer is to go All Programs; Accessories, Windows Explorer.

3. Select drive C, then double-click on the Program Files (x86) folder to open it. (If you are using Vista, open the Program Files folder.) The address field shows Computer, Local Disk (C), Program Files (x86). Now open the Intuit folder so that the Address field shows Computer, Local Disk (C), Program Files (x86), Intuit. This is the location (program path) of QuickBooks 2014 on your computer.

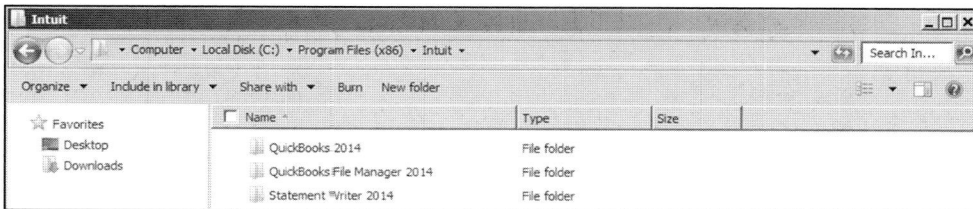

4. Right-click on the QuickBooks 2014 folder. A drop-down list appears. Left-click on Properties. The QuickBooks 2014 Properties window appears. Compare your QuickBooks 2014 Properties window to the one shown. Your files sizes may differ. The date shown in the Created field will also differ.

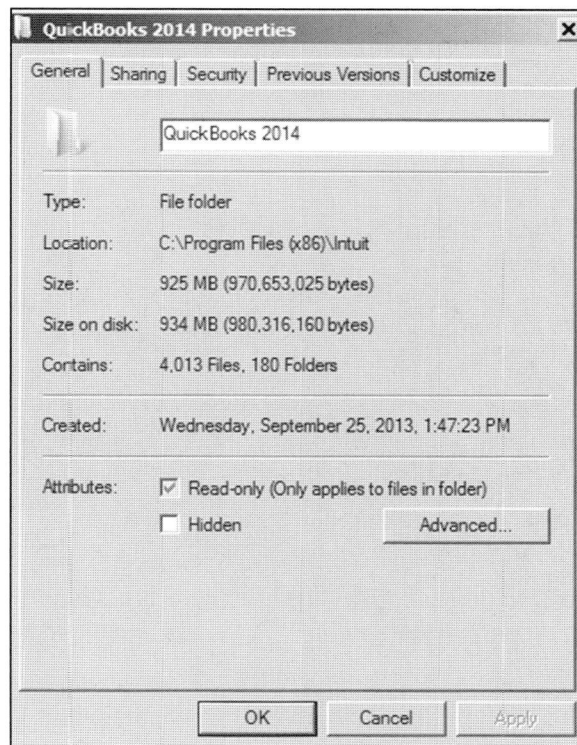

5.   Click [OK] to close the QuickBooks 2014 Properties window. Close Windows Explorer.

6.   Exit Sample Rock Castle Construction.

👓   **Read me: QuickBooks Login window requires password**

After exiting Sample Rock Castle Construction, I started QB and opened the company again. Why am I getting a QuickBooks Login window?

1.   Start QuickBooks. From the menu bar, select File, Open Previous Company, C:\Users\...\....\Your Name sample_product-based buisness.QBW. The QuickBooks Login window appears. *OR,* restore the Your Name Chapter 2 End (Portable).qbm file.

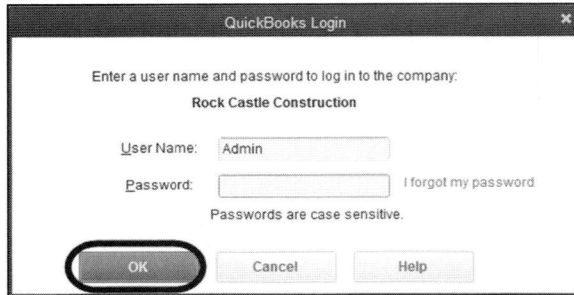

2.   Click <OK> and Sample Rock Castle Construction opens.

The authors suggest that you do <u>not</u> set up a password. Since you did set up a cashier role, the QuickBooks Login window appears. (*Hint:* Refer to Add User Roles, pages 52-58.

SUMMARY AND REVIEW

OBJECTIVES:

1.   Start QuickBooks 2014 (QB). If an Update Company window appears, refer to pages 271-272. The authors recommend installing the update.
2.   Open the sample product-based business,
3.   Backup and restore the sample business.
4.   Overview of QuickBooks 2014.

5.   Icon Bar and menu bar.
6.   Help, Preferences, and Product Information.
7.   Internal Control features.
8.   Using Windows Explorer.

RESOURCEFUL QUICKBOOKS

Read Me: Learning Center Tutorials.

1.   From the QuickBooks menu bar,
     Select Help; Learning Center
     Tutorials.
2.   The QuickBooks Learning Center
     window appears. Select

     New to
     QuickBooks?

Help	
QuickBooks Help	F1
Ask Intuit	
What's New	
Quick Start Center	
Find Training...	
Learning Center Tutorials	

3.   Watch the video, Getting Around in QuickBooks (3:40).
4.   Link to Using the home page.

From the Using the home page link, answer these questions.

1.   What does the Home page show?

2.   Is there a difference between the menus and Home page?

3.   What does the Icon Bar include?

4.   What selections do you use to customize the Home page?

5.   How do you go to centers?

Multiple Choice Questions: The Online Learning Center includes the multiple-choice questions at www.mhhe.com/QBessentials2014, select Student Edition, Chapter 2, Multiple Choice.

_____ 1. How do you check your software registration status?

      a. Select File; Restore previous backup.
      b. Select Edit; Preferences.
      c. Software is automatically registered.
      d. With company open, press <F2>.

_____ 2. What happens to the QuickBooks Student Trial Edition once the trial period expires?

      a. Becomes QuickBooks Online Edition.
      b. Becomes QuickBooks Basic Edition.
      c. Becomes QuickBooks Premier Edition.
      d. Becomes inoperable.

_____ 3. When using the sample companies today's date is set to:

      a. 12/15/2015.
      b. 12/15/2016.
      c. 12/15/2017.
      d. 12/15/2018.

_____ 4. QuickBooks Student Trial Edition can be backed up to:

      a. Hard drive.
      b. Network drive.
      c. External media.
      d. All of the above.

_____ 5. Back up files may be saved as:

      a. Back up copy.
      b. Portable company file.
      c. Accountant copy.
      d. All of the above.

_A_ 6. Which of the following appears on the Menu Bar:

    a. Help.
    b. Find.
    c. Search.
    d. Feedback.

_C_ 7. All of the following Centers appear on the Icon Bar except:

    a. Customer Center.
    b. Employee Center.
    c. Help Center.
    d. Vendor Center.

_B_ 8. The File menu contains all the following except:

    a. Exit.
    b. Preferences.
    c. Utilities.
    d. All of the above.

_D_ 9. The Edit menu contains all the following except:

    a. Use Register.
    b. Preferences.
    c. Use Calculator.
    d. List.

_A_ 10. The Reports menu contains all the following except:

    a. Loans.
    b. Purchases.
    c. Inventory.
    d. Budgets.

Short-answer questions: To answer these questions, go online to www.mhhe.com/QBessentials2014, link to Student Edition, Chapter 2, QA Templates. The analysis question on the next page is also included.

1. What are the names of the two sample businesses?

2. What is the purpose of Backup and Restore?

3. List eight Icon Bar selections for Sample Rock Castle Construction.

4. How can a user access QuickBooks Help?

5. Preferences can be customized two ways, list them.

6. List steps to display QuickBooks product information.

7. What rights and permissions does a QuickBooks Administrator have?

8. When a user is set up, list some of the access rights that can be granted.
9. Why is an audit trail important for good internal control?

10. What Windows program is used to view QuickBooks 2014 properties?

Exercise 2-1: Follow the instructions below to complete Exercise 2-1:

1. Start QB.[1] (*Hint:* If Rock Castle Construction is shown on your title bar, select File; Close Company).

2. Open the sample service-based business.

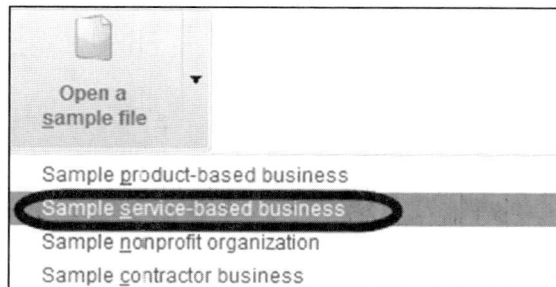

3. The QuickBooks Information window appears. Read it, then click
    OK . The title bar shows Sample Larry's Landscaping & Garden Supply - QuickBooks 2014.

4. Backup the sample service-based business to the USB drive folder named Your Name QB Backups. Select File; Create Copy. On the Save Copy or Backup window, select Portable company file. The suggested file name is **Your Name sample_service-based business**. Use your first and last name.

5. Exit or continue.

Exercise 2-2: Follow the instructions below to complete Exercise 2-2.

1. Start your e-mail program.

2. Create an e-mail message to your professor. Type **Your Name Chapter 2 End** for the Subject. (Use your first and last name.)

3. Attach the file you backed up on pages 61-62, **Your Name Chapter 2 End (Portable)**. Recall it is located on your USB drive. (*Hint:* If you

---

[1]If an Update Company window appears, refer to pages 271-272. The authors recommend installing the update.

created a password, remember to send to instructor. If you did <u>not</u> create a password, when the file is restored a QuickBooks Login window appears. Select | OK | to restore the file. Refer to the Read Me box on page 64.)

4. CC yourself on the message to be sure the message sends.

5. Send the message to your professor. You should receive a copy of it as well.

ANALYSIS QUESTION: Why is it important to set up user roles and permissions?

Chapter 3 — New Company Setup for a Merchandising Business

OBJECTIVES: In Chapter 3, you learn to:

1. Open company called Your Name Retailers Inc.
2. Set preferences.
3. Edit the chart of accounts.
4. Enter beginning balances.
5. Record check register entries.
6. Edit to correct an error.
7. Complete account reconciliation.
8. Display the trial balance.
9. Display the financial statements.
10. Make backup of work.[1]

Additional textbook related resources are on the textbook website at www.mhhe.com/QBessentials2014. The website includes chapter resources, including troubleshooting tips, online quizzes, QA templates, narrated PowerPoints, etc.

In this text you are the sole stockholder and manager of a merchandising corporation that sells inventory. Merchandising businesses are retail stores that resell goods and services.

In this chapter, you open your merchandising business called Your Name Retailers Inc. that you set up in Chapter 1. Then, you complete the accounting tasks for the month of October using your checkbook register and bank statement as source documents.

In accounting, you learn that source documents are used to show written evidence of a business transaction. In this chapter the source documents used are your checkbook register and bank statement.

---

[1]The chart in the Preface, page xii, shows the file name and size of each backup file. Refer to this chart for backing up data. Remember, you can back up to a hard drive location or external media.

GETTING STARTED

1.   Start QuickBooks 2014.[2]

2.   You should see Your Name Retailers Inc. on the title bar

> Your Name Retailers Inc. - QuickBooks Accountant 2014

   a.   If not, Select File; Close Company. From the No Company Open window, select Open or restore an existing company.

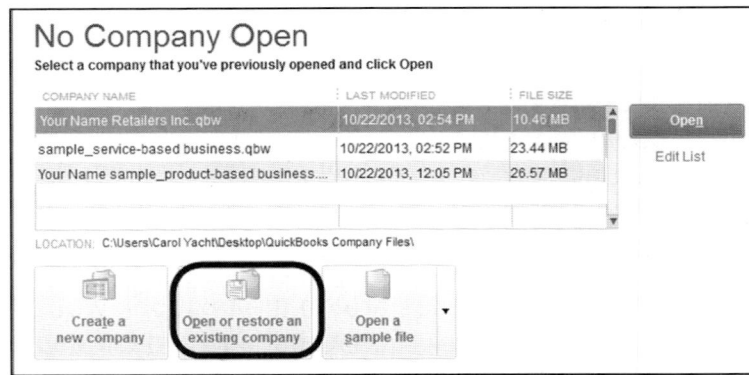

   b.   On the Open or Restore Company window, select Restore a backup copy. Go to the location of the Your Name Retailers Inc. backup file that you made in Chapter 1, pages 16-18.

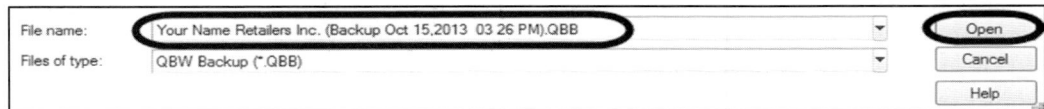

   c.   Click [Open]. In the Where do you want to restore the file? window, click [Next].

   d.   Rename Your Name Retailers Inc. to **Your Name Retailers Inc. Chapter 3** in the Save Company File window. (*Hint:* Company files have a .QBW extension.)

---

[2] If an Update Company window appears, refer to pages 271-272. The authors recommend installing the update.

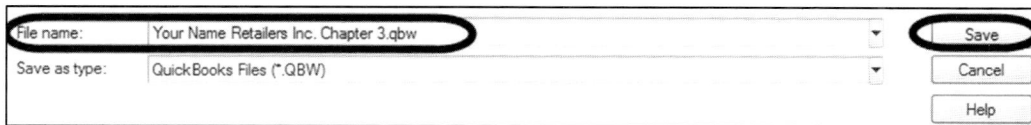

e. Click [Save]. When the screen prompts Your data has been restored successfully, click [OK]. The title bar shows Your Name Retailers Inc. - QuickBooks Accounting 2014.

COMPANY PREFERENCES

By setting **preferences**, you can customize QuickBooks to suit the needs of your business and personal style of working. Preferences allow you to configure the way in which some functions and keys work in QuickBooks. In the example that follows you set preferences for account numbers.

Follow these steps to set the company preferences for Your Name Retailers Inc.

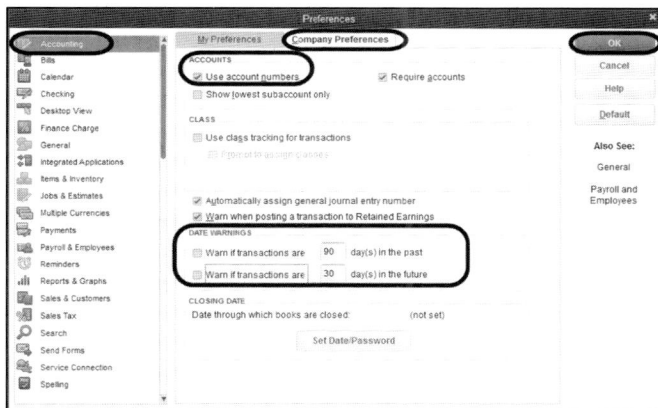

1. From the menu bar, select Edit; Preferences. Company Preferences tab and select Accounting.

2. Check the box next to Use account numbers. Uncheck the boxes next to Date Warnings. Compare your screen with the one shown here.

3. Click [OK].

4. From the menu bar, select Edit; Preferences. Click on My Preferences tab; Desktop View. Select a Color Scheme of your choice.

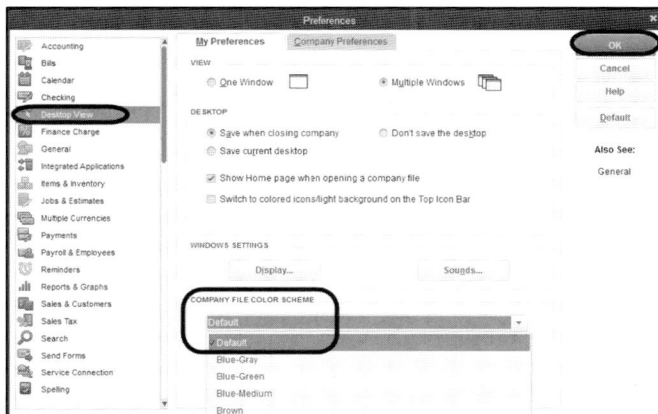

5. Click [OK].

6. Select Edit; Preferences. Click on My Preferences tab, Checking.
   Put a check mark next to Open the Write Checks form
   with…account, the Open the Pay Bills form with…account, and
   Open the Make Deposits form with…account. Make sure you have
   the three checkmarks shown below.

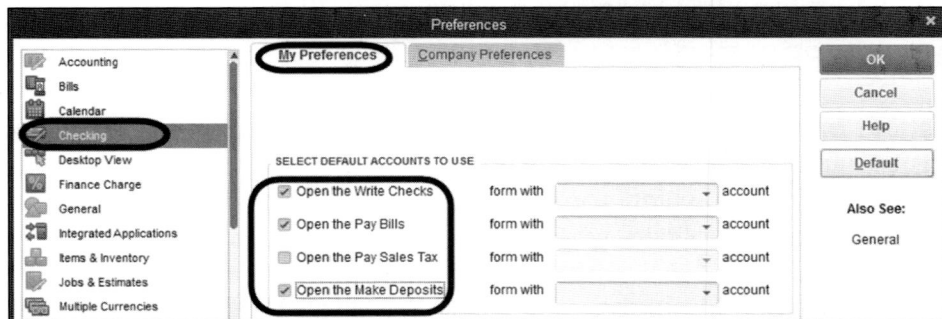

a. For Open the Write Checks form with….account, use the
   drop-down menu to select the **Home State Bank** account.

b. Use the drop-down menu to pick **Home State Bank** for Open
   the Pay Bills form with…account.

c. Use the drop-down menu to pick **Home State Bank** for Open
   the Make Deposits form with…account.

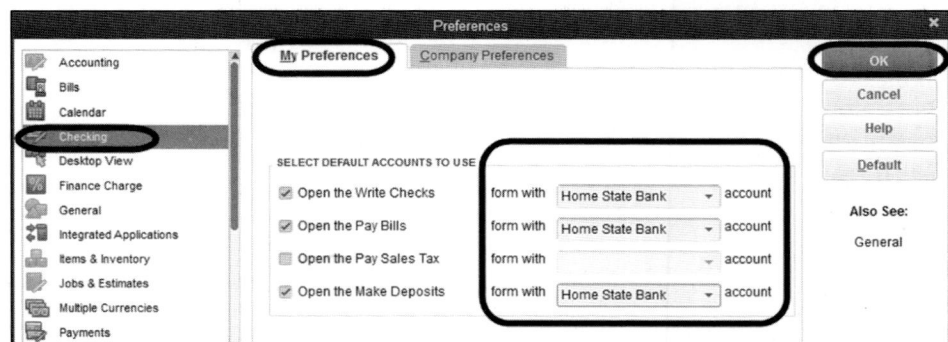

d. Make sure Home State Bank appears in the form with fields
   for Write Checks, Pay Bills, Make Deposits. Click
   [OK].

7.   Select Edit; Preferences. Click on My Preferences tab and select Send Forms. Uncheck box next to Auto-check the Email Later checkbox if customer's Preferred Delivery Method is e-email. In the Send E-Mail using section, select Web Mail Click [OK]. (Since the author has Outlook, that e-mail selection is shown.)

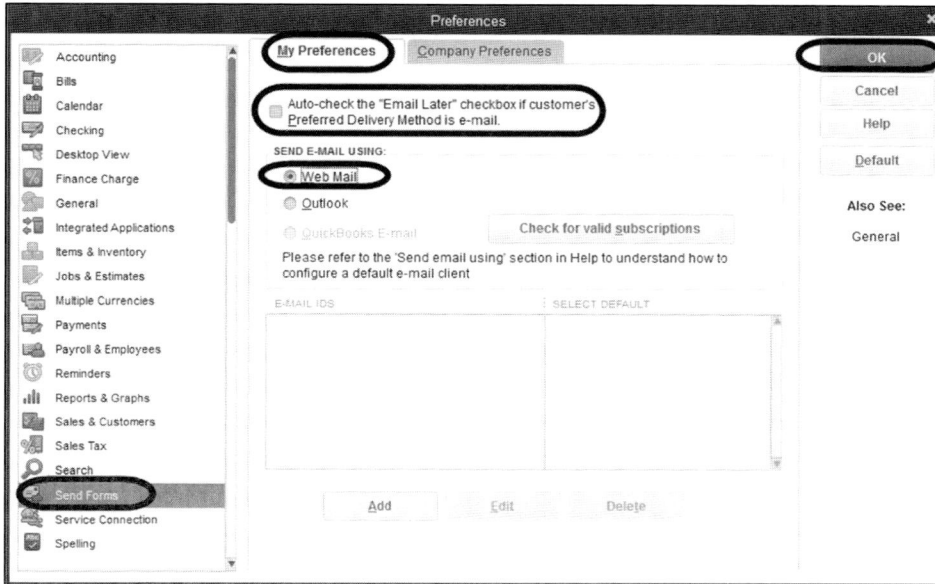

When the Warning window appears, read it, then click [OK]. Click [Home] to see the Home page.

CHART OF ACCOUNTS

Examine the Home page to learn there are many ways to access a company's chart of accounts. In accounting you learn that the ***chart of accounts*** is a list of all accounts in the company's general ledger. Notice you can click on the Home page's icon; use <Ctrl>+<A>; or from the menu bar, select Lists, Chart of Accounts; or Company, Chart of Accounts.

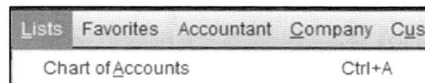

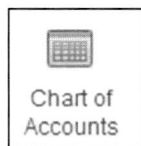

Lists	Favorites	Accountant	Company	Cust
Chart of Accounts			Ctrl+A	

1.   From Home page, click [Chart of Accounts].

2. The Chart of Accounts appears. If necessary, resize it so you can
    view all accounts. Notice all have 0.00 balance totals.

Follow these steps to add, edit, and change accounts.

Delete Accounts

Follow these steps to delete accounts.

1. Highlight Account No.
    48300, Sales Discounts.
    Right-click on the
    highlighted account,
    left-click Delete.

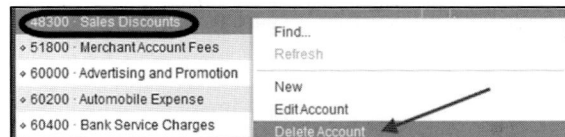

2. When the window prompts "Are you sure that you want to delete this
    account?," click [OK] Account No. 48300, Sales Discounts, is
    removed.

3. Your Name Retailers Inc. chart of accounts is extensive. For now, delete the accounts shown on the table below.

No.	Name
18700	Security Deposits Asset
63500	Janitorial Expense
64300	Meals and Entertainment
66700	Professional Fees
68500	Uniforms
80000	Ask My Accountant

Make Accounts Inactive

Follow these steps to make Account No. 24000, Payroll Liabilities, inactive.

1. Highlight Account No. 24000, Payroll Liabilities and right-click. Left-click Make Account Inactive.

2. Repeat step 1 to make Account 66000, Payroll Expenses inactive.

3. Check Include inactive box at bottom of the Chart of Accounts to reveal all inactive accounts. Notice inactive accounts have an X beside them.

| Account ▼ | Activities ▼ | Reports ▼ | Attach ☑ Include inactive |

◦ Home State Bank	Bank	0.00
◦ 15000 · Furniture and Equipment	Fixed Asset	0.00
◦ 17000 · Accumulated Depreciation	Fixed Asset	0.00
✗ ◦ 24000 · Payroll Liabilities	Other Current Liability	0.00
◦ 30000 · Opening Balance Equity	Equity	0.00
◦ 30100 · Capital Stock	Equity	0.00
◦ 30200 · Dividends Paid	Equity	0.00
◦ 32000 · Retained Earnings	Equity	
◦ 46000 · Merchandise Sales	Income	
◦ 51800 · Merchant Account Fees	Cost of Goods Sold	
◦ 60000 · Advertising and Promotion	Expense	
◦ 60200 · Automobile Expense	Expense	
◦ 60400 · Bank Service Charges	Expense	
◦ 61700 · Computer and Internet Expenses	Expense	
◦ 62400 · Depreciation Expense	Expense	
◦ 63300 · Insurance Expense	Expense	
◦ 63400 · Interest Expense	Expense	
◦ 64900 · Office Supplies	Expense	
✗ ◦ 66000 · Payroll Expenses	Expense	
◦ 67100 · Rent Expense	Expense	
◦ 67200 · Repairs and Maintenance	Expense	
◦ 68100 · Telephone Expense	Expense	
◦ 68600 · Utilities	Expense	

Change/Edit Accounts

Follow these steps to change or edit an account.

1. Right-click on Account No. 30000, Opening Balance Equity.

2. Left-click Edit Account.

3. Change the Account name field to **Common Stock**. Change Description field to **Common Stock par value.**

4. For Tax-Line Mapping select: B/S-Liabs/Eq.: Capital Stock-Common Stock.

5. Click [Save & Close]. Observe that Account No. 30000 name is Common Stock.

6. Change the following accounts.

No.	New Name	Change
30100	Paid in Capital	Description: Paid in Capital Tax-Line Mapping: B/S-Liabs/Eq.: Paid in or capital surplus.
30200	Dividends	
46000	Sales	
51800	Freight In	Description: FOB shipping
60000	Advertising and Promotion Exp.	
60400	Bank Service Charges Expense	
64900	Supplies Expense	Description: Supplies expense
67200	Repairs and Maintenance Expense	
68600	Utilities Expense	
10000	Home State Bank (*Hint:* In the Number field, type **10000**)	Description: Cash in bank Tax Line Mapping: B/S-Assets: Cash
17000	Accumulated Depreciation-F&E	Tax Line Mapping: B/S-Assets: Accumulated Depreciation

Add Accounts

1. To add Account No. 14000, Computer Equipment, click on the down-arrow next to Account, select New.

2. On the Add New Account: Choose Account Type window, select Fixed Asset (major purchases).

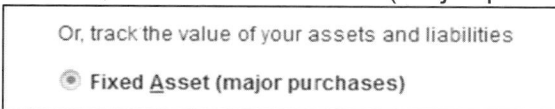

   Or, track the value of your assets and liabilities

   ⦿ Fixed Asset (major purchases)

3. Click [Continue]. The Add New Account window appears. In Number field, type **14000**, in Account Name field type **Computer Equipment**. For Description, type **Computer equipment.**

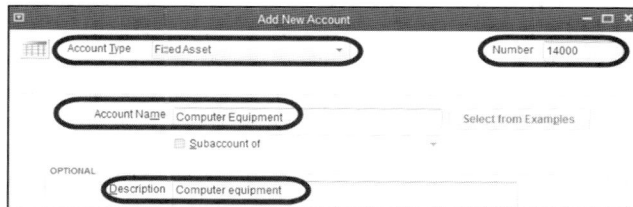

4. Click Save & New . Add the following accounts.

No.	Name	Account Type	Tax-Line Mapping
13000	Supplies	Other current asset	B/S-Assets: Other current assets
16000	Accumulated Depreciation-CEqmt.	Fixed asset	B/S-Assets: Accumulated Depreciation
18000	Prepaid Insurance	Other current asset	B/S-Assets: Other current assets
22000	Accounts Payable	Accounts Payable	B/S-Liabs/Eq.: Accounts payable
26000	Your Name Notes Payable	Long Term Liability	B/S-Liabs/Eq.: Loans from Stockholders

5. When done adding each account, click Save & Close .

6. View your chart of accounts list.

BEGINNING BALANCES

The *Balance Sheet* establishes the beginning balances as of October 1, 20XX (current year). In accounting you learn that a Balance Sheet lists the types and amounts of assets, liabilities, and equity as of a specific date. A balance sheet is also called a *statement of financial position*. Since QuickBooks asks you to enter the account balances on the day prior to your start date, the September 30 balance sheet is shown here.

Your Name Retailers Inc. Balance Sheet, September 30, 20XX (current year)		
ASSETS		
Current Assets:		
10000 - Home State Bank	$51,000.00	
Other Current Assets:		
13000 - Supplies	2,500.00	
18000 -Prepaid Insurance	2,500.00	
Total Current Assets		$56,000.00
Fixed Assets:		
14000 - Computer Equipment	1,000.00	
15000 - Furniture and Equipment	4,000.00	
Total Fixed Assets		5,000.00
Total Assets		$61,000.00
LIABILITIES AND STOCKHOLDERS' EQUITIES		
Long-Term Liabilities:		
26000 – Your Name Notes Payable	20,000.00	
Total Long-Term Liabilities		$20,000.00
Stockholders' Equities:		
30000 - Common Stock		41,000.00
Total Liabilities & Equities		$61,000.00

Follow the steps shown to enter opening balances for Your Name Retailers Inc. on September 30, 20XX, the day before your QuickBooks start date. If your chart of accounts is not on your desktop, click on the Chart of Accounts icon. Notice all accounts have 0.00 balance totals.

1. Right-click on Account No. 13000 Supplies.

2. Select Edit Account.

3. Click Enter Opening Balance... .

4. In Opening Balance field type **2,500.00** as of **09/30/20XX. (Use your current year)**.

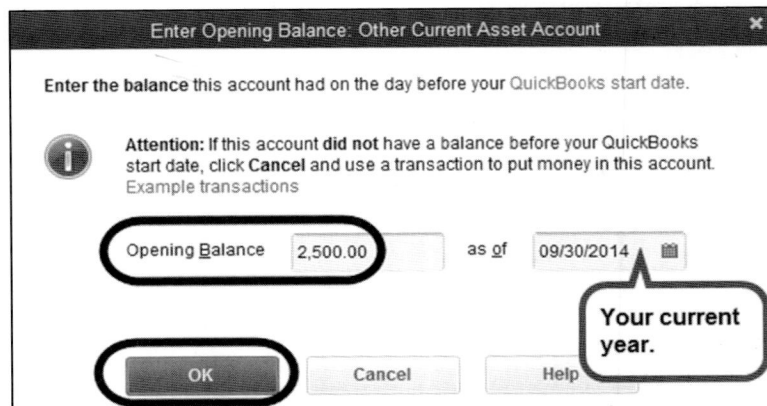

5. Click OK .

6. When returned to the Edit Account screen, click Save & Close .

7. Edit the following accounts to add their beginning balances:

No.	Name	Opening Balance as of 09/30/20XX
10000	Home State Bank	51,000.00
14000	Computer Equipment	1,000.00
15000	Furniture and Equipment	4,000.00
18000	Prepaid Insurance	2,500.00
26000	Your Name Notes Payable	20,000.00

8. Compare your chart of accounts to the one shown. Edit yours until it agrees.

NAME ▲	TYPE	BALANCE TOTAL	ATTACH
10000 · Home State Bank	Bank	51,000.00	
◆13000 · Supplies	Other Current Asset	2,500.00	
◆14000 · Computer Equipment	Fixed Asset	1,000.00	
◆15000 · Furniture and Equipment	Fixed Asset	4,000.00	
◆16000 · Accumulated Depreciation-CEqmt.	Fixed Asset	0.00	
◆17000 · Accumulated Depreciation-F&E	Fixed Asset	0.00	
◆18000 · Prepaid Insurance	Other Current Asset	2,500.00	
◆22000 · Accounts Payable	Accounts Payable	0.00	
◆24000 · Payroll Liabilities	Other Current Liability	0.00	
◆26000 · Your Name Notes Payable	Long Term Liability	20,000.00	
◆30000 · Common Stock	Equity	41,000.00	
◆30100 · Paid in Capital	Equity	0.00	
◆30200 · Dividends	Equity	0.00	
◆32000 · Retained Earnings	Equity		
◆46000 · Sales	Income		
◆51800 · Freight In	Cost of Goods Sold		
◆60000 · Advertising and Promotion Exp.	Expense		
◆60200 · Automobile Expense	Expense		
◆60400 · Bank Service Charges Expense	Expense		
◆61700 · Computer and Internet Expenses	Expense		
◆62400 · Depreciation Expense	Expense		
◆63300 · Insurance Expense	Expense		
◆63400 · Interest Expense	Expense		
◆64900 · Supplies Expense	Expense		
◆66000 · Payroll Expenses	Expense		
◆67100 · Rent Expense	Expense		
◆67200 · Repairs and Maintenance Expense	Expense		
◆68100 · Telephone Expense	Expense		
◆68600 · Utilities Expense	Expense		

Account ▼   Activities ▼   Reports ▼   Attach   ☑ Include inactive

October 1 Balance Sheet

To make sure that you have entered the October 1 balances correctly, display a balance sheet and compare it to the balance sheet on the previous page. Follow these steps to do that.

1. From the Icon Bar, click **Reports**. Company & Financial is selected.

    Scroll down the Report Center to the Balance Sheet & Net Worth area. Select Balance Sheet Standard. In the Dates field, type or select **10/1/20XX**. (*Hint:* Type your current year. The date appears in both fields.)

Balance Sheet & Net Worth

Balance Sheet Standard

Dates: Custom ▼

10/1/2014   10/1/2014

Run   Info   Fave   Help

2. Click [Run]. The Balance Sheet for October 1, 20XX (your current year) displays. Compare it to the one shown on page 81.

Balance Sheet		
Customize Report	Share Template	Memorize	Print ▼	E-mail ▼	Excel ▼	Hide Header	Collapse	Refresh

Dates Custom ▼   As of 10/01/2014 🛗   Columns Total only ▼   Sort By Default ▼

Your Name Retailers Inc.
Balance Sheet
As of October 1, 2014

	◇ Oct 1, 14 ◇
▼ASSETS	
▼ Current Assets	
▼ Checking/Savings	
10000 · Home State Bank	▶ 51,000.00 ◀
Total Checking/Savings	51,000.00
▼ Other Current Assets	
13000 · Supplies	2,500.00
18000 · Prepaid Insurance	2,500.00
Total Other Current Assets	5,000.00
Total Current Assets	56,000.00
▼ Fixed Assets	
14000 · Computer Equipment	1,000.00
15000 · Furniture and Equipment	4,000.00
Total Fixed Assets	5,000.00
TOTAL ASSETS	61,000.00
▼ LIABILITIES & EQUITY	
▼ Liabilities	
▼ Long Term Liabilities	
26000 · Your Name Notes Payable	20,000.00
Total Long Term Liabilities	20,000.00
Total Liabilities	20,000.00
▼ Equity	
30000 · Common Stock	41,000.00
Total Equity	41,000.00
TOTAL LIABILITIES & EQUITY	61,000.00

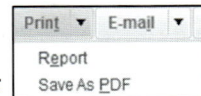

3. Click Print, then select either Report of Save as PDF [Print ▼ | E-mail ▼ / Report / Save As PDF]. If you Save as PDF, browse to your USB drive and name file: **Your Name October 1 BS.pdf.**

4. From the menu bar, select Window, Close All. Click [🏠 Home] to return to the Home page.

BACKUP BEGINNING COMPANY DATA

Follow these steps to backup Your Name Retailers Inc. October 1 data.

1. From menu bar, select File; Back Up Company, Create Local Backup. The Create Backup window appears

    > ◉ Local backup
    > Save locally to a removable storage device (such as a CD or USB flash drive) or to a folder on your network.

2. Make sure Local backup is selected. On the Create Backup window, select [Options].

3. The Backup Options window appears. Type your USB drive letter and create a folder labeled **Your Name Chapter 3**. (Substitute your drive letter for H and type your name.)

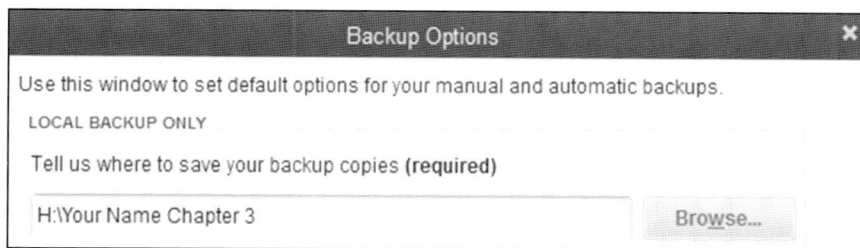

Backup Options	✕
Use this window to set default options for your manual and automatic backups.	
LOCAL BACKUP ONLY	
Tell us where to save your backup copies (required)	
H:\Your Name Chapter 3	Browse...

4. Click [OK]. When the screen prompts "The directory you have selected doesn't exist. Do you want to create it?," select [Yes]. On the Create Backup window select [Next].

5. Select Save it now to question, When do you want to save your

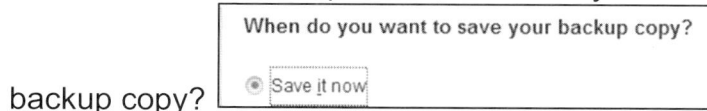

    > When do you want to save your backup copy?
    > ◉ Save it now

    backup copy?

6. Click [Next]. The Save Backup Copy window appears. In the File name field, type **Your Name Chapter 3 October 1**.

File name:	Your Name Chapter 3 October 1.QBB		Save
Save as type:	QBW Backup (*.QBB)		Cancel
			Help

7. Click [Save]. While the file is being backed up, a Working window appears. When the window prompts, QuickBooks has saved a backup of the company file . . . ., click [OK]. You are returned to the Home page.

ACCOUNT REGISTER

An account register for cash transactions is a listing of all deposits and checks. It is similar to your checkbook's transaction register. Your Name Retailers Inc. transaction register is shown here. Your Name Retailers Inc. writes checks and deposits manually in their checkbook and then records them in QuickBooks 2014.

Check Number	Date	Description of Transaction	Payment	Deposit	Balance
					51,000.00
	10/2	Deposit (Acct. No. 30000, Common Stock)		1,500.00	52,500.00
4002	10/4	The Business Store (Acct.14000, Computer Equipment) for computer storage	1,000.00		51,500.00
4003	10/25	Office Supply Store (Acct. No. 13000, Supplies)	200.00		51,300.00

In accounting, you learn that source documents are used to show written evidence of a business transaction. Examples of source documents are sales invoices, purchase invoices, and in this case, the checkbook's transaction register for the Home State Bank account.

Make Deposits

Follow these steps to use your checkbook's transaction register to record your October entries relating to cash.

1. On the Home page in the Banking section, notice there are task icons to record deposits, write checks, print checks, reconcile bank, and check register.

2. Since the first transaction is a deposit, click on the Record Deposits

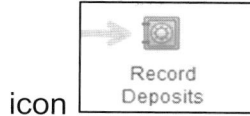

    icon

3. The Make Deposits window appears. For Deposit To, make sure Account No. 10000 Home State Bank is selected. Type **10/02/20XX** (your current year) as the Date. For From Account select **30000 Common Stock**. For Pmt Meth. select **Cash**. For Amount type **1500.00.**

4. For Received From select <Add New> . The Select Name Type window appears. In Select Name Type window pick **Other**

5. Click **OK** .

6. The New Name window appears. Type **Your Name, address,** and **phone number**.

7. Click **OK** .

8. The Received From field shows Your Name. Compare your Make Deposits screen with the one shown on the next page.

9. Click [Save & Close]. You are returned to the Home page.

10. Click on the icon for Check Register [Check Register].

11. Compare your Check Register to the one shown. Notice both the opening cash balance and the 10/2 deposit are shown. The updated cash balance in account 10000 is $52,500.00 which agrees with the checkbook's transaction register on page 86.

12.   Close the Check Register.

Write Checks for Assets

Follow these steps to record a purchase of computer storage.

1.   From the Home page, click on the Write Checks icon.

2.   The Write Checks window appears. The Bank Account field shows Account No. 10000, Home State Bank. Observe that the Ending Balance field shows $52,500. This is the same balance as on the checkbook's transaction register.

3.   Click on the Print Later box to uncheck it.

4.   Type **4002** in the No. field.

5.   Type **10/4/20XX (use your current year)** in the Date field.

6.   Type **1000** in the Amount field.

7.   In the Pay to the Order of field, select <Add New> . The Select Name Type window appears, pick Vendor and click **OK** .

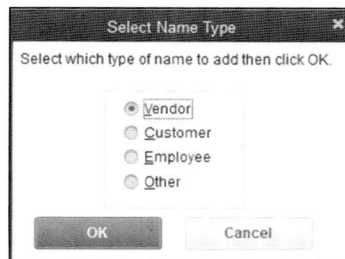

8.   The New Vendor wincow appears. Type **The Business Store** for Vendor Name, **0.00** for the Opening Balance as of **10/04/20XX.**

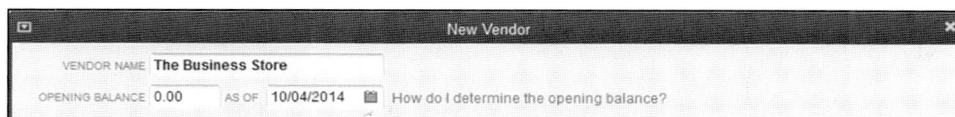

9.   Click **OK** . You are returned to the Write Checks window.

10.   In the Items and expenses table, Expenses should be selected. In the Account field, select Account No. 14000, Computer Equipment. In Memo field type **Computer storage.**

11.   Compare your Check window to the one shown here.

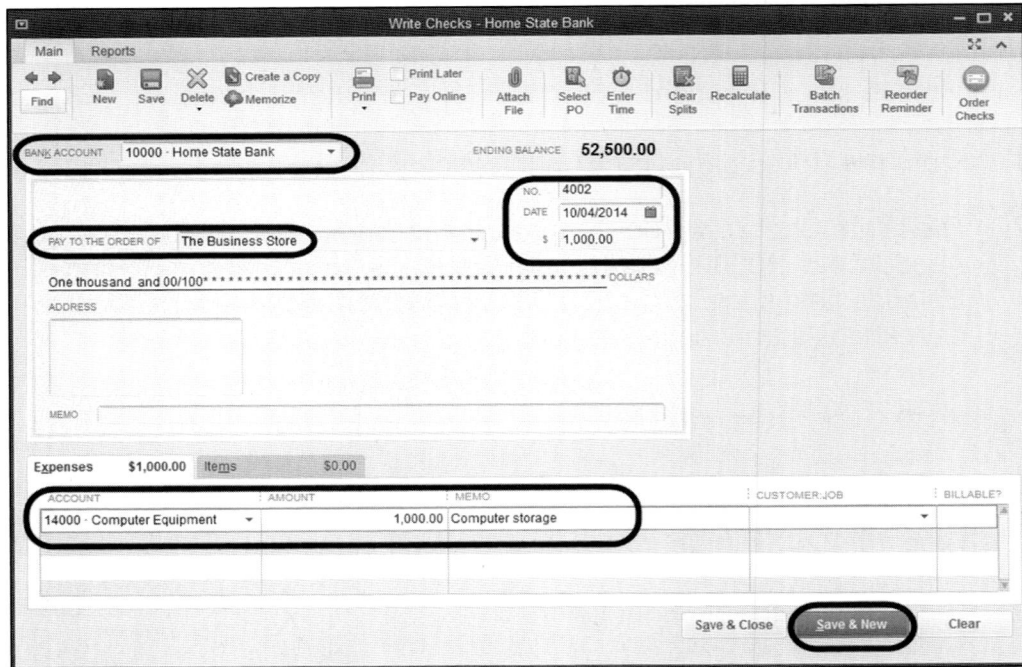

12.   Click **Save & New**. The Write Checks window is ready for the next transaction.

13.   In the Bank Account field Account No. 10000, Home State Bank should appear. If not, select it. Observe that the Ending Balance field shows $51,500.00. The same balance shown earlier in your checkbook's transaction register.

14.   The Print Later box should be unchecked.

15.   The No. field displays 4003.

16.   Type **10/25/20XX (use your current year)** in the Date field.

17.   Type **300** in the Amount field.

18.   In the Pay to field, type **The Office Supply Store**. Press <Tab>. When the Name Not Found window appears. Click **Quick Add**,

then select Vendor. Click OK . You are returned to the Write Checks window.

19. The Expenses tab should be selected. In the Account field, select Account No. 13000, Supplies. The Amount field should show 300.00. Type **Store Supplies** in the memo field.

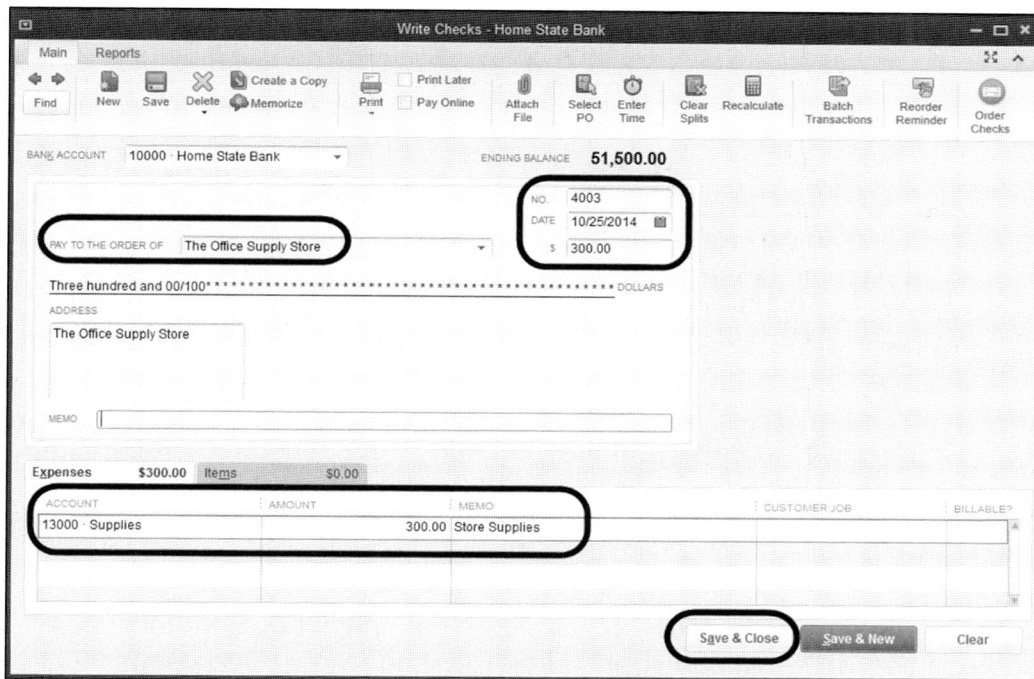

20. Click Save & Close .

Home State Bank Check Register

Periodically view the check register to confirm the account balance equals what is shown on the checkbook register and that there are no errors. To view the Check Register, follow these steps.

1. From the Banking section of the Home page, click Check Register .

2. The 10000 Home State Bank window appears.

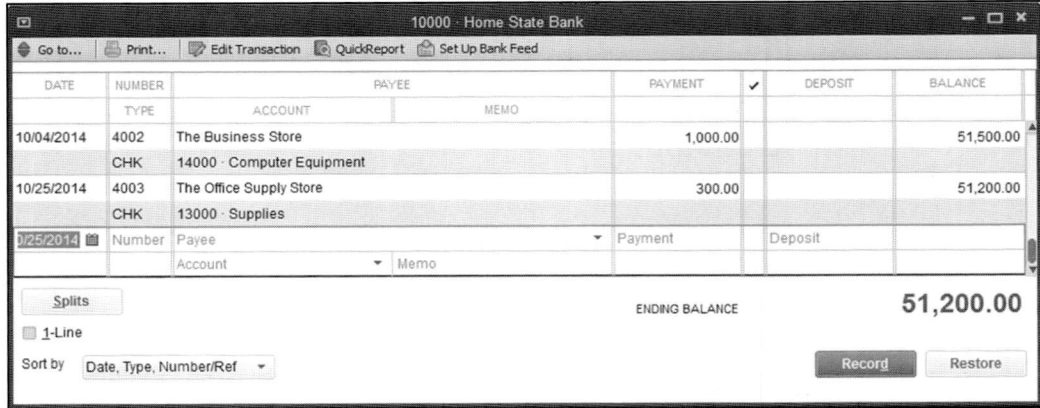

DATE	NUMBER	PAYEE		PAYMENT	✔	DEPOSIT	BALANCE
	TYPE	ACCOUNT	MEMO				
10/04/2014	4002	The Business Store		1,000.00			51,500.00
	CHK	14000 · Computer Equipment					
10/25/2014	4003	The Office Supply Store		300.00			51,200.00
	CHK	13000 · Supplies					
0/25/2014	Number	Payee		Payment		Deposit	
		Account	Memo				

Splits

ENDING BALANCE   **51,200.00**

☐ 1-Line

Sort by   Date, Type, Number/Ref ▾   Record   Restore

3. Compare the above check register to your checkbook's transaction register shown on page 86. Notice the balances are not the same. An error was made in writing check # 4003. The check was written incorrectly for $300 instead of $200.

4. To correct, you must void the check in your checkbook and edit the entry.

EDIT AN ENTRY

When you notice a mistake, you can void the check in your checkbook and edit the transaction in your Check Register. Since QuickBooks 2014 includes an audit trail, it tracks every transaction and shows when and how an entry was changed. You can view this audit trail using Menu Bar Reports; Accountant & Taxes, Audit Trail. When you void a check and edit a transaction, the audit trail shows the original entry (Prior) and the edited entry (Latest). Follow these steps to correct the error.

1. You should be viewing the Check Register. If not, from the Banking section of the Home page, click on Check Register icon.

2. Using the mouse, click on the 10/25 transaction. Click on ☑ **Edit Transaction** . This takes you to the original 10/25 entry. To edit the entry, type the correct check No. **4004** and amount **200.00** over the incorrect entries (*HINT:* Press <Tab> to move between fields.)

4003 4004	10/25	Office Supply Store (Acct. No. 13000, Store Supplies)	200.00		51,300.00

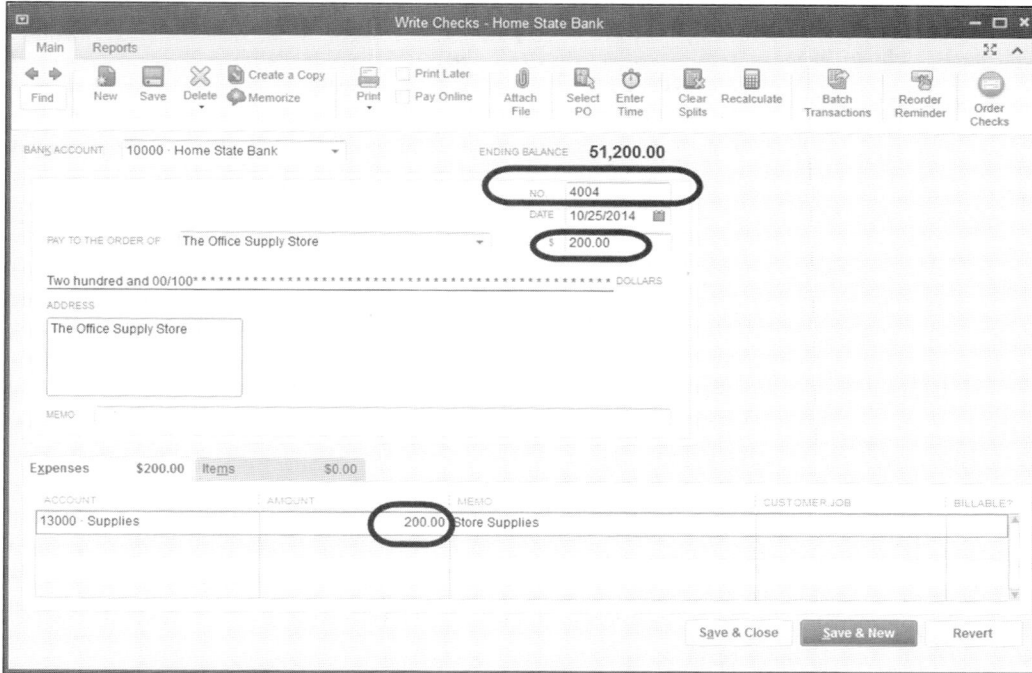

3. Make sure the 10/25 check has been edited. Click Save & Close . The Recording Transaction window appears. Read the information.

4. Click Yes . You are returned to the Check Register. Notice Home State Bank balance is now $51,300.00.

5. Close the Check Register.

6. To view the audit trail of this edit, go to the Report Center or the Reports menu; select Accountant & Taxes, Audit Trail (Dates: All).

Notice edited check 4003 is not in bold and its State is labeled Prior, meaning it has been replaced.

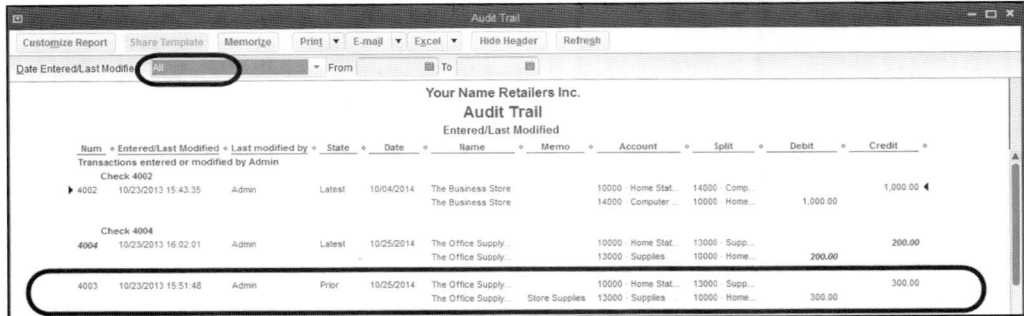

7. Close the Audit Trail. Do not memorize the report.

Write Check for Dividends

Follow these steps to record the payment of a cash dividend to the sole stockholder, Your Name. Your register states:

4005	10/30	Your Name (Acct. No. 30200 Dividends)	200.00		51,100.00

1. Select [Write Checks].

2. The Bank Account field shows Account No. 10000, Home State Bank. Observe that the Ending Balance field shows $51,300, the same as the checkbook's transaction register. The Print Later box should be unchecked.

3. Type **4005** in the No. field.

4. Type **10/30/20XX (use your current year)** in the Date field.

5. Type **200** in the Amount field.

6. In the Pay to field, type **Your Name**. Press <Tab>.

7. The Expenses tab should be selected. For the Account, select Account No. 30200, Dividends.

8. In Memo field type **Cash dividend to stockholder.**

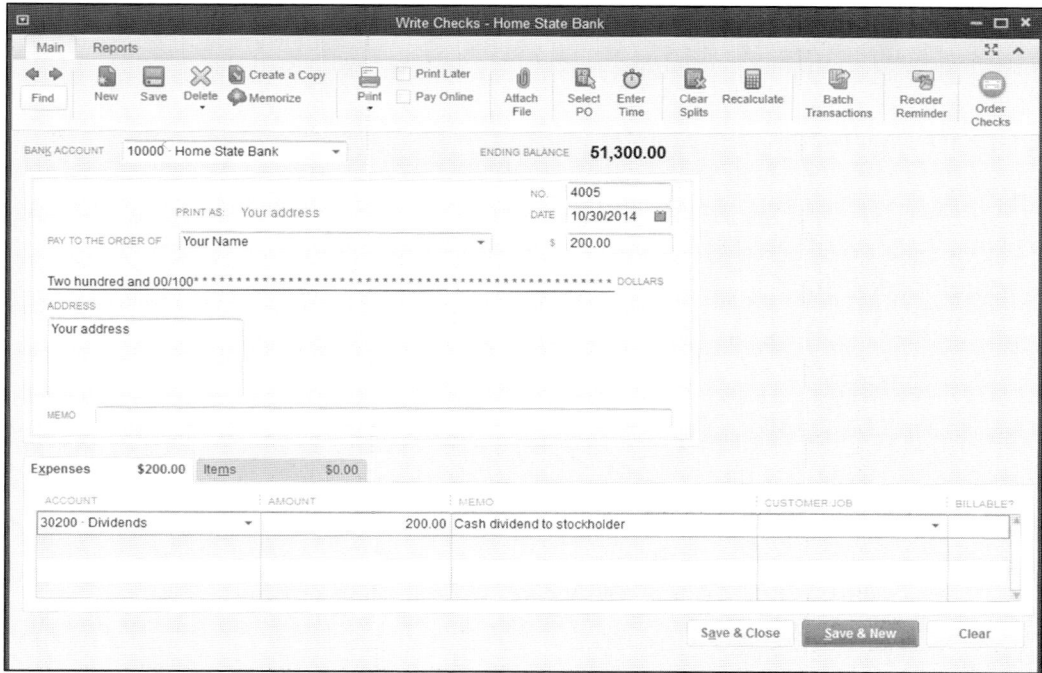

9. Click [S̲ave & Close]. You are returned to the Home page.

BACKUP THE OCTOBER CHECK REGISTER

Before you complete account reconciliation, back up your data.

1. From menu bar, select File; Backup Up Company, Create Local Backup.

2. Create a local backup and click [**Next**].

3. Select Save it now, click [**Next**].

4. Browse to your USB drive to Your Name Chapter 3 folder and name file **Your Name Chapter 3 October Check Register.** Click [Save].

5. When the window prompts, QuickBooks has saved a backup of the company file...., click **OK**.

6. Exit QuickBooks 2014 or continue to the next section.

ACCOUNT RECONCILIATION

You receive a bank statement every month for your Home State Bank account (Account No. 10000) which shows the checks and deposits that have cleared the bank. Your bank statement for Home State Bank Account is shown here.

Statement of Account		Your Name Retailers	
Home State Bank		Your address	
October 1 to October 31 Account # 923-121368			
		Reno, NV	
REGULAR HOME STATE BANK			
Previous Balance		$ 51,000.00	
1 Deposits (+)		1,500.00	
2 checks (-)		1,200.00	
Service Charges (-)	10/31	10.00	
Ending Balance	10/31	**$51,290.00**	
DEPOSITS			
	10/4	1,500.00	
CHECKS (Asterisk * indicates break in check number sequence)			
	10/5	4002	1,000.00	
	10/30	4005*	200.00	

Follow these steps to reconcile your bank statement balance to Account No. 10000, Home State Bank.

1. In the Banking section of the Home page, click **Reconcile** .

2. The Begin Reconciliation window appears. If necessary, in the Account field, select **10000, Home State Bank**.

3. Type **10/31/20XX (use your current year)** in the Statement Date field.

4. Confirm 51,000.00 appears as the Beginning Balance.

5. Type **51290.00** in the Ending Balance field.

6. In Service Charge field, type **10.00** for amount and **10/31/20XX** for Date and select account **60400 Bank Service Charge Expense**.

7. Compare your Begin Reconciliation window to the one shown here. (*Hint:* Your year may differ, as well as the date in the Interest Earned field.)

	Begin Reconciliation	✕

Select an account to reconcile, and then enter the ending balance from your account statement.

Account   10000 · Home State Bank   ▾

Statement Date   10/31/2014 📅
Beginning Balance   51,000.00   What if my beginning balance doesn't match my statement?
Ending Balance   51,290.C0

Enter any service charge or interest earned.

Service Charge   Date   Account
10.00   10/31/2014 📅   60400 · Bank Service Charges Expe ▾

Interest Earned   Date   Account
0.00   09/30/2013 📅   ▾

| Locate Discrepancies | Undo Last Reconciliation | Continue | Cancel | Help |

8. Click [**Continue**]. The Reconcile – Home State Bank window appears.

9. Click on the rows next to the checks and deposits that have cleared the bank. Make sure the checks that have *not* cleared the bank remain unchecked; for example, Check No. 4004 should *not* be checked.

10. Compare your Reconcile Account – Home State Bank window to the one shown on the next page. Notice the Difference is 0.00. (*Hint:* Only Reconcile if Difference is 0.00!)

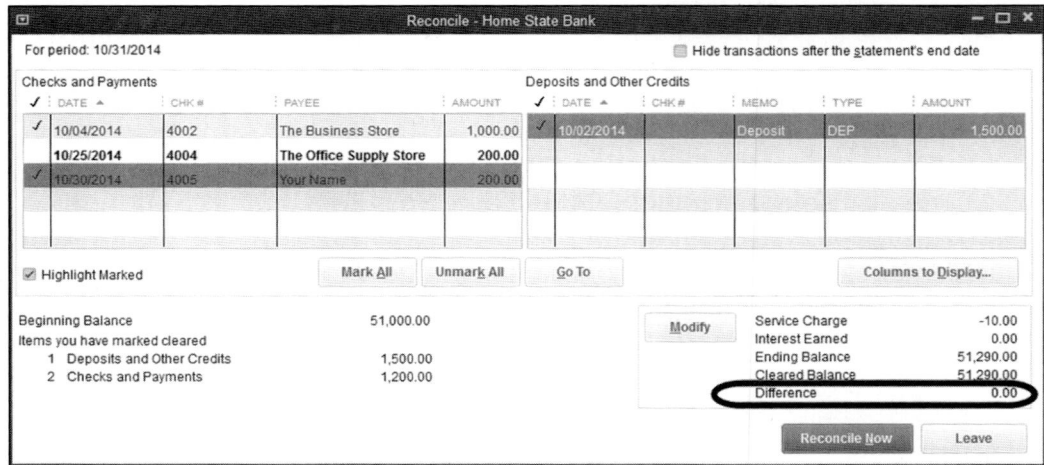

11. Click **Reconcile Now**. (When the Information window appears, read it, then click <OK>.) The Select Reconciliation Report window appears. Display both the summary and detail reports.

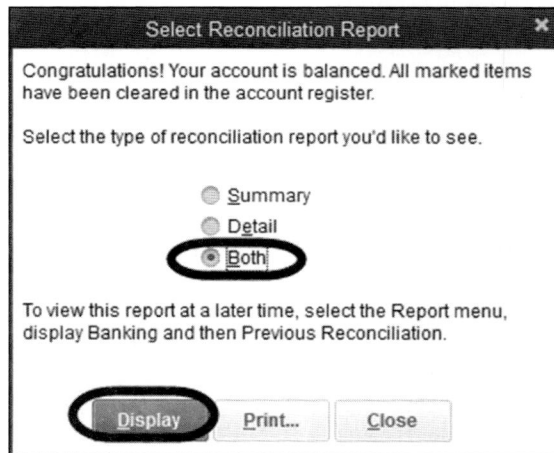

12. Click **Display**. (Select <OK> to the message.) The Reconciliation Summary report appears. Both the Reconciliation Detail and the Reconciliation Summary report display. If necessary, move them around your screen. Compare your Reconciliation Detail report with the one shown on the next page.

Your Name Retailers Inc.
Reconciliation Detail
10000 · Home State Bank, Period Ending 10/31/2014

Type	◇	Date	◇	Num	◇	Name	◇ Clr ◇	Amount	◇	Balance	◇
Beginning Balance										51,000.00	
Cleared Transactions											
Checks and Payments - 3 items											
▶ Check		10/04/2014		4002		The Business Store	✓	-1,000.00		-1,000.00 ◀	
Check		10/30/2014		4005		Your Name	✓	-200.00		-1,200.00	
Check		10/31/2014					✓	-10.00		-1,210.00	
Total Checks and Payments								-1,210.00		-1,210.00	
Deposits and Credits - 1 item											
Deposit		10/02/2014					✓	1,500.00		1,500.00	
Total Deposits and Credits								1,500.00		1,500.00	
Total Cleared Transactions								290.00		290.00	
Cleared Balance								290.00		51,290.00	
Uncleared Transactions											
Checks and Payments - 1 item											
Check		10/25/2014		4004		The Office Supply...		-200.00		-200.00	
Total Checks and Payments								-200.00		-200.00	
Total Uncleared Transactions								-200.00		-200.00	
Register Balance as of 10/31/2014								90.00		51,090.00	
Ending Balance								90.00		51,090.00	

13. Compare your Reconciliation Summary window to the one shown.

Your Name Retailers Inc.
Reconciliation Summary
10000 · Home State Bank, Period Ending 10/31/2014

	◇	Oct 31, 14	◇
Beginning Balance		51,000.00	
▼ Cleared Transactions			
Checks and Payments - 3 items		-1,210.00	
Deposits and Credits - 1 item		1,500.00	
Total Cleared Transactions		290.00	
Cleared Balance		**51,290.00**	
▼ Uncleared Transactions			
Checks and Payments - 1 item		-200.00	
Total Uncleared Transactions		-200.00	
Register Balance as of 10/31/2014		**51,090.00**	
Ending Balance	▶	**51,090.00** ◀	

14. Close the reports.

You have successfully completed your transactions for October. Now let's look at how these transactions were debited and credited.

PRINTING THE JOURNAL

To see the journal, follow these steps.

1. From the Report Center or Reports menu, select Accountant & Taxes, Journal. If the Collapsing and Expanding window appears, click <OK>.

2. For the Date, type **9/30/20XX** to **10/31/20XX**. If necessary, click
   Refresh. (*Hint:* If you select Reports from the Icon Bar to go to the Report Center, after typing or selecting dates, click <Run>. If you go to Reports from the menu bar, after typing the date range, select <Refresh>).

Your Name Retailers Inc.
Journal
September 30 through October 31, 2014

Trans #	Type	Date	Num	Adj	Name	Memo	Account	Debit	Credit
1	Deposit	09/30/2014				Account Op...	13000 · Supplies	2,500.00	
						Account Op...	30000 · Common S...		2,500.00
								2,500.00	2,500.00
2	Deposit	09/30/2014				Account Op...	10000 · Home Stat...	51,000.00	
						Account Op...	30000 · Common S...		51,000.00
								51,000.00	51,000.00
3	General Journal	09/30/2014	1			Account Op...	14000 · Computer ...	1,000.00	
						Account Op...	30000 · Common S...		1,000.00
								1,000.00	1,000.00
4	General Journal	09/30/2014	2			Account Op...	15000 · Furniture a...	4,000.00	
						Account Op...	30000 · Common S...		4,000.00
								4,000.00	4,000.00
5	Deposit	09/30/2014				Account Op...	18000 · Prepaid In...	2,500.00	
						Account Op...	30000 · Common S...		2,500.00
								2,500.00	2,500.00
6	General Journal	09/30/2014	3			Account Op...	26000 · Your Nam...		20,000.00
						Account Op...	30000 · Common S...	20,000.00	
								20,000.00	20,000.00
7	Deposit	10/02/2014				Deposit	10000 · Home Stat...	1,500.00	
					Your Name	Deposit	30000 · Common S...		1,500.00
								1,500.00	1,500.00
8	Check	10/04/2014	4002		The Business Store		10000 · Home Stat...		1,000.00
					The Business Store	Computer st...	14000 · Computer ...	1,000.00	
								1,000.00	1,000.00
9	Check	10/25/2014	4004		The Office Supply...		10000 · Home Stat...		200.00
					The Office Supply...	Store Supplies	13000 · Supplies	200.00	
								200.00	200.00
10	Check	10/30/2014	4005		Your Name		10000 · Home Stat...		200.00
					Your Name	Cash dividen...	30200 · Dividends	200.00	
								200.00	200.00
11	Check	10/31/2014				Service Cha...	10000 · Home Stat...		10.00
						Service Cha...	60400 · Bank Serv...	10.00	
								10.00	10.00
TOTAL								83,910.00	83,910.00

The first six transactions are the beginning balances that you
entered from the October 1 balance sheet earlier in the chapter.
Scroll down the Transaction Detail report to see all of it. Notice the
edited transaction does not appear.

3.   Close the Journal report. Do not memorize the report.

TRANSACTION DETAIL BY ACCOUNT

Transaction Detail by Account report is similar to a general ledger (GL).
For purposes of seeing each account balance, follow the steps below to
display the Transaction Detail by Account report.

1.   From the Report Center or Reports menu, select Accountant &
Taxes, Transaction Detail by Account.

2.   The date range is 9/30/20XX to 10/31/20XX. Scroll down the report
to see all the accounts. A partial Transaction Detail by Account
report is shown. (*Hint:* Use current year.)

Your Name Retailers Inc.
Transaction Detail by Account
September 30 through October 31, 2014

Type	Date	Num	Adj	Name	Memo	Clr	Split	Debit	Credit	Balance
10000 · Home State Bank										
Deposit	09/30/2014				Account Op...	✓	30000 · Comm...	51,000.00		51,000.00
Deposit	10/02/2014				Deposit	✓	30000 · Comm...	1,500.00		52,500.00
Check	10/04/2014	4002		The Business Store		✓	14000 · Comp...		1,000.00	51,500.00
Check	10/25/2014	4004		The Office Supply...			13000 · Supp...		200.00	51,300.00
Check	10/30/2014	4005		Your Name		✓	30200 · Divid...		200.00	51,100.00
Check	10/31/2014				Service Cha...	✓	60400 · Bank...		10.00	51,090.00
Total 10000 · Home State Bank								52,500.00	1,410.00	51,090.00
13000 · Supplies										
Deposit	09/30/2014				Account Op...	✓	30000 · Comm...	2,500.00		2,500.00
Check	10/25/2014	4004		The Office Supply...	Store Supplies		10000 · Home...	200.00		2,700.00
Total 13000 · Supplies								2,700.00	0.00	2,700.00
18000 · Prepaid Insurance										
Deposit	09/30/2014				Account Op...	✓	30000 · Comm...	2,500.00		2,500.00
Total 18000 · Prepaid Insurance								2,500.00	0.00	2,500.00
14000 · Computer Equipment										
General Journal	09/30/2014	1			Account Op...	✓	30000 · Comm...	1,000.00		1,000.00
Check	10/04/2014	4002		The Business Store	Computer st...		10000 · Home...	1,000.00		2,000.00
Total 14000 · Computer Equipment								2,000.00	0.00	2,000.00
15000 · Furniture and Equipment										
General Journal	09/30/2014	2			Account Op...	✓	30000 · Comm...	4,000.00		4,000.00
Total 15000 · Furniture and Equipment								4,000.00	0.00	4,000.00
26000 · Your Name Notes Payable										
General Journal	09/30/2014	3			Account Op...	✓	30000 · Comm...		20,000.00	-20,000.00
Total 26000 · Your Name Notes Payable								0.00	20,000.00	-20,000.00
30000 · Common Stock										
Deposit	09/30/2014				Account Op...			13000 · Supp...		2,500.00	-2,500.00
Deposit	09/30/2014				Account Op...			10000 · Home...		51,000.00	-53,500.00
General Journal	09/30/2014	1			Account Op...			14000 · Comp...		1,000.00	-54,500.00
General Journal	09/30/2014	2			Account Op...			15000 · Furn...		4,000.00	-58,500.00
Deposit	09/30/2014				Account Op...			18000 · Prep...		2,500.00	-61,000.00
General Journal	09/30/2014	3			Account Op...			26000 · Your...	20,000.00		-41,000.00
Deposit	10/02/2014			Your Name	Deposit			10000 · Home...		1,500.00	-42,500.00
Total 30000 · Common Stock								20,000.00	62,500.00	-42,500.00

3. Close the report. Do not memorize it.

TRIAL BALANCE

To display Your Name Retailers' trial balance follow these steps.

1. From the Report Center or Reports menu, select Accountant &
   Taxes, Trial Balance.

2. The date range is 9/30/20XX (current year) to 10/31/20XX. Compare
   your Trial Balance with the one shown. (*Hint:* Remember to use
   current year.)

Your Name Retailers Inc.
Trial Balance
As of October 31, 2014

	Oct 31, 14	
	◇ Debit ◇	Credit ◇
10000 · Home State Bank	▶ 51,090.00 ◀	
13000 · Supplies	2,700.00	
18000 · Prepaid Insurance	2,500.00	
14000 · Computer Equipment	2,000.00	
15000 · Furniture and Equipment	4,000.00	
26000 · Your Name Notes Payable		20,000.00
30000 · Common Stock		42,500.00
30200 · Dividends	200.00	
60400 · Bank Service Charges Expense	10.00	
TOTAL	62,500.00	62,500.00

3. Close the Trial Balance without saving or memorizing.

FINANCIAL STATEMENTS

To display Your Name Retailers' balance sheet follow these steps.

1. From the Report Center or Reports menu, select Company &
   Financial, Profit and Loss Standard.

2. The date range is 10/1/20XX (use current year) to 10/31/20XX.

```
                Your Name Retailers Inc.
                    Profit & Loss
                     October 2014
                                        ◇ Oct 14 ◇
    ▼ Expense
        60400 · Bank Service Charges Expense ▶  10.00 ◀
        Total Expense                           10.00

    Net Income                                 -10.00
```

3. Close the profit and loss without saving or memorizing.

4. From the Report Center or Reports menu, select Company &
    Financial, Balance Sheet Standard. The report date is **10/31/20XX**.

```
                Your Name Retailers Inc.
                    Balance Sheet
                 As of October 31, 2014
                                        ◇ Oct 31, 14 ◇
    ASSETS
    Current Assets
        Checking/Savings
            10000 · Home State Bank        ▶  51,090.00 ◀
        Total Checking/Savings                51,090.00

        Other Current Assets
            13000 · Supplies                   2,700.00
            18000 · Prepaid Insurance          2,500.00
        Total Other Current Assets             5,200.00

    Total Current Assets                      56,290.00

    Fixed Assets
        14000 · Computer Equipment            2,000.00
        15000 · Furniture and Equipment       4,000.00
    Total Fixed Assets                        6,000.00

    TOTAL ASSETS                             62,290.00

    ▼ LIABILITIES & EQUITY
    ▼ Liabilities
        ▼ Long Term Liabilities
            26000 · Your Name Notes Payable  20,000.00
            Total Long Term Liabilities      20,000.00

        Total Liabilities                    20,000.00

    ▼ Equity
        30000 · Common Stock                 42,500.00
        30200 · Dividends                      -200.00
        Net Income                             -10.00
        Total Equity                         42,290.00

    TOTAL LIABILITIES & EQUITY               62,290.00
```

5. Close the balance sheet without saving or memorizing.

6. From the Company & Financial menu, select Statement of Cash Flow. The date range is 10/01/20XX to 10/31/20XX **(use your current year)**.

Your Name Retailers Inc.

Statement of Cash Flows

October 2014

	◇ Oct 14 ◇
▼ OPERATING ACTIVITIES	
Net Income	▶ -10.00 ◀
▼ Adjustments to reconcile Net Income	
▼ to net cash provided by operations:	
13000 · Supplies	-200.00
Net cash provided by Operating Activities	-210.00
▼ INVESTING ACTIVITIES	
14000 · Computer Equipment	-1,000.00
Net cash provided by Investing Activities	-1,000.00
▼ FINANCING ACTIVITIES	
30000 · Common Stock	1,500.00
30200 · Dividends	-200.00
Net cash provided by Financing Activities	1,300.00
Net cash increase for period	90.00
Cash at beginning of period	51,000.00
Cash at end of period	51,090.00

---

7. Close reports without saving or memorizing.

BACKUP CHAPTER 3 DATA

Before completing the end-of-chapter exercises, follow these steps to backup Chapter 3 data.

1. From menu bar, select File; Backup Company, Create Local Backup.

2. Create a local backup and click [Next].

3. Select Save it now and click Next.

4. Browse to your USB drive to Your Name Chapter 3 folder and name file **Your Name Chapter 3 October End.** Click Save.

5. When the window prompts, QuickBooks has saved a backup of the company file…., click OK.

6. Exit QuickBooks 2014 or continue to the next section.

SUMMARY AND REVIEW

OBJECTIVES: In Chapter 3, you used the software to:

1. Open company called Your Name Retailers Inc.
2. Set preferences.
3. Edit the chart of accounts.
4. Enter beginning balances.
5. Record check register entries.
6. Edit to correct an error.
7. Complete account reconciliation.
8. Display the trial balance.
9. Display the financial statements.
10. Make backup of work.[3]

Additional textbook related resources are on the textbook website at www.mhhe.com/QBessentials2014. It includes chapter resources, including troubleshooting tips, narrated PowerPoints, QA Templates, online quizzes, etc.

[3]The chart in the Preface shows you the size of each backup file. Refer to this chart for backing up data. Remember, you can back up to a hard drive location or external media.

RESOURCEFUL QUICKBOOKS

Read Me: QuickBooks Learning Center Tutorials

Access the QuickBooks Tutorials: From the menu bar, Select Help; Learning Center Tutorials.

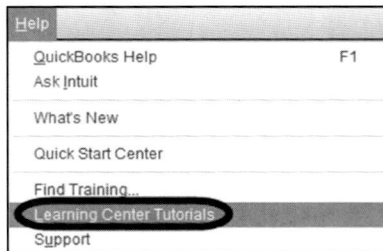

Help	
QuickBooks Help	F1
Ask Intuit	
What's New	
Quick Start Center	
Find Training...	
Learning Center Tutorials	
Support	

Watch the QuickBooks Learning Center video tutorials about Reports (2:03).

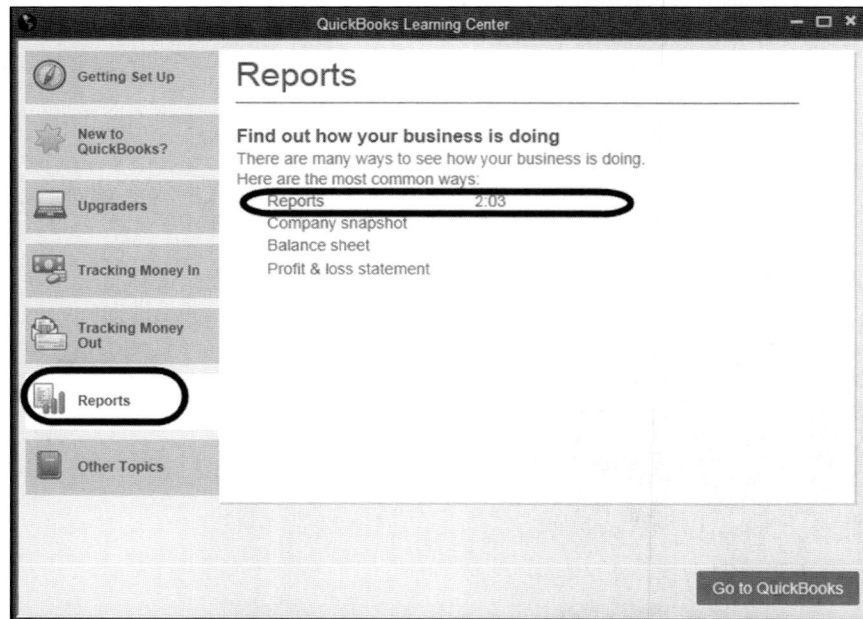

QuickBooks Learning Center

Getting Set Up

New to QuickBooks?

Upgraders

Tracking Money In

Tracking Money Out

Reports

Other Topics

Reports

Find out how your business is doing
There are many ways to see how your business is doing. Here are the most common ways:
Reports   2:03
Company snapshot
Balance sheet
Profit & loss statement

Go to QuickBooks

1. How many reports does QB have?

2. What does memorizing a report do?

3. How does the report center organize reports? Explain.

4. How does the Report Center help you understand what the reports include?

Multiple Choice Questions: The Online Learning Center includes the multiple-choice questions at www.mhhe.com/QBessentials2014, select Student Edition, Chapter 3, Multiple Choice.

_____ 1. How many backups were made of company data in Chapter 3?

      a. One.
      b. Two.
      c. Three.
      d. Four.

_____ 2. The Business Store is a:

      a. Vendor.
      b. Customer.
      c. Employee.
      d. Other.

_____ 3. The Home page area that includes write checks is:

      a. Employees.
      b. Vendors.
      c. Banking.
      d. Company.

_____ 4. An Audit Trail report shows:

      a. All transactions.
      b. Only edited transactions.
      c. Only voided transactions.
      d. Only duplicate transactions.

C 5. How often should an account be reconciled?

 a. Daily.
 b. Weekly.
 c. Monthly.
 d. Quarterly.

C 6. Reconciliation reports generated when an account is reconciled include:

 a. Summary.
 b. Detail.
 c. Both.
 d. No report is generated.

D 7. In Report Center under Accountant & Taxes, all of the following reports can be generated except:

 a. Transaction Detail by Account.
 b. Transaction List by Date.
 c. Audit Trail.
 d. Unclassified.

D 8. In the Report Center under Company & Financial all of the following reports can be found for Profit & Loss except:

 a. Prev Year Comparison.
 b. By Job.
 c. By Class.
 d. By Date.

B 9. In the Report Center under Company & Financial all of the following reports can be found for Balance Sheet & Net Worth except:

 a. Summary.
 b. YTD Comparison.
 c. Prev Year Comparison.
 d. Net Worth Graph.

10. In the Report Center under Company & Financial all of the following reports can be found for Cash Flow Report except:

    a. Statement of Cash Flows.
    b. Cash Flow Forecast.
    c. All of the above.
    d. None of the above.

True/Make True: To answer these questions, go online to www.mhhe.com/QBessentials2014, link to Student Edition, Chapter 3, QA Templates. The analysis question is also included.

1. In Chapter 3, the checkbook's transaction register and September 30, 20XX balance sheet are used as source documents.

2. In accounting, written evidence of a business transaction is called an account register.

3. Two actions are necessary when a company writes a check in error, the check must be voided and the entry must be edited in QuickBooks.

4. Two backups were made in Chapter 3 of Your Name Retailers Inc. company data.

5. The first date for recording transactions is 10/01/20XX.

6. The company preference for write checks and record deposits is Account No. 10000, Home State Bank.

7. The total cash balance on 10/31/20XX is $50,000.00.

8. The 10/31/20XX Profit & Loss report for Your Name Retailers Inc. had a net income.

9. The total assets on the 10/31/20XX Balance Sheet for Your Name Retailers Inc. were $100,000.00.

10. Your Name Retailers Inc. had a positive cash flow for the month of October.

Exercise 3-1: Follow the instructions to complete Exercise 3-1. You must complete Chapter 3 activities *before* you can do Exercise 3-1.

1. Print the Chart of Accounts. (Refer to the Read me box for saving reports as PDF files.)

2. Print the 9/30/20XX to 10/31/20XX journal.

3. Print the 9/30/20XX to 10/31/20XX transaction detail by account.

Exercise 3-2: Follow the instructions below to complete Exercise 3-2.

1. Print the 9/30/20XX to 10/31/20XX trial balance.

2. Print the 10/01/20XX to 10/31/20XX profit and loss report.

3. Print the 10/31/20XX balance sheet.

4. Print the 10/01/20XX to 10/31/20XX statement of cash flows.

Read Me: Save QB reports as PDF Files

Your instructor may want you to email the QB reports as PDF attachments. To do that, follow these steps:

1. Display the report.
2. Click the Print button; select Save as PDF. If report is emailed to your instructor, select E-mail, then Send report as PDF.
3. The suggested file name is **Exercise 3-1 Chart of Accounts.pdf**, etc.

You need Adobe Reader to save as PDF files. If needed, download the free Adobe Reader, www.adobe.com.

If your instructor prefers receiving reports as an Excel file, refer to page 266, Use Excel with QuickBooks, Appendix B, Troubleshooting.

Analysis Question: Why are the trial balance totals different from the balance sheet totals?

Chapter 4

Working with Inventory, Vendors, and Customers

OBJECTIVES:

1. Open the company, Your Name Retailers Inc.
2. Enter items and inventory preferences.
3. Enter vendor records.
4. Enter inventory items.
5. Print the vendor list and item list.
6. Enter bills and record purchase returns.
7. Pay bills.
8. Add a vendor and non-inventory item on the fly.
9. Enter customer records and defaults.
10. Record customer sales on account and sales returns.
11. Receive customer payments.
12. Make backups.[1]

Additional textbook resources are on the textbook website at www.mhhe.com/QBessentials2014 including chapter resources, online quizzes, etc.

GETTING STARTED

Your Name Retailers Inc. started operations on October 1, 20XX (use your current year) in Reno, NV and is organized as a corporation. Customers purchase three products from Your Name Retailers Inc. The three products sold by Your Name Retailers are:

➢ Podcasts (audio files).
➢ ebooks (PDF files). PDF is an abbreviation of portable document format.
➢ TV programs (video files).

---

[1] The chart in the Preface, page xii, shows the file name and size of each backup file. Refer to this chart for backing up data. Remember, you can back up to a hard drive location or external media.

Follow these steps to open Your Name Retailers Inc.

1. Start QuickBooks.[2] You should see Your Name Retailers Inc. - QuickBooks Accountant 2014 on the title bar.

Your Name Retailers Inc. - QuickBooks Accountant 2014

2. If you do <u>not</u> see Your Name Retailers Inc. on the title bar, follow these steps.

    a. Select File; Close Company. From the No Company Open window, select Open or restore an existing company.

    b. On the Open or Restore Company window, select Restore a backup copy. Go to the location of the Your Name Chapter 3 October End.QBB backup file that you made in Chapter 3. (This backup was made on pages 104-105). Click Open .

    c. In the Where do you want to restore the file? window, click Next .

    d. Rename Your Name Retailers Inc.Chapter 3.qbw file to **Your Name Chapter 4 October Begin** in the Save Company File as

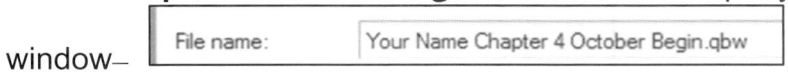

        window—

File name:	Your Name Chapter 4 October Begin.qbw

---

[2]If an Update Company window appears, refer to pages 271-272. The authors recommend installing the update.

e. Click [Save]. When the screen prompts Your data has been restored successfully, click [OK]. The title bar shows Your Name Retailers Inc. - QuickBooks Accounting 2014.

3. To confirm that you are starting in the correct place, display the 10/31 trial balance. (Your year may differ.) Compare your trial balance account balances with the one shown at the end of Chapter 3 on page 102.

4. Close the trial balance without saving.

ITEMS & INVENTORY PREFERENCES

Follow these steps to set preferences for items and inventory.

1. From the menu bar, select Edit; Preferences.

2. Select Items & Inventory, then the Company Preferences tab.

3. Click on the box next to Inventory and purchase orders are active to place a checkmark in the box. Compare your Items & Inventory Preferences to the screen image on the next page.

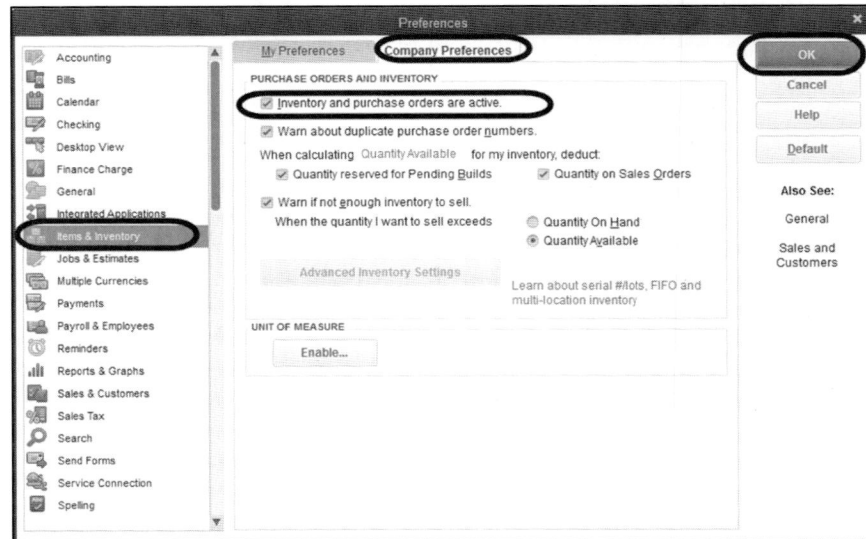

4. Click [OK]. When the Warning window prompts, QuickBooks must close all its open windows to change this preference, click [OK].

5. Click [Home].

MERCHANDISING BUSINESSES

Merchandising businesses purchase the merchandise they sell from suppliers known as *vendors*. A vendor is a person or company from whom Your Name Retailers buys products or services. When Your Name Retailers makes a purchase on account from vendors, the transaction is known as an *accounts payable transaction*. Purchases made on account involve payment terms; for example, Your Name Retailers purchases inventory on account from a vendor. The vendor offers the Your Name Retailers 30 days to pay for the purchase. This is shown as Net 30 in the Payment terms field of the vendor record.

QuickBooks organizes and monitors Your Name Retailers' *accounts payable*. Accounts Payable is a group of accounts that show the amounts owed to vendors or creditors for goods, supplies, or services purchased on account.

When entering a purchase, you select the vendor's name and item. The vendor's address information, payment terms, and appropriate accounts are automatically debited and credited. This works similarly for accounts receivable.

The Vendors section of the Home page illustrates the work flow of entering and paying a vendor bill as well as the tracking of any inventory items purchased on account.

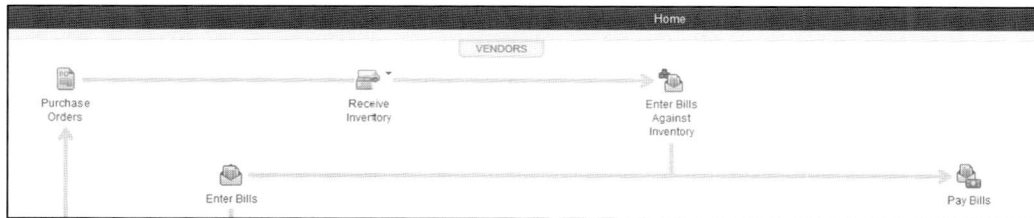

VENDORS

The Vendor Center gives you quick access to your vendors, their contact and billing information, and vendor transactions. In the Vendor Center, you perform all the tasks related to vendors and payables. The Vendor Center is the starting point for managing vendor purchases and the tracking of inventory items purchased.

To see the Vendor Center, select [Vendors]. You can also select Vendors; Vendor Center from the menu bar.

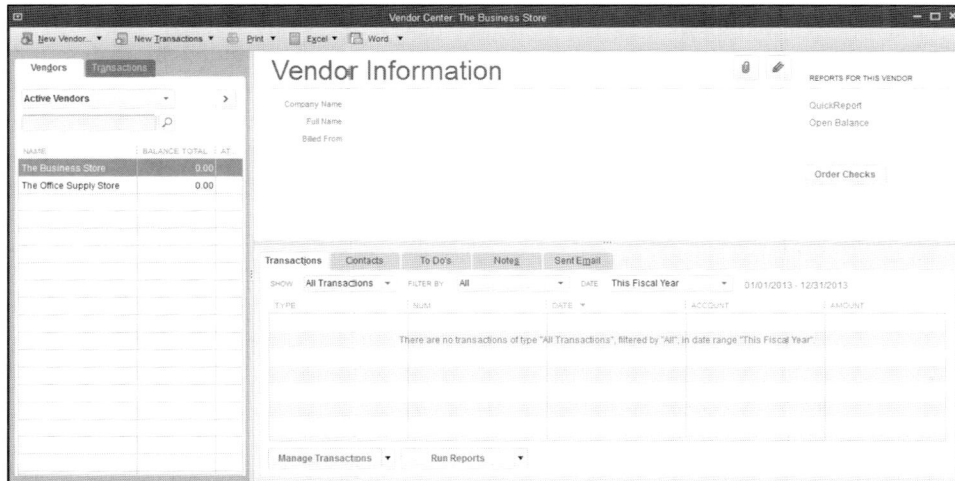

The next section shows you how to set up vendors. Follow these steps to enter vendor default information.

1. If necessary, on the Icon Bar, select [Vendors].

2. Select the down-arrow next to New Vendor, then select New Vendor.

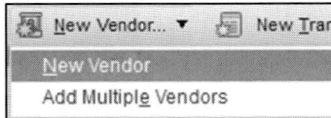

   New Vendor... ▼   New Tran
   New Vendor
   Add Multiple Vendors

3. If a window pops up, read it then click <OK>. The New Vendor window appears.

   Complete the following fields:

   Vendor Name: **Podcast Ltd.**
   Opening Balance: **0** as of **10/01/20XX** (use your current year)
   Company Name: **Podcast Ltd.**
   Full Name   **Howie Hansen**
   Work Phone: **213-555-0100**
   Fax: **213-555-0300**
   Main Email: **howie@podcast.net**
   Website: **www.podcast.net**
   In the Address Details, Billed From field, type the following:
                           1341 Barrington Road
                           Los Gatos, CA 90046 USA

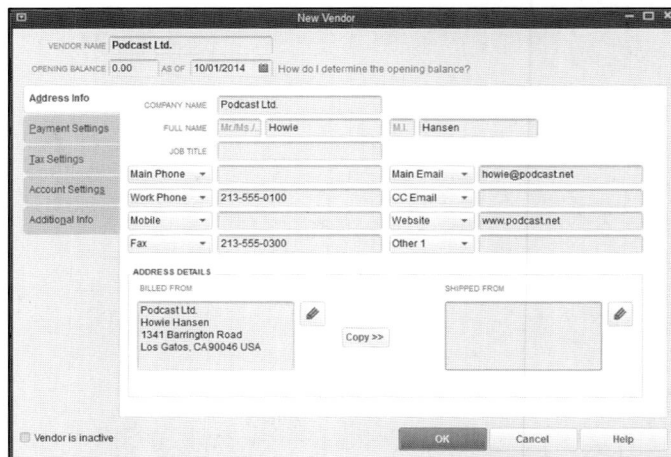

4.   Click Payment Settings. Complete the following fields:

Account No.:	**22000**
Payment Terms:	**Net 30**
Credit limit:	**10,000.00**
Print Name on Check as:	Podcast Ltd.

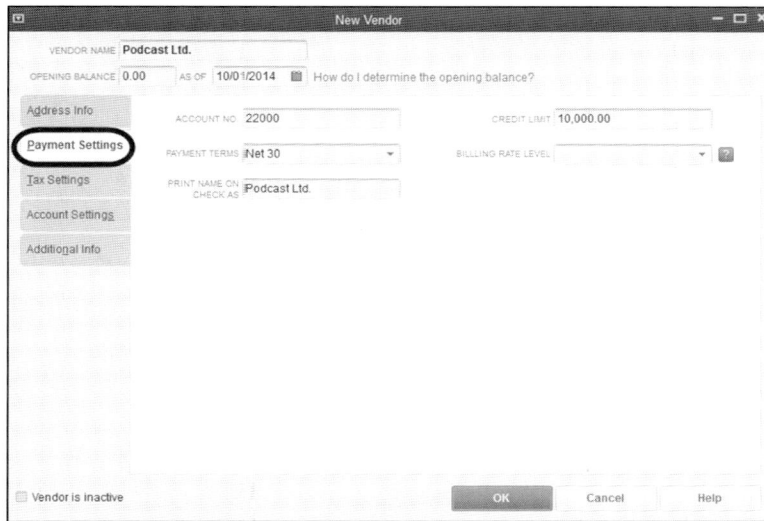

5.   Click Additional Info. In the Vendor Type field, select **Suppliers**.

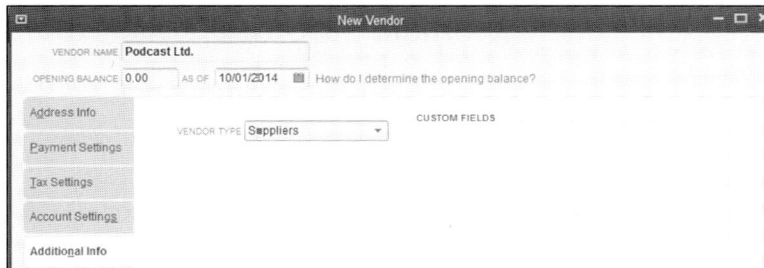

6.   Review data under Address Info, Payment Settings, and Additional Info. When satisfied, click OK .

7.   Set up the next vendor record:

Vendor Name:	**eBooks Express**
Opening Balance:	**0** as of **10/01/20XX** (use your current year)

Company Name:	**eBooks Express**
Full Name:	**Nancy Noel**
Work Phone:	**541-555-4320**
Fax:	**541-555-8808**
Main Email:	**nancy@ebooks.com**
Website:	**www.ebooks.com**
Address:	**10756 NW First Street**
	Gig Harbor, OR 97330 USA

Payment Settings:

Account	**22000**
Payment Terms:	**Net 30**
Credit limit:	**10,000.00**
Print Name on Check as:	eBooks Express

Additional Info:

Vendor Type:	**Suppliers**

8. Review data under Address Info, Payment Settings, and Additional Info. When satisfied, click [OK].

9. Set up the next vendor record.

Vendor Name:	**TV Flix**
Opening Balance:	**0** as of **10/01/20XX** (use your current year)
Company Name:	**TV Flix**
Full Name:	**Hugo Saybrook**
Work Phone:	**213-555-1690**
FAX:	**213-555-6320**
Main Email:	**hugo@tvflix.com**
Website:	**www.tvflix.com**
Address:	**7709 Sunset Boulevard**
	Burbank, CA 91501 USA

Payment Settings:

Account	**22000**
Payment Terms:	**Net 30**
Credit limit:	**10,000.00**
Print Name on Check as:	TV Flix

Additional Info:

Vendor Type:	**Suppliers**

10. Click [OK] to return to the Vendor Center.

Notice all of your vendors, the three you added this chapter plus the two you added previously when you purchased supplies and furniture (Chapter 3) are listed in the left pane of the Vendor Center window with account balances of zero.

Vendors	Transactions	
Active Vendors	▾	>
	🔍	
NAME	BALANCE TOTAL	A...
eBooks Express	0.00	
Podcast Ltd.	0.00	
The Business Store	0.00	
The Office Supply Store	0.00	
TV Flix	0.00	

11. Close the Vendor Center.

INVENTORY ITEMS

An *inventory item* is a product that is purchased for sale and is tracked in Account No. 12100, Inventory Asset, on the balance sheet. Because the Inventory account is increased or decreased for every purchase, sale or return, its balance in the general ledger is current. In QuickBooks when you purchase and receive inventory items, they are added to inventory. When you sell these items and they are added to an invoice, the items are subtracted from inventory.

Complete the following steps to add a new item to inventory.

1. From the Home page's Company area, click on the down-arrow next to Inventory Activities, then Inventory Center.

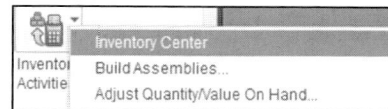

2. From the Inventory Center, select New Inventory Item, New Inventory Item.

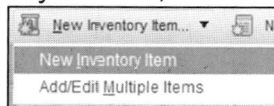

3. If necessary, in the Type field, select Inventory part. Complete these fields:

Item Name/Number: **Podcast**
Description on Purchase Transactions and Sales Transactions:
                audio files (Sales automatically fills)

Cost:	**15.00**
COGS Account:	**Account No. 50000, Cost of Goods Sold**
Preferred Vendor:	**Podcast Ltd.**
Sales Price:	**30.00**
Income Account:	**Account No. 46000, Sales**
Asset Account:	**12100, Inventory Asset**
On Hand:	0.00
Total Value:	0.00
As of:	**10/01/20XX** (use your current year)

4. When satisfied, click [Next]. When the New Item window appears, make sure Inventory Part is selected.

5. The New Item window is ready for the next inventory item. Complete these fields.

Item Name/Number:	**eBook**
Description on Purchase Transactions and Sales Transactions:	**PDF files**

Cost:	**25.00**
COGS Account:	Account No. 50000, Cost of Goods Sold
Preferred Vendor:	**eBooks Express**
Sales Price:	**50.00**
Income Account:	Account No. 46000, Sales
Asset Account:	Account No. 12100, Inventory Asset
On Hand:	0.00
Total Value:	0.00
As of:	**10/01/20XX** (use your current year)

6.   Click [<u>Next</u>] when satisfied.

7.   If Check Spelling on Form window appears checking the spelling of PDF, select [Ignore All].

8.   The New Item window is ready for the next inventory part. Complete these fields.

Item Name/Number:	**TV Programs**
Description on Purchase Transactions and Sales Transactions:	
	video files
Cost:	**30.00**
COGS Account:	Account No.50000, Cost of Goods Sold
Preferred Vendor:	TV Flix
Sales Price:	**60.00**
Income Account:	Account No. 46000, Sales
Asset Account:	Account No. 12100, Inventory Asset
On Hand:	0.00
Total Value	0.00
As of:	**10/01/20XX** (use your current year)

9.   When satisfied, click [OK] to return to the Inventory Center.

NAME	PRICE
◇ eBook	50.00
◇ Podcast	30.00
◇ TV Programs	60.00

To accommodate inventory tracking, two accounts are automatically added to the Chart of Accounts — Account No. 12100 Inventory Asset and Account No. 50000, Cost of Goods Sold. Display the chart of accounts to see these accounts. A partial chart of accounts is shown.

NAME ▲	TYPE	BALANCE TOTAL	ATTACH
◦10000 · Home State Bank	Bank	51,090.00	
◦12100 · Inventory Asset	Other Current Asset	0.00	
◦13000 · Supplies	Other Current Asset	2,700.00	
◦14000 · Computer Equipment	Fixed Asset	2,000.00	
◦15000 · Furniture and Equipment	Fixed Asset	4,000.00	
◦16000 · Accumulated Depreciation-CEqmt.	Fixed Asset	0.00	
◦17000 · Accumulated Depreciation-F&E	Fixed Asset	0.00	
◦18000 · Prepaid Insurance	Other Current Asset	2,500.00	
◦22000 · Accounts Payable	Accounts Payable	0.00	
◦24000 · Payroll Liabilities	Other Current Liability	0.00	
◦26000 · Your Name Notes Payable	Long Term Liability	20,000.00	
◦30000 · Common Stock	Equity	42,500.00	
◦30100 · Paid in Capital	Equity	0.00	
◦30200 · Dividends	Equity	-200.00	
◦32000 · Retained Earnings	Equity		
◦46000 · Sales	Income		
◦50000 · Cost of Goods Sold	Cost of Goods Sold		

Account No. 12100, Inventory Asset, tracks the current value of inventory. QuickBooks automatically adds the Inventory Asset account to the Chart of Accounts the first time you create an inventory item.

Account No. 50000, Cost of Goods Sold, is also added to your Chart of Accounts the first time you add an inventory item. QuickBooks uses this account to track how much you paid for goods and materials that were held in inventory and then sold.

The New Item window on page 120 includes two fields for these accounts, COGS Account and Asset Account.

LISTS

You just added three vendors and three inventory items. QuickBooks' list feature shows the details of each record.

Vendor List

The vendor list shows information about the vendors with whom you do business. Follow these steps to display the vendor list.

1. From the Icon Bar, select [Vendors] ; click on the Vendors tab . The Vendor List appears. Observe you can view list by All Vendors, Active Vendors, Vendors with Open Balances, or Custom Filter.

2. To see The Business Store vendor record, drill down. (*Hint:* Double-click on The Business Store vendor.)

3. Since this vendor was added on the fly in the previous chapter, you need to add vendor information. The Business Store is located at 1234 Front Range Road, Reno, NV 89555; Work Phone, 775-555-3300; Fax is 775-555-1020; Main Email, jimmy@tbs.com; and Website is www.tbs.com. Payment Settings include Account No. 22000; Payment Terms, Net 30; Print name on check as The Business Store; and Credit Limit, 5,000.00. Additional Info includes Suppliers as the Vendor Type.

4. To see The Office Supply Store vendor record, drill down. Add the following vendor information: The Office Supply Store is located at 9876 Hogback Road, Reno, NV 89555; Work Phone 775-555-9876; Fax, 775-555-9798; Main Email: sophie@oss.com; Website, www.oss.com. Payment Settings include Account No. 22000, Payment Terms Net 30, Print Name on Check as The Office Supply Store, Credit Limit 5,000.00. Additional Info includes Suppliers as the Vendor Type. Click [OK] to return to the Vendors List.

5. If you need to edit Vendor Information, click on the pencil icon [pencil] .

6. Click on the arrow button [>] at the top of the Vendor list to show the full list.

7. Click [<] to return to the Vendor Center.

Item List

The Item List shows information about inventory items including name, description, type, account, on hand, and price. When you open the list, you view the active items.

Follow the steps on below to display the item list.

1. From the Menu Bar, select Vendors; Items List. The Item List appears. If necessary, click on the Name column to list the items in alphabetic order.

2. Notice there are several items listed that you did not add, Total Sales - Non-taxable and Total Sales - Taxable. Since Your Name Retailers Inc. is located in Nevada, there is no sales tax.

3. To delete Total Sales - Non-Taxable, highlight it. Use the Item down-arrow to select Delete Item. When asked "Are you sure you want to delete this item?" Select [OK].

4. Delete Total Sales - Taxable, too.

5.   Now the three items you added appear in the list.

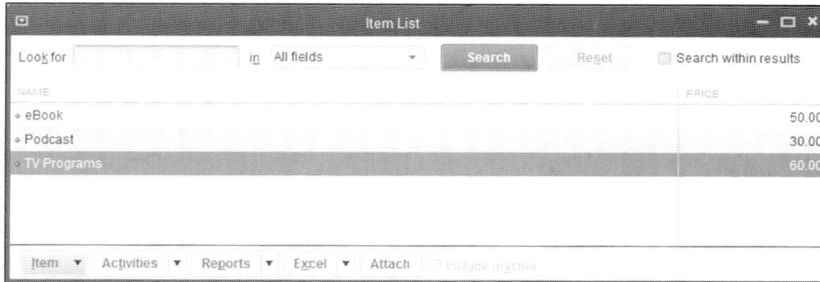

6.   To see an item record, drill-down by double-clicking on it.

7.   Close all Windows. (*HINT:* Select Window, Close all. Then, click

🏠 Home
.

8.   Backup if you are working in a computer lab to your USB drive or
      continue to the next section. The suggested file name is **Your
      Name Chapter 4 Vendors and Inventory.QBB.** (*Hint:* From the
      menu bar, select File; Backup Company, Create Local Backup. You
      may want to set up a Chapter 4 folder.)

Read Me: Delete Extra Backups

If a window appears that asks you to delete backups, select No, Don't Delete .
To allow for more backups to the same folder, select File; Back Up Company,
Create Local Backup, select the <Options> button. Increase the number of

☑ Limit the number of backup copies in this folder to   25

backup copies .

VENDOR TRANSACTIONS

In the Vendors section of the Home page, you perform all the tasks related to vendors and payables. It is the starting point for managing vendor purchases and inventory. In this section, you work with some of these features.

In the Vendors area of the Home page, notice you can enter purchase orders placed with vendors, receive inventory, enter bills against inventory, enter bills, and pay bills.

Vendor and Payable Reports

In the Report Center, there are many Vendors & Payables reports, including those that focus on A/P Aging, Vendor Balances, Lists, and related reports. In this chapter you will use them to gain quick access to vendor or payable information.

A/P Aging (due and overdue bills)

Vendor Balances

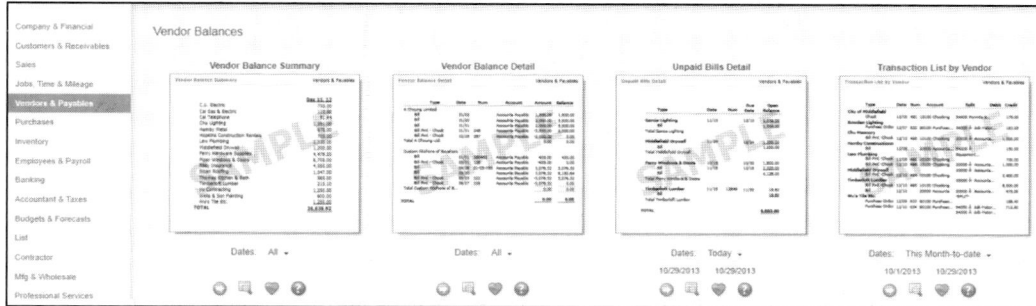

Accounts Payable Tasks

In QuickBooks, all information about a purchase is recorded in the Vendors area of the Home page. Then, QuickBooks takes the necessary information from the Vendors pane and automatically does the accounting debits and credits.

There are two ways to make a purchase on account in QuickBooks. You can use a purchase order tracking system where a purchase is followed from its initial request until payment. In the accounting work flow diagram, Purchase Order to Receive Inventory to Enter Bills Against Inventory to Pay Bills is shown. (To illustrate, the work flow was altered slightly.)

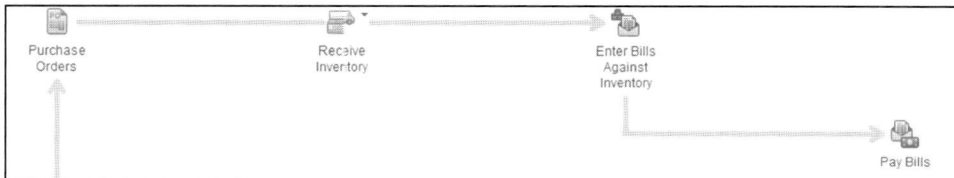

Or, a purchase on account can be tracked from when the bill is received until it is paid. In the accounting work flow diagram, Enter Bill to Pay Bill is shown.

In the following section, you use the Enter Bill and Pay Bill icons to purchase inventory on account from vendors. Transaction processing is dependent on which defaults are set for vendors and inventory items.

Since vendor defaults were set up earlier in this chapter, this means that vendor information is completed automatically in the Enter Bills window. Purchases from vendors are posted to both the General Ledger and to detailed vendors and payables accounts. In accounting, vendors and payables details are shown in the *accounts payable ledger*.

When Your Name Retailers pays vendors, QuickBooks' Pay Bills feature is used. Purchases work hand in hand with payments. Once you have entered a bill, it is available when you pay bills. Then, QuickBooks distributes the appropriate amounts.

The next section explains how to enter bills. The term bill and invoice are used interchangeably. A *bill* or *invoice* is a request for payment for products or services.

Enter Bills

The transaction you are going to record is:

Date   *Description of Transaction*

11/02   Invoice No. 5 received from Podcast Ltd. for the purchase of 20 audio files, $15 each, for a total of $300.

Follow these steps to record this transaction.

1. From the Vendors area on the Home page, select the Enter Bills icon.

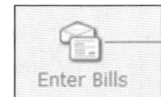

2. When the Enter Bills window appears, complete the following fields:

    Date: **11/02/20XX (use your current year)**
                       (Press <Tab> between fields)
    Vendor: Podcast Ltd.
    Memo: Invoice No. 5

    Click on Items Tab, complete the following fields:

    Item: Podcast
    Description: audio files is completed automatically
    Qty: **20**

Cost: 15.00 is completed automatically
Amount: 300.00 is completed automatically

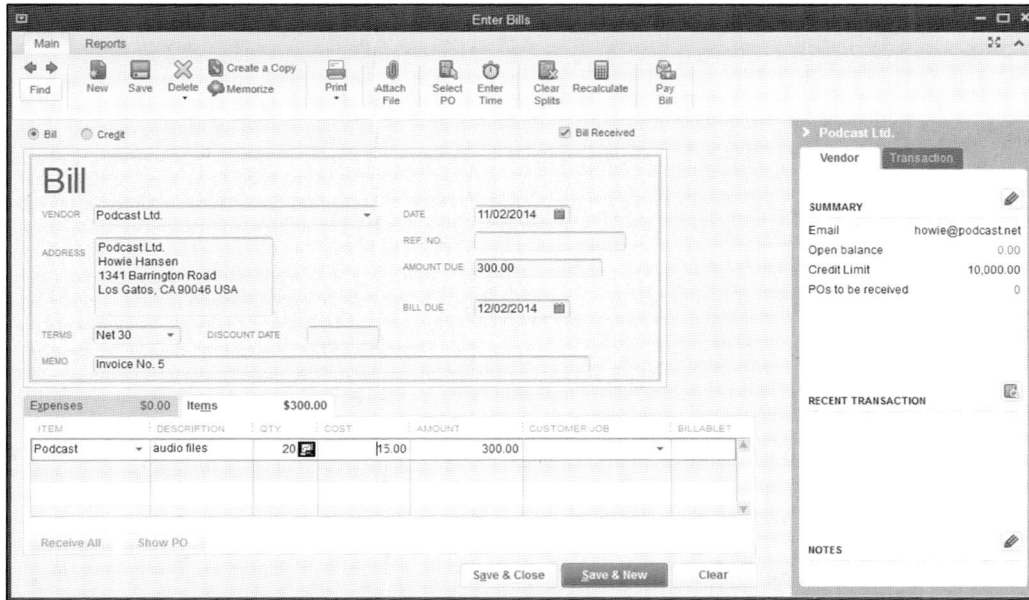

3.   Click [Save & Close]. Before completing the next transaction, let's
     see how QuickBooks debited and credited this information.

4.   Select the Report Center (from either the Icon Bar or menu bar);
     Select Accountant & Taxes, Journal. Select Custom for Dates. Type
     11/01/20XX (your current year) in the From field and **11/02/20XX**
     (your current year) in the To field. Click Run (or Refresh) to display
     the report.

5.   The transaction was debited and credited as follows:

When the 12100 Inventory Asset account is debited, it is increased. When the 22000 Accounts Payable account is credited it is also increased. Your Name Retailers owes Podcast Ltd. $300 for this purchase. Close the Journal without saving.

6. To see how this transaction is recorded in the accounts payable ledger, go to the Vendor Center, Podcast Ltd., link to QuickReport, From 11/1/XX to 11/2/XX. The Vendor QuickReport appears.

7. Double click Bill to drill down to the original entry on the Enter Bills window. Close windows.

8. Enter the following bills. (*Hint:* Select the Enter Bills icon.) Remember to click Save & New after each transaction. Saving posts the transaction to the appropriate accounts in the general ledger and accounts payable ledger.

Date	Description of Transaction
11/03	Invoice No. 90eB received from eBooks Express for the purchase of 15 PDF files, $25 each, for a total of $375. (*Hint:* In the Item field, select eBook.)
11/03	Invoice No. 210TV received from TV Flix for the purchase of 25 video files, $30 each, for a total of $750. (*Hint:* In the Item field, select TV Programs.)
11/05	Invoice No. 78PS received from Podcast Ltd. for the purchase of 18 audio files, $15 each, for a total of $270.

Purchase Returns

Sometimes it is necessary to return merchandise that has been purchased from a vendor. When entering a purchase return, you need to record it as a Credit instead of a Bill in the Enter Bills window.

The following transaction is for merchandise returned to a vendor.

Date   *Description of Transaction*

11/10   Returned two video files to TV Flix from Invoice No. 210TV, Credit Memo No. CM1, for a total of $60.

Follow these steps to record a credit memo.

1. If Enter Bills window is not displayed, click on the Home page's Enter Bills icon.

2. When the Enter Bills window appears, select the Credit radio button and complete the following fields:

    Date: **11/10/20XX (use your current year)**
    Vendor: TV Flix
    Ref. No.   **CM1**
    Memo: **Invoice No. 210TV**
    Item: TV Programs
    Qty: **2**

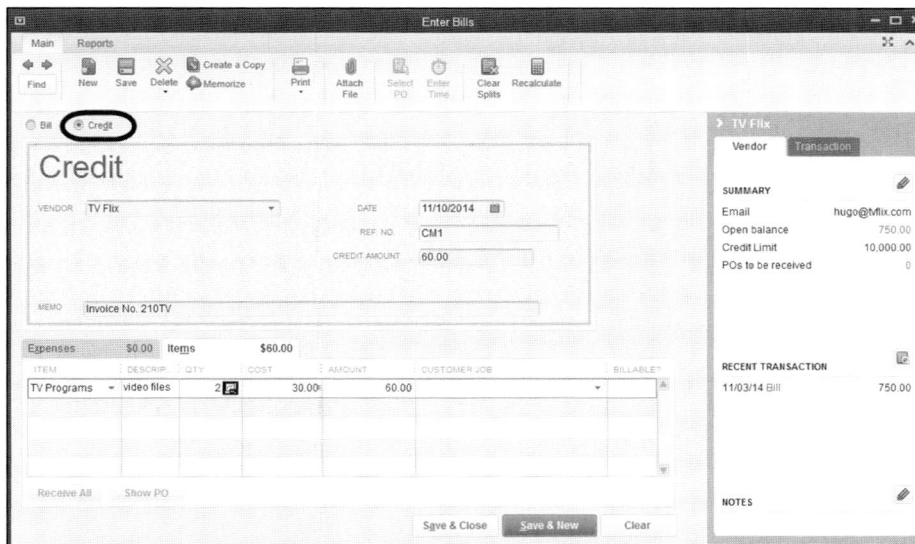

3. After comparing your Enter Bills; Credit window click [Save & New].

4. Let's see how this entry is journalized. Go to Report Center; Accountant & Taxes, Journal, date is 11/10/20XX. Observe that 22000 Accounts Payable TV Flix is debited for $60. This reduces the accounts payable account balance by $60. Also, 12100 Inventory Asset is credited for $60. This reduces the inventory account balance by the amount of the return. After viewing, close Journal without saving it.

5. To see the return on a QB report, display the Vendor Center. In Vendors tab, highlight TV Flix. Link to QuickReport. Type **11/1/20XX** to **11/10/20XX**, [Refresh]. Observe that Account 22000 Accounts Payable is debited for 60.00 on 11/10/20XX.

6. To determine the balance in the Accounts Payable account on 11/10/20XX, go to Report Center, Vendors & Payables, Vendor Balance Summary. Select All Dates. Observe that the Total of all Vendor Balances is $1,635.

```
              Your Name Retailers Inc.
            Vendor Balance Summary
                  All Transactions
                     ◇ Nov 10, 14 ◇
          eBooks Express ▶    375.00 ◀
          Podcast Ltd.        570.00
          TV Flix             690.00
          TOTAL             1,635.00
```

7. This should agree with the 11/10/20XX Balance Sheet for Accounts Payable. (Report Center; Company & Financial, Balance

```
     LIABILITIES & EQUITY
        Liabilities
          Current Liabilities
            Accounts Payable        1,635.00
            Total Current Liabilities  1,635.00
```

Sheet & Net Worth, Balance Sheet Summary. Custom Dates as of 11/10/20XX.) The general ledger balance for accounts payable is 1,635.00. This is the *same* amount that is shown on the Vendor Balance Summary report.

8. Close all windows. Do not save reports. Click 🏠 Home .

Vendor Payments

Use the Pay Bills icon on the Home page to pay vendor bills. The Pay Bills form will display a list of the company's unpaid bills. You can choose to pay individual bills or pay all of them.

In the transaction that follows, all vendor bills are paid.

Date   *Description of Transaction*

11/20   Your Name Retailers pays all outstanding vendor bills for a total of $1,635.

1. Click [Pay Bills].

2. When the Pay Bills window appears, if necessary select the Show all bills radio button. Click [Select All Bills].

3. Confirm Method field shows Check.

4. Confirm the Account field shows 10000, Home State Bank.

5. Type Payment Date, **11/20/20XX** (use your current year).

6. Since Your Name Retailers returned merchandise to TV Flix, highlight TV Flix. The Discount & Credit Information for Highlighted Bill appears. Observe that the Total Credits Available field shows $60.00.

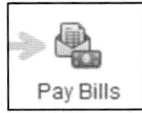

7. Click on [Set Credits]. The Discounts and Credits window appears.

8. Click [Done]. Cbserve that the Credits used for TV Flix shows $60.00 and the Amt. To Pay shows 690 (750 – 60 = 690).

9. Compare your Pay Bills window to the one below. Observe that the Totals row shows $1,635. This agrees with the accounts payable balance shown on page 133.

10. Click [Pay Selected Bills].

11. Payment Summary window appears. Scroll down to see all the vendor payments. Observe that the Total shows 1,635 which is in agreement with the Accounts Payable balance.

```
PAYMENT DETAILS
Payment Date       11/20/2014
Payment Account    10000 · Home State Bank
Payment Method     Check
```

Payments have been successfully recorded for the following 4 of 4 bills:

DATE DUE	VENDOR	AMOUNT PAID
12/05/2014	Podcast Ltd.	270.00
12/03/2014	TV Flix	690.00
	Total	1,635.00

How do I find and change a bill payment?

You can print checks now or print them later from Print Forms on the File menu.

[Pay More Bills] [Print Checks] [Done]

12. Click [Done]. (*NOTE:* If this were a real business you would have printed and mailed the checks.)

13. Display the detailed account balance for Account No. 22000, Accounts Payable. (Report Center; Company & Financial, Balance Sheet & Net Worth, Balance Sheet Detail. Custom Dates From 10/01/20XX To 11/20/20XX.) Observe that the Balance Sheet Detail shows that the balance in Accounts Payable is 0.00 as of 11/20/20XX. Close report without saving it.

14. Display the Vendor Center. Observe that each vendor shows a zero balance.

15. To see how the vendor payments are journalized, display the 11/20/20XX Journal. (Report Center; Accountant & Taxes, Journal, date is 11/20/20XX) Observe that each vendor payment

is journalized separately; for example, the November 20 vendor payment to eBooks Express shows a debit to Account No. 22000 for $375; and a credit to Account No. 10000, Home State Bank for $375. If you add the three payments together they equal, $1,635, which is the total of the three payments—375+690+570=1,635.

Purchasing Assets from Vendors

In the previous chapter you purchased assets for cash and used the check register as your source document. Now, along with credit purchases for inventory, assets can also be purchased on account from vendors. To see how to purchase assets on account, complete the following steps.

Date   *Description of Transaction*

11/21   Purchased notebook computer equipment on account from The Business Store, Invoice BOS44, for a total of $400, terms Net 30 days.

1. Record the 11/21/20XX credit purchase using Enter Bills. In the Vendor name field, select The Business Store, Memo: Invoice No. BOS 44.

2. If necessary, click on Expenses tab and complete the following fields:

   Account: 14000, Computer Equipment
   Amount: 400.00
   Memo: Notebook computer

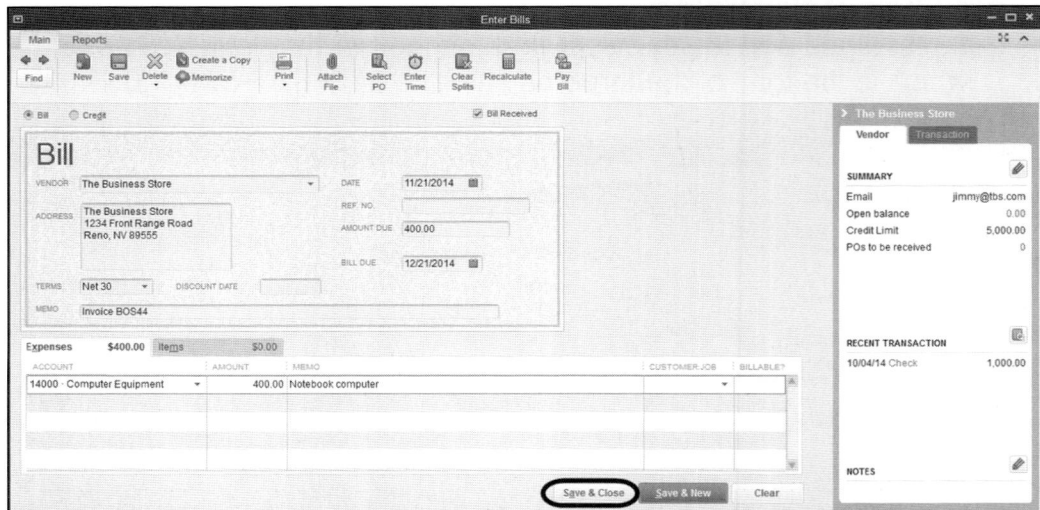

3. When satisfied, click Save & Close.

4.   Backup your work. (*Hint:* File; Back Up Company, Create Local Backup.) Name backup file **Your Name Chapter 4 Vendors.QBB**.

CUSTOMERS

Now that you have purchased items from vendors, you are ready to sell that inventory. To do that, you need to learn how to use QuickBooks' customers and receivables tasks. This section shows you how to establish customer records and defaults and explains how QuickBooks' customer work flows are organized. *Accounts receivable* is a group of accounts that show the amounts customers owe for services or products sold on credit. Credit transactions from customers are called *accounts receivable transactions*.

Customer receipts work similarly to paying vendor invoices. A *customer invoice* is defined as a request for payment to a customer for products or services sold.

The Home page's Customers area is where you perform all the tasks related to customers and receivables. The Customers area shows the work flow of customer tasks. You will work with some of these Customers work flow icons.

Once a new invoice is recorded using the Create Invoices icon, the Receive Payments icon is used to record customer payments or collections. The Create Sales Receipts icon is used for cash sales. The Refunds & Credits icon is used when dissatisfied customers receive a refund or some kind of consideration resulting from a previous sale.

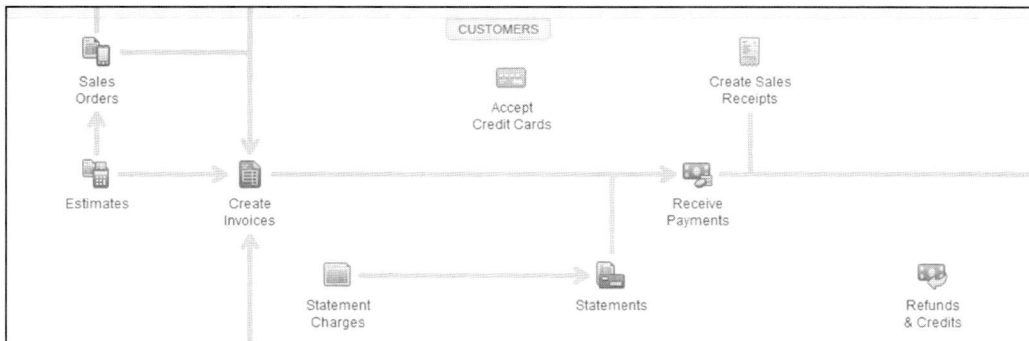

QuickBooks has a Customer Center (Icon Bar, [Customers icon] ; or menu bar, Customers) to track tasks related to customers and receivables. The center provides easy access to customer records, contact information, transaction details, and history. The Customer Center is the starting point for managing customers and the tracking of items sold.

Customer Records

On the Customer Center, you set up customers and receivables. Follow these steps to set up customer records and defaults.

1. From the Icon Bar, select [Customers] , New Customer & Job, New Customer. The New Customer window appears.

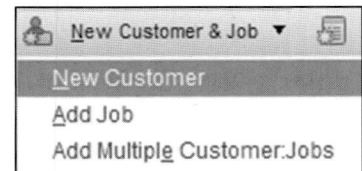

   New Customer & Job ▼
   New Customer
   Add Job
   Add Multiple Customer:Jobs

2. Complete the Address Info fields shown here.

Customer Name:	**Audio Answers**
Opening Balance:	**0.00** as of **10/01/20XX (current year)**
Company Name:	**Audio Answers**
Full Name:	**Cathleen McClure**
Work Phone:	**303-555-9312**
Fax:	**303-555-1234**
Main Email:	**cathleen@audio.biz**
Address:	**113 Aspen Drive**
	Telluride, CO 80010

   Click [Copy >>]. The Add Shipping Address Information window appears. Check the information, then click [OK].

Payment Settings tab:

Account No.:	**AA1**
Credit Limit:	**7,500.00**
Payment Terms:	Net 30
Preferred Delivery Method:	Mail
Preferred Payment Method:	Check

Additional Info tab:

Customer Type: Retail

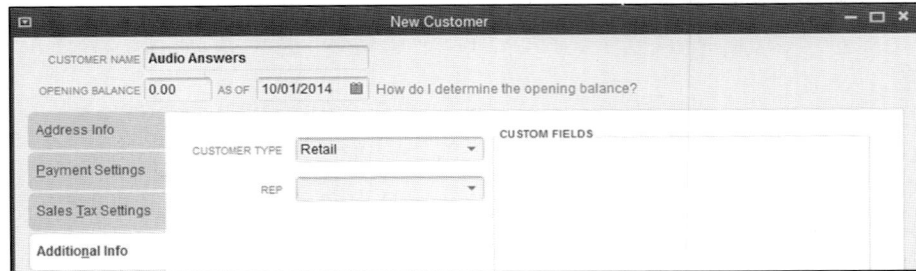

3.   Check the information entered. Click [OK] .

4.   Enter the following customers:

Customer Name:	**iPrint Design**
Opening Balance:	**0.00** as of **10/01/20XX (current year)**
Company Name:	**iPrint Design**
Full Name:	**Rolo Kalm**
Work Phone:	**310-555-2367**
Fas:	**310-555-2368**
Main Email:	**rolo@iprint.com**
Address:	**4900 Springer Drive**
	Palos Verdes, CA 90212
Account No.:	**IP2**
Credit Limit:	**7,500.00**
Payment Terms:	Net 30
Preferred Delivery Method:	Mail
Preferred Payment Method:	Check
Type:	Retail

Customer Name:	**Video Solutions**
Opening Balance:	**0.00** as of **10/01/20XX (current year)**
Company Name:	**Video Solutions**
Full Name:	**Lyman Hudson**
Work Phone:	**727-555-0613**
Fax:	**727-555-0615**
Main Email:	**lh@video.com**

Address:	**86113 Ginnie Blvd.**
	Fanning Springs, FL 34688
Account No.:	**VS3**
Credit Limit:	**7,500.00**
Payment Terms:	Net 30
Preferred Delivery Method:	Mail
Preferred Payment Method:	Check
Type:	Retail

5. Click [OK] to return to Customer Center.

Customer List

The customer list shows information about the customers with whom you do business. Follow these steps to display the customer list.

1. If necessary, go to the Customer Center; click on the Customers & Jobs tab. The Customer List appears. Observe you can view list by All Customers, Active Customers (the default), Customers with Open Balances, Customers with Overdue Invoices, Customers with Almost Due Invoices, or Custom Filter.

2. Click on the [>] button show the full list.

3. Click on the [<] button to return to the Customer Center.

4. To see the detailed record and transaction history of a specific customer, double click on the customer name in the customer list. Information about the customer will appear in the right pane of the Customer Center.

Customers & Accounts Receivables and Sales Reports

QuickBooks' Report Center provides many customer, receivable, and sales reports that are used in this chapter. Customers & Receivables reports provide information about A/R Aging, Customer Balance, Lists, and other related reports.

Customers & Receivables: A/R Aging (what my customers owe me and what is overdue). A partial window is shown below. Scroll down the Customers & Receivables report center to see more.

Lists:

Sales reports include many Sales by Customer, Sales by Item, and Sales by Rep types of reports. In the Report Center, select Sales. A partial list of reports is shown on the next page. Scroll down the Sales Report Center to see more.

Sales
Sales by Customer

CUSTOMER TRANSACTIONS

In the Customers section of the Home page, you perform the tasks related to customers and accounts receivables. In this section, you work with some of these features.

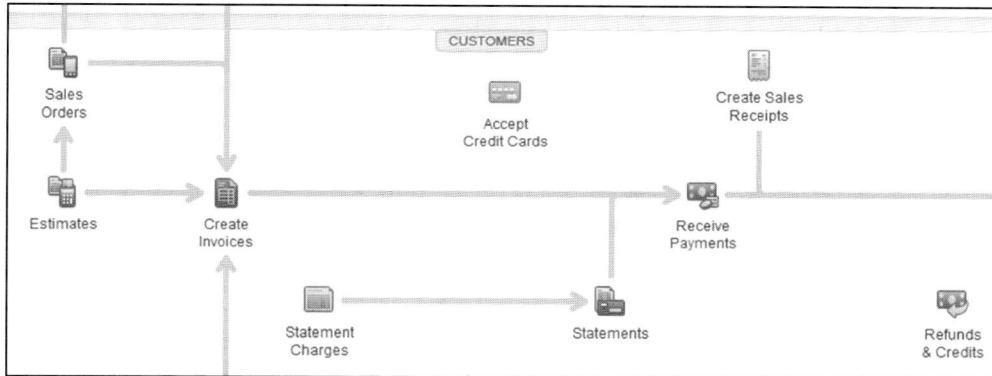

In QuickBooks, all information about a sale on account is recorded on the Create Invoice form. Then, QuickBooks takes the necessary information from the Invoice window and automatically creates the transaction's debits and credits. Credit sales from customers are posted to both the General Ledger and to the customers and receivables accounts. In accounting, customers and receivables accounts grouped together are called the **accounts receivable ledger**.

You use QuickBooks' Create Invoices icon to record credit sales to customers. **Credit sales** or sales on account refer to sales made to customers that will be paid for later. Your Name Retailers offers customers payment terms of Net 30 days.

Sales Invoices

The transaction you are going to record is:

Date	*Description of Transaction*
11/15/20XX	Sold 5 eBooks (PDF files) on account to iPrint Design for a total credit sale of $250, Invoice # 1.

Follow these steps to enter the transaction.

1. Click [Create Invoices]. The Create Invoices window appears.

2. Complete these fields.

Customer:Job:	iPrint Design
Date:	**11/15/20XX**
Invoice #:	1 is completed automatically
Qty.:	**5**
Item Code:	eBook
Description:	PDF files is completed automatically
Unit Price:	50.00 is completed automatically
Amount:	250.00 is completed automatically

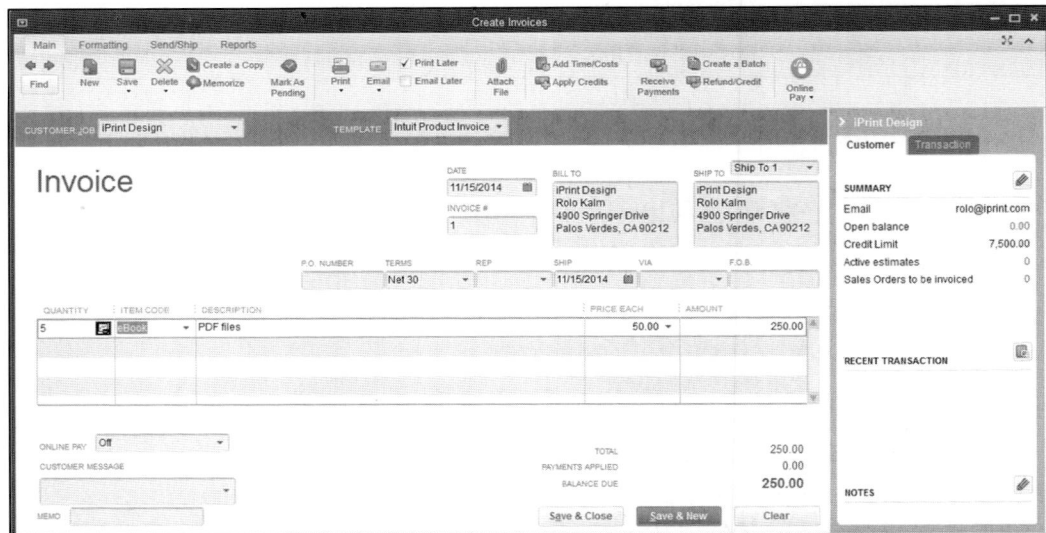

3. When satisfied, click [Save & New].

4. If Check Spelling on Form window appears, select [Ignore All]. The
    Create Invoices window is ready for the next two transactions.

Date   *Description of Transaction*

11/15/20XX   Sold 15 Podcasts (audio files) on account to Audio
                Answers for a total credit sale of $450, Invoice # 2.

11/15/20XX   Sold 8 TV Programs (video files) on account to Video
                Solutions for a total credit sale of $480, Invoice # 3.

5. Click [Save & Close].

6. Look at how QuickBooks journalizes these sales by displaying the
    11/15/20XX Journal. (Report Center; Accountant & Taxes, Journal,
    date is 11/15/20XX)

					Your Name Retailers Inc.					
					Journal					
					November 15, 2014					
Trans #	Type	Date	Num	Adj	Name	Memo	Account		Debit	Credit
21	Invoice	11/15/2014	1		iPrint Design		11000 · Accounts Receivable		250.00	
					iPrint Design		46000 · Sales			250.00
					iPrint Design		12100 · Inventory Asset			125.00
					iPrint Design		50000 · Cost of Goods Sold		125.00	
									375.00	375.00
22	Invoice	11/15/2014	2		Audio Answers		11000 · Accounts Receivable		450.00	
					Audio Answers		46000 · Sales			450.00
					Audio Answers		12100 · Inventory Asset			225.00
					Audio Answers		50000 · Cost of Goods Sold		225.00	
									675.00	675.00
23	Invoice	11/15/2014	3		Video Solutions		11000 · Accounts Receivable		480.00	
					Video Solutions		46000 · Sales			480.00
					Video Solutions		12100 · Inventory Asset			240.00
					Video Solutions		50000 · Cost of Goods Sold		240.00	
									720.00	720.00
TOTAL									1,770.00	1,770.00

7. Look closely at the accounts debited and credited for the sale made
    to iPrint Design.

    Observe that *both* the sales price, $250, and the cost of the
    inventory item are debited and credited. When Your Name Retailers
    sells PDF files the customer pays $50 each (5 PDF files were sold
    for a total of $250). When Your Name Retailers buys PDF files from

the vendor, it pays $25 x 5 = $125. QuickBooks tracks both the sales price *and* the purchase price when items are sold. The sales price is debited and credited to AR/customer and Sales; the cost of the item is debited and credited to Cost of Goods Sold and Inventory, respectively. This entry keeps the Inventory account perpetually up to date.

8. Close the Journal without saving.

Inventory

Before recording more sales, let's look at the status of inventory as of November 15, 20XX (use your current year). Follow these steps to do that.

1. From the menu bar or Icon Bar, select Reports, Inventory, Inventory Valuation Detail. The dates are 10/1/20XX to 11/15/20XX. Observe that the following quantities are on hand.

eBook	PDF files	10
Podcast	audio files	23
TV Programs	video files	15

Your Name Retailers Inc.
Inventory Valuation Detail
October 1 through November 15, 2014

Type	Date	Name	Num	Qty	Cost	On Hand	Avg Cost	Asset Value
Inventory								
eBook (PDF files)								
Bill	11/03/2014	eBooks Express		15	375.00	15	25.00	375.00
Invoice	11/15/2014	iPrint Design	1	-5		10	25.00	250.00
Total eBook (PDF files)						10		250.00
Podcast (audio files)								
Bill	11/02/2014	Podcast Ltd.		20	300.00	20	15.00	300.00
Bill	11/05/2014	Podcast Ltd.		18	270.00	38	15.00	570.00
Invoice	11/15/2014	Audio Answers	2	-15		23	15.00	345.00
Total Podcast (audio files)						23		345.00
TV Programs (video files)								
Bill	11/03/2014	TV Flix		25	750.00	25	30.00	750.00
Credit	11/10/2014	TV Flix	CM1	-2	-60.00	23	30.00	690.00
Invoice	11/15/2014	Video Solutions	3	-8		15	30.00	450.00
Total TV Programs (video files)						15		450.00
Total Inventory						48		1,045.00
TOTAL						48		1,045.00

2. Close windows without saving.

Sales Returns

When a customer returns a product or requires a refund, you can create a customer credit memo with the Credit Memo/Refunds form.

The following transaction is for a sales return.

Date   *Description of Transaction*

11/17/20XX   Audio Answers returned 2 Podcasts (audio files).

Follow these steps to enter the sales return.

1.   Click 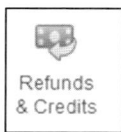.

2.   Select Audio Answers as the Customer.

3.   Type **11/17/20XX** in the date field.

4.   In the Item field, select Podcast.

5.   Type **2** in the Qty. field.

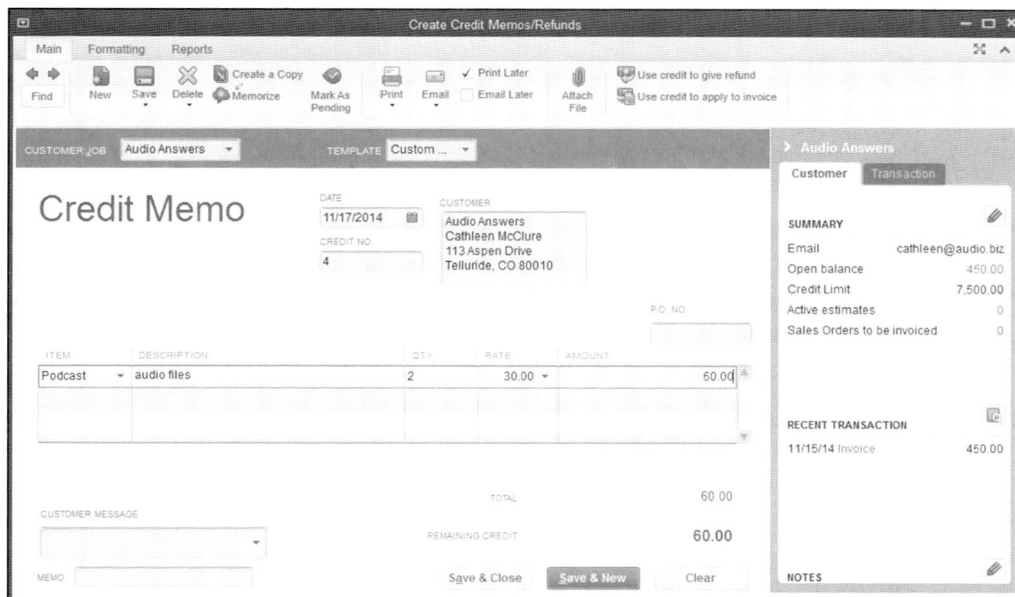

6. When satisfied, click [Save & Close].

7. When the Available Credit window appears, select Apply to an invoice, then [OK].

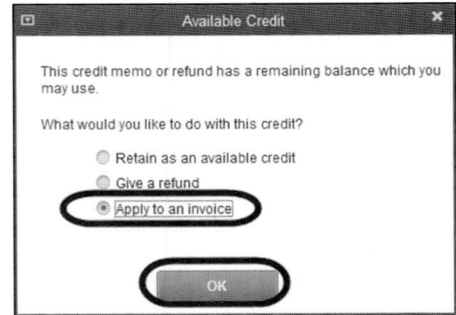

Available Credit

This credit memo or refund has a remaining balance which you may use.

What would you like to do with this credit?

○ Retain as an available credit
○ Give a refund
● Apply to an invoice

OK

8. When Apply Credits to Invoices window appears, confirm the Audio Answers 11/15/20XX Invoice is checked.

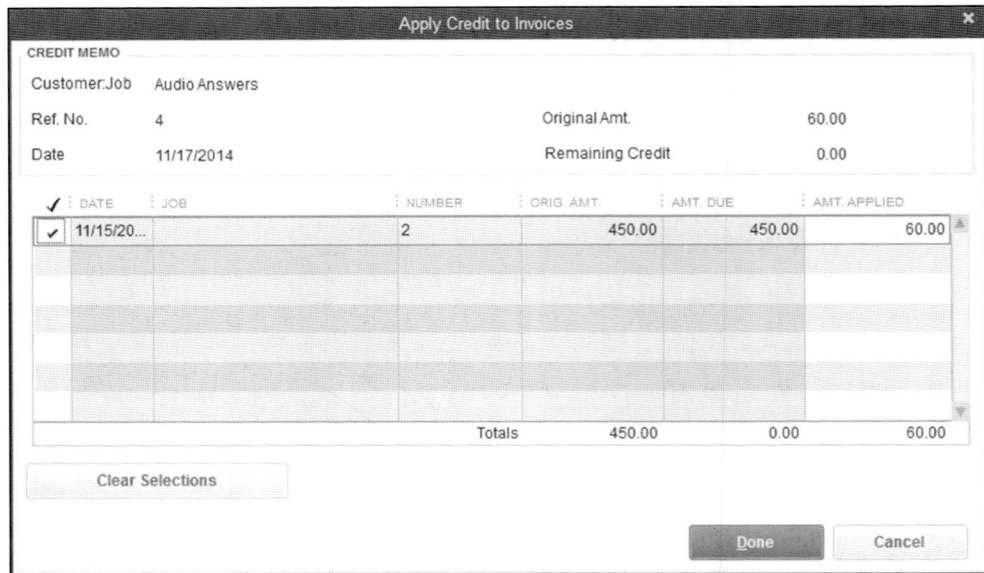

Apply Credit to Invoices

CREDIT MEMO

Customer:Job	Audio Answers				
Ref. No.	4	Original Amt.	60.00		
Date	11/17/2014	Remaining Credit	0.00		

✓	DATE	JOB	NUMBER	ORIG. AMT.	AMT. DUE	AMT. APPLIED
✓	11/15/20...		2	450.00	450.00	60.00
			Totals	450.00	0.00	60.00

Clear Selections

Done   Cancel

9. Click [Done] to apply the credit to the invoice.

10. To see how this entry is journalized. Display the 11/17/20XX Journal. (Report Center; Accountant & Taxes, Journal, date is 11/17/20XX) Close Journal without saving it.

Your Name Retailers Inc.
Journal
November 17, 2014

Trans #	Type	Date	Num	Adj	Name	Memo	Account	Debit	Credit
24	Credit Memo	11/17/2014	4		Audio Answers		11000 · Accounts Receivable		60.00
					Audio Answers		46000 · Sales	60.00	
					Audio Answers		12100 · Inventory Asset	30.00	
					Audio Answers		50000 · Cost of Goods Sold		30.00
								90.00	90.00
TOTAL								90.00	90.00

11.   Display the Customer Balance Detail Report to see how the accounts receivable account records customer transactions. (*Hint:* Report Center, Customers & Receivables, Customer Balance Detail, All Dates) Observe that the balance in the Audio Answers account is reduced by the amount of the 11/17/20XX return. Also, notice that the Total on the report is $1,120. This total should agree with the 11/17 balance for Account No. 11000, Accounts Receivable.

Your Name Retailers Inc.
Customer Balance Detail
All Transactions

Type	Date	Num	Account	Amount	Balance
Audio Answers					
Invoice	11/15/2014	2	11000 · Accounts Receivable	450.00	450.00
Credit Memo	11/17/2014	4	11000 · Accounts Receivable	-60.00	390.00
Total Audio Answers				390.00	390.00
iPrint Design					
Invoice	11/15/2014	1	11000 · Accounts Receivable	250.00	250.00
Total iPrint Design				250.00	250.00
Video Solutions					
Invoice	11/15/2014	3	11000 · Accounts Receivable	480.00	480.00
Total Video Solutions				480.00	480.00
TOTAL				1,120.00	1,120.00

12.   Close the Customer Balance Detail report without saving.

13.   Display the Balance Sheet Detail Report From 10/01/20XX To 11/20/20XX. (*Hint:* Report Center, Company & Financial, Balance Sheet Detail.) Notice the Account No. 11000, Accounts Receivable, shows the same balance as the Customer Balance Detail, $1,120.00.

					Your Name Retailers Inc.				
					Balance Sheet Detail				
					As of November 20, 2014				
Type	Date	Num	Adj	Name	Memo	Clr	Split	Debit	Credit	Balance
11000 · Accounts Receivable										0.00
Invoice	11/15/2014	1		iPrint Design			46000 · Sales	250.00		250.00
Invoice	11/15/2014	2		Audio Answers			46000 · Sales	450.00		700.00
Invoice	11/15/2014	3		Video Solutions			46000 · Sales	480.00		1,180.00
Credit Memo	11/17/2014	4		Audio Answers			46000 · Sales		60.00	1,120.00
Total 11000 · Accounts Receivable								1,180.00	60.00	1,120.00
Total Accounts Receivable								1,180.00	60.00	1,120.00

14.   Close the report without saving.

Credit Card Sales

Your Name Retailers accepts credit cards for customer sales but does not use QuickBooks' credit card processing service. (QuickBooks charges a fee for processing credit card sales.) Observe that on the Icon Bar, there is a Credit Cards selection [Credit Cards]. Also, within the Home page's Customers area, there is an Accept Credit Cards. Since there is a charge for using the Credit Cards selections, do *not* make these selections.

Your Name Retailers Inc. is set up to accept credit cards for customer payments and processes credit card sales at their bank, Home State Bank. For our purposes, you will see how a company can process credit cards but you will *not* set up the online credit card processing.

The transaction you are going to record is:

Date   *Description of Transaction*

11/18   Sold 5 eBooks for $250; 8 Podcasts for $240; and 6 TV Programs for $360; for total credit card sales of $850, Sale No. 1.

Follow these steps to enter a new customer on the fly and record credit card sales.

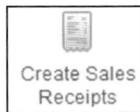

1.   Click [Create Sales Receipts]. The Enter Sales Receipts window appears.

2.   Type **11/18/20XX** in the Date field.

3. Accept the default Sale No.

4. In the Customer:Job field, select <Add New>. On the New Customer form, complete these fields.

Customer Name:	**Credit Card Sales**
Opening Balance	**0.00** as of **10/01/20XX**
Company Name:	**Credit Card Sales**

    CUSTOMER NAME | Credit Card Sales

    OPENING BALANCE | 0.00 | AS OF | 10/01/2014 | How do I determine the opening balance?

    Address Info

    COMPANY NAME | Credit Card Sales

    Payment Settings:

    Account No.: **CCS**
    Preferred Payment Method: Select
    <Add New>. In the Payment Method
    field, type **Credit Card**. The Payment
    Type is Cash. Click <OK>.

    New Payment Method

    Payment Method
    Credit Card
    Payment Type
    Cash

    OK
    Cancel
    Help
    ☐ Method is inactive

    The New Customer window looks like
    this:

    New Customer

    CUSTOMER NAME | Credit Card Sales
    OPENING BALANCE | 0.00 | AS OF | 10/01/2014 | How do I determine the opening balance?

Address Info	ACCOUNT NO. CCS		CREDIT LIMIT
Payment Settings	PAYMENT TERMS		PRICE LEVEL
Sales Tax Settings	PREFERRED DELIVERY METHOD	None	ADD ONLINE PAYMENT LINK TO INVOICES	Follow Company Default
Additional Info	PREFERRED PAYMENT METHOD	Credit Card		

5. Click [OK]. You are returned to the Enter Sales Receipts window. Credit Cards Sales is shown in the Customer:Job field. Observe that the Sale No. field is completed automatically with the number 1.

6. In the Item field, select eBook.

7. Type **5** in the Qty. field.

8. Go to the Item field, select Podcast.

9. Type **8** in the Qty. field.

10. Go to the Item field, select TV Programs.

11. Type **6** in the Qty. field.

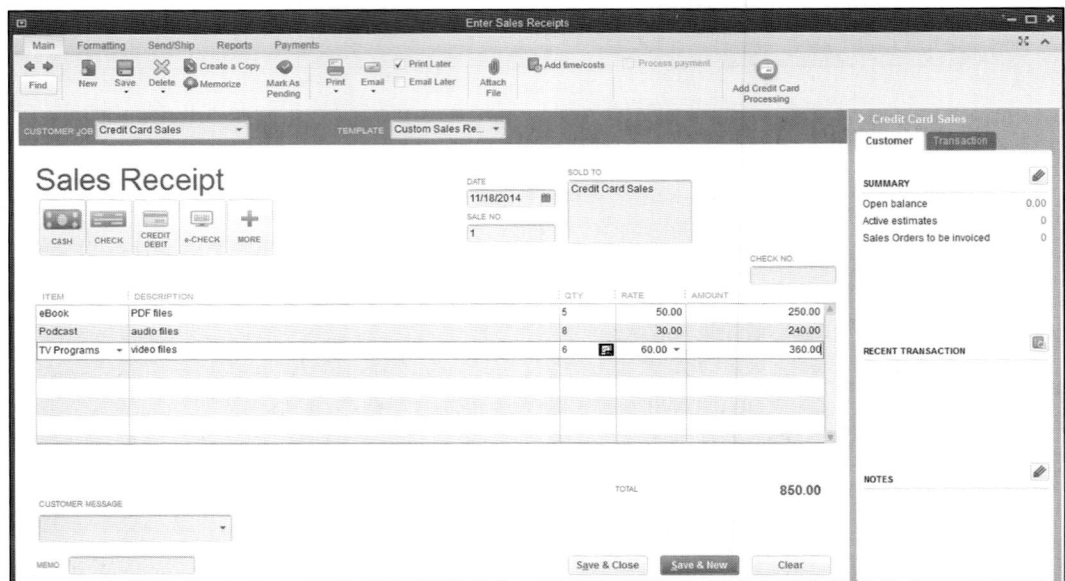

12. Click [Save & Close]. Ignore the spelling window about PDF.

13. To see how this transaction is journalized, display the Journal for 11/18/20XX. Observe that each item amount is individually debited and credited to Undeposited Funds, Sales, Costs of Goods Sold, and Inventory.

Your Name Retailers Inc.
Journal
November 18, 2014

Trans #	Type	Date	Num	Adj	Name	Memo	Account	Debit	Credit
25	Sales Receipt	11/18/2014	1		Credit Card Sales		12000 · Undeposited Funds	850.00	
					Credit Card Sales	-MULTIPLE-	46000 · Sales		850.00
					Credit Card Sales	-MULTIPLE-	12100 · Inventory Asset		425.00
					Credit Card Sales	-MULTIPLE-	50000 · Cost of Goods Sold	425.00	
								1,275.00	1,275.00
TOTAL								1,275.00	1,275.00

The Memo column shows MULTIPLE. This indicates more than one inventory item. Drill down (double-click) MULTIPLE to see the Enter Sales Receipts window which indicates the three items sold: eBooks (5 PDF files), Podcast (8 audio files), and TV Programs (6 video files). Close the Enter Sales Receipts window and the Journal without saving.

Customer Payments

When a customer sends you a payment, enter the customer payment on the Receive Payment window. You can then apply the payment to the invoices that are due. A payment might cover one or more invoice, or it may be for part of the invoice. You can select which invoice to settle against a payment as well as the amount to apply to each invoice. *Or,* you can have QuickBooks automatically apply the payment to invoices in chronological order from the oldest outstanding invoice.

In the following transactions, customers pay their outstanding invoices.

Date   *Description of Transaction*

11/23   Received a check in full payment of Audio Answers' account, $390.

Using the payment from Audio Answers as an example, follow these steps to record a customer payment.

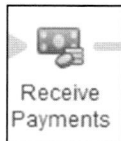

1.   Click **Receive Payments**.

2.   Complete the following fields on the Receive Payments form:

Received From: Audio Answers
Payment Amount: **390.00**
Date: **11/23/20XX**

3.   A check mark is placed next to the 11/15 invoice automatically. Notice the original amount $450.00 was reduced to $390.00 by the previously applied credit memo for $60.00 since Audio Answers returned merchandise.

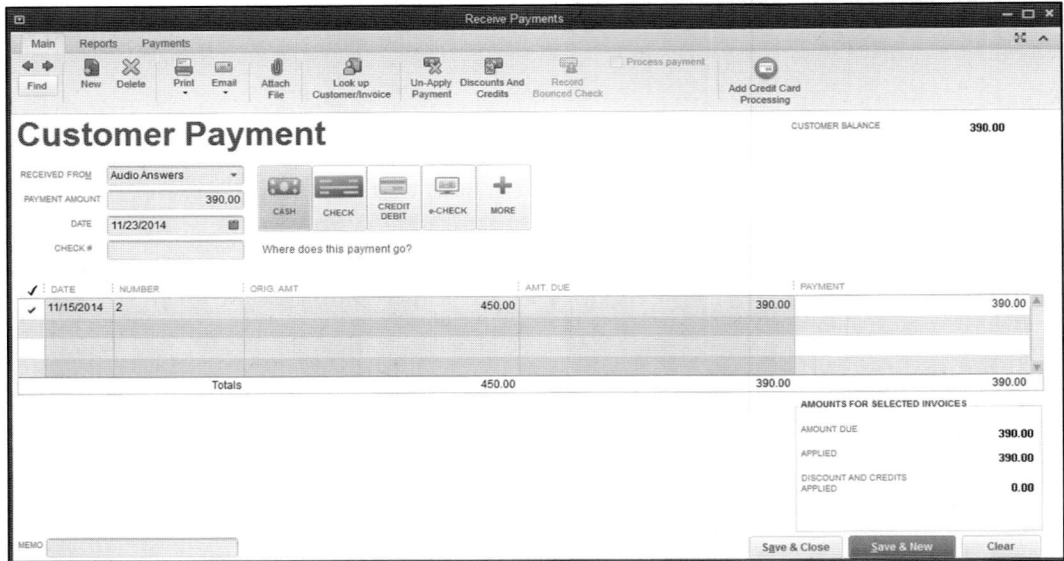

4.   Click   Save & Close .

5.   Display the 11/23/20XX Journal. When a customer payment is received, Undeposited Funds and Accounts Receivable are debited and credited respectively. (The example shows the customer payment received from Audio Answers.)

Trans #	Type	Date	Num	Adj	Name	Memo	Account	Debit	Credit
26	Payment	11/23/2014			Audio Answers		12000 Undeposited Funds	390.00	
					Audio Answers		11000 Accounts Receivable		390.00
								390.00	390.00
TOTAL								390.00	390.00

Your Name Retailers Inc.
Journal
November 23, 2014

What are undeposited funds? Account No. 12000, Undeposited Funds, is a cash account for amounts received from customers but not yet deposited to the bank account. When bank deposits are made, Undeposited Funds will be credited and Home State Bank will be debited. You can think of undeposited funds as a clearing account. The undeposited funds account holds the cash until they are deposited and cleared by the bank. The November bank statement will show which customer payments cleared Account No. 10000, Home State Bank, which is Your Name Retailers' bank account.

6. Record the two November 24, 20XX payments received from customers.

    Date   *Description of Transaction*

    11/24   Received a check in full payment of iPrint Design's account, $250.

    11/24   Received a check in full payment of Video Solutions' account, $480.

7. Click [Save & Close] to return to Home page. After you record the customer payments received on 11/23 and 11/24, you deposit those the checks receive.

8. Click [Record Deposits]. The Payments to Deposit window appears.

9. Place a check mark next to the 11/23 and 11/24 checks included in the deposit. (Customer checks for $390.00 +$250.00 +$480.00.) Place a check mark next to Credit Card Sales of $850.00, too.

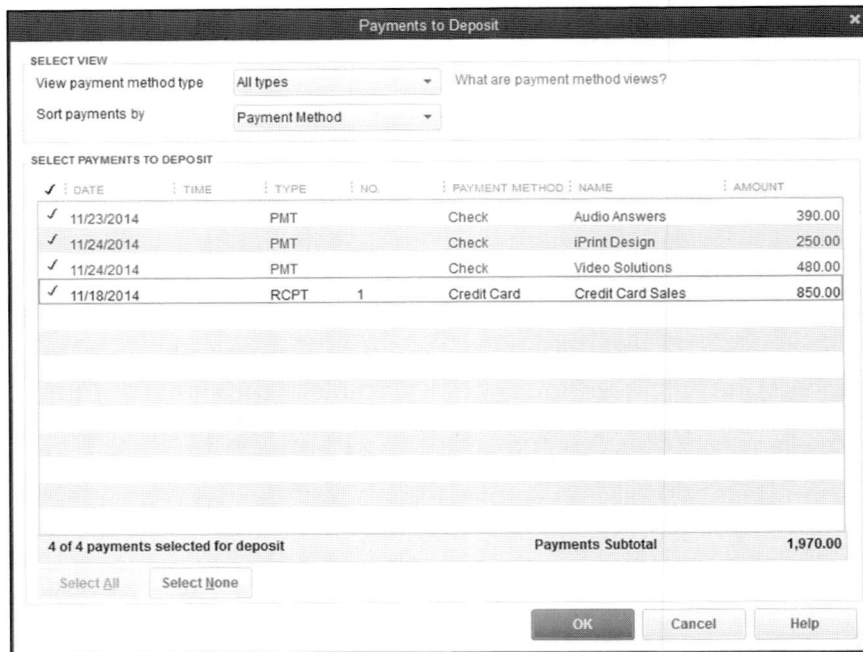

10. The Total amount of the deposit is $1,970.00. Click .

11. The Make Deposits window appears. Observe that the Deposit To field shows Home State Bank.

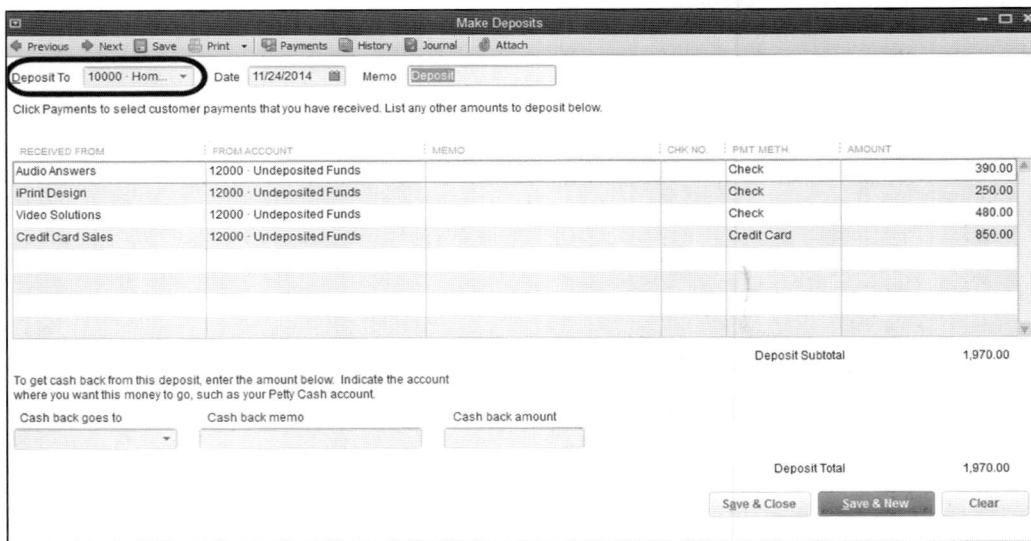

12. Click [S̲ave & Close]. You are returned to the Home page.

13. Backup your work. The suggested file name is **Your Name Chapter 4 November.QBB**. Exit QuickBooks or continue to the next section.

Comment:
Separation of duties means work is divided between different employees to insure data integrity and minimize the opportunity for wrongdoing. This is a basic internal control. For example, to keep employees from stealing customer payments, the tasks opening the mail, recording customer payments, and making deposits at the bank are assigned to three different employees.

ACCOUNT RECONCILIATION

To reconcile Account No. 10000 for November, use the bank statement below. (*Hint:* See previous chapter for October's Account Reconciliation steps.) Check numbers are shown on the following bank statement. Depending on whether you recorded a check number for each vendor payment, check numbers may or may not be included on the Reconcile window shown on page 160.

Statement of Account Home State Bank November 1 to November 30		Account # 923-121368	Your Name Retailers Your address Reno, NV	
REGULAR CHECKING				
Previous Balance	10/31	**$51,290.00**		
Deposits(+)		1,970.00		
Checks (-)		1,835.00		
Service Charges (-)	11/30	10.00		
Ending Balance	11/30	51,415.00		
DEPOSITS				
	11/24	1,120.00	Customers	
	11/24	850.00	Credit Card	
CHECKS (Asterisk * indicates break in check number sequence)				
	11/3	200.00	4004	
	11/25	375.00	4006*	
	11/25	570.00	4007	
	11/25	690.00	4008	

1. After placing check marks beside the cleared deposits and checks per the bank statement, compare your window to the following.

2. The Reconcile - Home State Bank window shows a Difference of 0.00.

3. Click [Reconcile Now]. Select Both. Compare your Reconciliation Detail report to the one shown.

4. Close the Reconciliation Detail and Reconciliation Summary windows. (*Hint:* The Reconciliation Summary report is not shown.)

REPORTS

Print the following reports. If you have made errors in your entries, void and edit your original entries to correct your reports. (*Hint:* See pages 92-94.)

1. Trial Balance from 10/01/20XX to 11/30/20XX.

Your Name Retailers Inc.
Trial Balance
As of November 30, 2014

	Nov 30, 14	
	Debit	Credit
10000 · Home State Bank	51,415.00	
11000 · Accounts Receivable	0.00	
12000 · Undeposited Funds	0.00	
12100 · Inventory Asset	650.00	
13000 · Supplies	2,700.00	
18000 · Prepaid Insurance	2,500.00	
14000 · Computer Equipment	2,400.00	
15000 · Furniture and Equipment	4,000.00	
22000 · Accounts Payable		400.00
26000 · Your Name Notes Payable		20,000.00
30000 · Common Stock		42,500.00
30200 · Dividends	200.00	
46000 · Sales		1,970.00
50000 · Cost of Goods Sold	985.00	
60400 · Bank Service Charges Expense	20.00	
TOTAL	64,870.00	64,870.00

2.   Journal 11/01/20XX to 11/30/20XX.

Your Name Retailers Inc.
Journal
November 2014

Trans #	Type	Date	Num	Adj	Name	Memo	Account	Debit	Credit
12	Bill	11/02/2014			Podcast Ltd.	Invoice No. 5	22000 · Accounts Payable		300.00
					Podcast Ltd.	Invoice No. 5	12100 · Inventory Asset	300.00	
								300.00	300.00
13	Bill	11/03/2014			eBooks Express	Invoice No. 90eB	22000 · Accounts Payable		375.00
					eBooks Express	Invoice No. 90eB	12100 · Inventory Asset	375.00	
								375.00	375.00
14	Bill	11/03/2014			TV Flix	Invoice No. 210TV	22000 · Accounts Payable		750.00
					TV Flix	Invoice No. 210TV	12100 · Inventory Asset	750.00	
								750.00	750.00
15	Bill	11/05/2014			Podcast Ltd.	Invoice No. 78PS	22000 · Accounts Payable		270.00
					Podcast Ltd.	Invoice No. 78PS	12100 · Inventory Asset	270.00	
								270.00	270.00
16	Credit	11/10/2014	CM1		TV Flix	Invoice No. 210TV	22000 · Accounts Payable	60.00	
					TV Flix	Invoice No. 210TV	12100 · Inventory Asset		60.00
								60.00	60.00
17	Bill Pmt -Check	11/20/2014			eBooks Express	22000	10000 · Home State Bank		375.00
					eBooks Express	22000	22000 · Accounts Payable	375.00	
								375.00	375.00
18	Bill Pmt -Check	11/20/2014			Podcast Ltd.	22000	10000 · Home State Bank		570.00
					Podcast Ltd.	22000	22000 · Accounts Payable	570.00	
								570.00	570.00
19	Bill Pmt -Check	11/20/2014			TV Flix	22000	10000 · Home State Bank		690.00
					TV Flix	22000	22000 · Accounts Payable	690.00	
								690.00	690.00
20	Bill	11/21/2014			The Business Store	Invoice BOS44	22000 · Accounts Payable		400.00
					The Business Store	Invoice BOS44	14000 · Computer Equipm...	400.00	
								400.00	400.00
21	Invoice	11/15/2014	1		iPrint Design		11000 · Accounts Receiv...	250.00	
					iPrint Design		46000 · Sales		250.00
					iPrint Design		12100 · Inventory Asset		125.00
					iPrint Design		50000 · Cost of Goods Sold	125.00	
								375.00	375.00
22	Invoice	11/15/2014	2		Audio Answers		11000 · Accounts Receiv...	450.00	
					Audio Answers		46000 · Sales		450.00
					Audio Answers		12100 · Inventory Asset		225.00
					Audio Answers		50000 · Cost of Goods Sold	225.00	
								675.00	675.00

Continued on the next page

23	Invoice	11/15/2014	3	Video Solutions		11000 · Accounts Receiv...	480.00	
				Video Solutions		46000 · Sales		480.00
				Video Solutions		12100 · Inventory Asset		240.00
				Video Solutions		50000 · Cost of Goods Sold	240.00	
							720.00	720.00
24	Credit Memo	11/17/2014	4	Audio Answers		11000 · Accounts Receiv...		60.00
				Audio Answers		46000 · Sales	60.00	
				Audio Answers		12100 · Inventory Asset	30.00	
				Audio Answers		50000 · Cost of Goods Sold		30.00
							90.00	90.00
25	Sales Receipt	11/18/2014	1	Credit Card Sales		12000 · Undeposited Funds	850.00	
				Credit Card Sales	-MULTIPLE-	46000 · Sales		850.00
				Credit Card Sales	-MULTIPLE-	12100 · Inventory Asset		425.00
				Credit Card Sales	-MULTIPLE-	50000 · Cost of Goods Sold	425.00	
							1,275.00	1,275.00
26	Payment	11/23/2014		Audio Answers		12000 · Undeposited Funds	390.00	
				Audio Answers		11000 · Accounts Receiv...		390.00
							390.00	390.00
27	Payment	11/24/2014		iPrint Design		12000 · Undeposited Funds	250.00	
				iPrint Design		11000 · Accounts Receiv...		250.00
							250.00	250.00
28	Payment	11/24/2014		Video Solutions		12000 · Undeposited Funds	480.00	
				Video Solutions		11000 · Accounts Receiv...		480.00
							480.00	480.00
29	Deposit	11/24/2014			Deposit	10000 · Home State Bank	1,970.00	
				-MULTIPLE-	Deposit	12000 · Undeposited Funds		1,970.00
							1,970.00	1,970.00
30	Check	11/30/2014			Service Charge	10000 · Home State Bank		10.00
					Service Charge	60400 · Bank Service Cha...	10.00	
							10.00	10.00
TOTAL							10,025.00	10,025.00

3. Inventory Valuation Detail 10/01/20XX to 11/30/20XX.

Your Name Retailers Inc.
Inventory Valuation Detail
October through November 2014

Type	Date	Name	Num	Qty	Cost	On Hand	Avg Cost	Asset Value
Inventory								
eBook (PDF files)								
Bill	11/03/2014	eBooks Express		15	375.00	15	25.00	375.00
Invoice	11/15/2014	iPrint Design	1	-5		10	25.00	250.00
Sales Receipt	11/18/2014	Credit Card Sales	1	-5		5	25.00	125.00
Total eBook (PDF files)						5		125.00
Podcast (audio files)								
Bill	11/02/2014	Podcast Ltd.		20	300.00	20	15.00	300.00
Bill	11/05/2014	Podcast Ltd.		18	270.00	38	15.00	570.00
Invoice	11/15/2014	Audio Answers	2	-15		23	15.00	345.00
Credit Memo	11/17/2014	Audio Answers	4	2		25	15.00	375.00
Sales Receipt	11/18/2014	Credit Card Sales	1	-8		17	15.00	255.00
Total Podcast (audio files)						17		255.00
TV Programs (video files)								
Bill	11/03/2014	TV Flix		25	750.00	25	30.00	750.00
Credit	11/10/2014	TV Flix	CM1	-2	-60.00	23	30.00	690.00
Invoice	11/15/2014	Video Solutions	3	-8		15	30.00	450.00
Sales Receipt	11/18/2014	Credit Card Sales	1	-6		9	30.00	270.00
Total TV Programs (video files)						9		270.00
Total Inventory						31		650.00
TOTAL						31		650.00

4. Transaction List by Vendor 11/01/20XX to 11/30/20XX.

Your Name Retailers Inc.
Transaction List by Vendor
November 2014

Type	Date	Num	Memo	Account	Clr	Split	Debit	Credit
eBooks Express								
Bill	11/03/2014		Invoice No. 90eB	22000 · Accounts Payable		12100 · Inventory Asset		375.00 ◄
Bill Pmt -Check	11/20/2014		22000	10000 · Home State Bank	✓	22000 · Accounts Payable		375.00
Podcast Ltd.								
Bill	11/02/2014		Invoice No. 5	22000 · Accounts Payable		12100 · Inventory Asset		300.00
Bill	11/05/2014		Invoice No. 78PS	22000 · Accounts Payable		12100 · Inventory Asset		270.00
Bill Pmt -Check	11/20/2014		22000	10000 · Home State Bank	✓	22000 · Accounts Payable		570.00
The Business Store								
Bill	11/21/2014		Invoice BOS44	22000 · Accounts Payable		14000 · Computer Equipment		400.00
TV Flix								
Bill	11/03/2014		Invoice No. 210TV	22000 · Accounts Payable		12100 · Inventory Asset		750.00
Credit	11/10/2014	CM1	Invoice No. 210TV	22000 · Accounts Payable		12100 · Inventory Asset	60.00	
Bill Pmt -Check	11/20/2014		22000	10000 · Home State Bank	✓	22000 · Accounts Payable		690.00

5. Purchase by Item Summary 11/01/20XX to 11/30/20XX. (*Hint:* This is a Purchases report.)

Your Name Retailers Inc.
Purchases by Item Summary
November 2014

		Nov 14	
		Qty	Amount
Inventory			
eBook (PDF files)	►	15 ◄	375.00
Podcast (audio files)		38	570.00
TV Programs (video files)		23	690.00
Total Inventory		76	1,635.00
TOTAL		76.00	1,635.00

6. Purchases by Vendor Detail 11/01/20XX to 11/30/20XX.

Your Name Retailers Inc.
Purchases by Vendor Detail
November 2014

Type	Date	Num	Memo	Name	Item	Qty	Cost Price	Amount	Balance
eBooks Express									
Bill	11/03/2014		Invoice No. 90eB	eBooks Express	eBook (PDF files)	15	25.00	375.00	375.00
Total eBooks Express						15		375.00	375.00
Podcast Ltd.									
Bill	11/02/2014		Invoice No. 5	Podcast Ltd.	Podcast (audio files)	20	15.00	300.00	300.00
Bill	11/05/2014		Invoice No. 78PS	Podcast Ltd.	Podcast (audio files)	18	15.00	270.00	570.00
Total Podcast Ltd.						38		570.00	570.00
TV Flix									
Bill	11/03/2014		Invoice No. 210TV	TV Flix	TV Programs (video files)	25	30.00	750.00	750.00
Credit	11/10/2014	CM1	Invoice No. 210TV	TV Flix	TV Programs (video files)	-2	30.00	-60.00	690.00
Total TV Flix						23		690.00	690.00
TOTAL						76		1,635.00	1,635.00

7. Transaction List by Customer 11/01/20XX to 11/30/20XX.

Your Name Retailers Inc.
Transaction List by Customer
November 2014

Type	Date	Num	Memo	Account	Clr	Split	Debit	Credit
Audio Answers								
Invoice	11/15/2014	2		11000 · Accounts Receivable		46000 · Sales	450.00	
Credit Memo	11/17/2014	4		11000 · Accounts Receivable		46000 · Sales		60.00
Payment	11/23/2014			12000 · Undeposited Funds	✓	11000 · Accounts Receivable	390.00	
Credit Card Sales								
Sales Receipt	11/18/2014	1		12000 · Undeposited Funds	✓	-SPLIT-	850.00	
iPrint Design								
Invoice	11/15/2014	1		11000 · Accounts Receivable		46000 · Sales	250.00	
Payment	11/24/2014			12000 · Undeposited Funds	✓	11000 · Accounts Receivable	250.00	
Video Solutions								
Invoice	11/15/2014	3		11000 · Accounts Receivable		46000 · Sales	480.00	
Payment	11/24/2014			12000 · Undeposited Funds	✓	11000 · Accounts Receivable	480.00	

8. Income by Customer Summary 11/01/20XX to 11/30/20XX. (*Hint:* Company & Financial reports.)

Your Name Retailers Inc.
Income by Customer Summary
November 2014

	Nov 14
Audio Answers	195.00
Credit Card Sales	425.00
iPrint Design	125.00
Video Solutions	240.00
TOTAL	985.00

9. Income and Expense Graph: *Hint:* Company & Financial, Income & Expense Graph, Dates 11/01/20XX to 11/30/20XX.

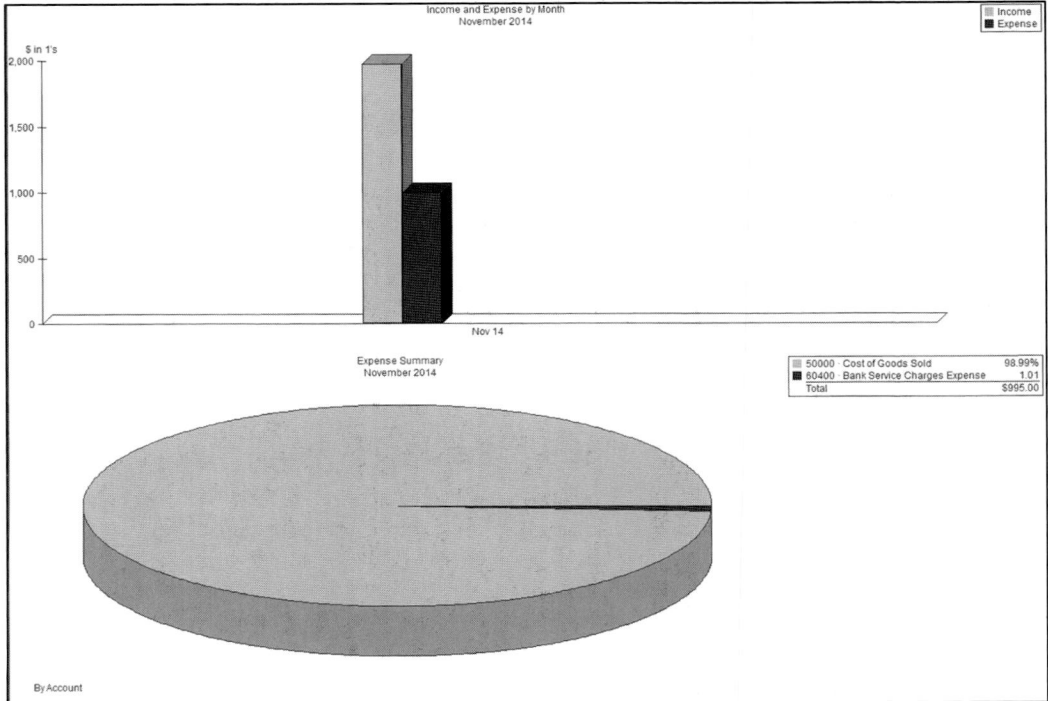

10. Sales by Item Summary 11/01/20XX to 11/30/20XX. (*Hint:* Sales report.)

	Qty	Amount	% of Sales	Avg Price	COGS	Avg COGS	Gross Margin	Gross Margin %
Your Name Retailers Inc. **Sales by Item Summary** November 2014								
				Nov 14				
▼ Inventory								
eBook (PDF files) ►	10 ◄	500.00	25.4%	50.00	250.00	25.00	250.00	50.0%
Podcast (audio files)	21	630.00	32%	30.00	315.00	15.00	315.00	50.0%
TV Programs (video files)	14	840.00	42.6%	60.00	420.00	30.00	420.00	50.0%
Total Inventory	45	1,970.00	100.0%	43.78	985.00	21.89	985.00	50.0%
TOTAL	45	1,970.00	100.0%	43.78		21.89		

BACKUP CHAPTER 4 DATA

1. Backup your work to your USB drive. (*Hint:* File; Back Up Company, Create Local Backup). Name your file **Your Name Chapter 4 End.QBB**

2. Exit QuickBooks or continue with the next section.

SUMMARY AND REVIEW

OBJECTIVES:

1. Open the company, Your Name Retailers Inc.
2. Enter items and inventory preferences.
3. Enter vendor records.
4. Enter inventory items.
5. Print the vendor list and item list.
6. Enter bills and record purchase returns.
7. Pay bills.
8. Add a vendor and non-inventory item on the fly.
9. Enter customer records and defaults.
10. Record customer sales on account and sales returns.
11. Receive customer payments.
12. Make backups.[3]

RESOURCEFUL QUICKBOOKS

Use the Learning Center Tutorials, Tracking Money In selection, to watch the following videos: Sales overview (2:55), Create an invoice (1:38), Receiving and depositing payments (2:30). Answer these questions.

1. Sales overview: What is the difference between an invoice and a sales receipt? What are items?

2. Create an invoice: What are the invoice steps?

3. Receiving and depositing payments: Where does the payment go?

---

[3] The chart in the Preface shows you the size of each backup file. Refer to this chart for backing up data. Remember, you can back up to a hard drive location or external media.

Multiple Choice Questions: The Online Learning Center includes the multiple-choice questions at www.mhhe.com/QBessentials2014, select Student Edition, Chapter 4, Multiple Choice.

_C_ 1. A group of posting accounts that shows the amounts owed to vendors or suppliers is called:

   a. Accounts receivable.
   b. Inventory.
   c. Accounts payable.
   d. Entering bills.
   e. All of the above.

_B_ 2. Your Name Retailers describes eBooks as:

   a. Video files.
   b. PDF files.
   c. Audio files.
   d. None of the above.
   e. All of the above.

_E_ 3. QuickBooks Lists include all of the following except:

   a. Items.
   b. Customers.
   c. Vendors.
   d. Accounts.
   e. All are QuickBooks Lists.

_C_ 4. Products that are purchased for sale are tracked in the following account:

   a. Account No. 46000, Sales.
   b. Account No. 11000, Accounts Receivable.
   c. Account No. 12100, Inventory Asset.
   d. Account No. 13000, Supplies.
   e. None of the above.

_C_

_____5. Which of the following shows information about inventory
items?

  a. Vendor list.
  b. Trial Balance.
  c. Item list.
  d. Vendor record.
  e. None of the above.

_A_

_____6. An in-depth view of the amounts the company owes its vendors
as of a selected date.

  a. Transaction list by vendor.
  b. Invoice.
  c. Purchases by item detail.
  d. A/P aging summary.
  e. All of the above.

_D_

_____7. When merchandise is returned to the vendor, the following
accounts are debited and credited:

  a. Dr. Account No. 12100, Inventory Asset; Credit Account No.
      50000, Cost of Goods Sold.
  b. Debit Account No. 50000, Cost of Goods Sold and Account
      No. 12100, Inventory Asset; Credit Account No. 50000,
      Cost of Goods Sold and Account No. 22000, Accounts
      Payable.
  c. Debit Account No. 50000, Cost of Goods Sold and Account
      No. 22000, Accounts Payable; Credit Account No. 50000,
      Cost of Goods Sold and Account No. 12100, Inventory
      Asset.
  d. Debit Account No. 22000 Accounts Payable; credit Account
      No. 12100, Inventory Asset.
  e. None of the above.

_A_ 8. When a vendor payment is made, the following accounts are debited and credited:

   a. Dr. Account No. 22000, Accounts Payable/vendor; Credit Account No. 10000, Home State Bank.
   b. Credit Account No. 10000, Home State Bank; Debit Account No. 12100, Inventory Asset
   c. Debit Account No. 50000, Cost of Goods Sold and Credit Account No. 10000, Home State Bank.
   d. Debit Account No. 22000 Accounts Payable; credit Account No. 50000, Cost of Goods Sold.
   e. None of the above.

_D_ 9. The term used for adding a new vendor to a transaction is called:

   a. Drill-down.
   b. A/P.
   c. Inventory item.
   d. On-the-fly.
   e. None of the above.

_E_ 10. Which report(s) shows the accounts payable balance?

   a. Purchases by vendor detail.
   b. Item list.
   c. Vendor transaction history.
   d. Trial balance.
   e. Both c. and d.

True/Make True: To answer these questions, go online to www.mhhe.com/QBessentials2014, link to Student Edition, Chapter 4, QA Templates. The analysis question at the end of the chapter is also included.

1.   Another term for vendor is supplier.

2.   A vendor of Your Name Retailers Inc is TV Flix.

3.   Credit card sales are recorded using the Pay Bills icon.

4.   Purchases from vendors are recorded using the Enter Bills icon.

5.   Sales to customers are recorded using the Create Invoice icon.

6.   Purchases returned to vendors are recorded using the Enter Bills icon.

7.   Returns from customers are recorded using the Refunds and Credits icon.

8.   Customer payments on account are recorded using the Receive Payments icon.

9.   Inventory purchased on account is recorded using the Enter Bills icon.

10. Vendor payments are recorded using the Create Cash Receipt icon.

Exercise 4-1: Follow the instructions below to complete Exercise 4-1.

1. Start QuickBooks and open Your Name Retailers. Restore the Your Name Chapter 4 End file. (*Hint:* If you are using your own PC, you may not need to restore. To check that you are starting in the right place, display the 11/30/20XX trial balance. Compare it to the one on page 161.)

2. Record the following transactions during the month of December:

Date	Description of Transaction
12/21	Pay BOS44 to The Business Store for the $400 laptop computer purchase on 11/21.
12/21	Invoice No. 101eB received from eBooks Express for the purchase of 16 PDF files, $25 each, for a total of $400.
12/21	Invoice No. 352TV received from TV Flix for the purchase of 22 video files, $30 each, for a total of $660.
12/21	Invoice No. 95PS received from Podcast Ltd. for the purchase of 12 audio files, $15 each, for a total of $180.
12/23	Returned two PDF files to eBooks Express, Credit Memo No. CM2 for a total of $50.
12/24	Sold 8 eBooks (PDF files) on account to iPrint Design for a total credit sale of $400, Invoice # 5.
12/24	Sold 10 Podcasts (audio files) on account to Audio Answers for a total credit sale of $300 Invoice # 6.
12/24	Sold 12 TV Programs (video files) on account to Video Solutions for a total credit sale of $720, Invoice # 7.
12/26	Sold 4 eBooks for $200; 8 Podcasts for $240; and 6 TV Programs for $360; for total credit card sales of $800, Sale No. 2.

12/27	Video Solutions returned 2 TV Programs (video files), $120. Apply to invoice.

12/27   Video Solutions returned 2 TV Programs (video files), $120. Apply to invoice.

12/30   Received a check in full payment of Audio Answers' account, $300.

12/30   Received a check in full payment of iPrint Design's account, $400.

12/30   Your Name Retailers pays all outstanding vendor bills for a total of $1,190. (*Hint:* Remember to Set Credit for the 12/23/20XX return to eBooks Express.)

12/30   Invoice No. 152PS received from Podcast Ltd. for the purchase of 10 audio files, $15 each, for a total of $150.

12/30   Make bank deposit into the Home State Bank account. Include all undeposited funds, $1,500.

3.   Continue with Exercise 4-2.

Exercise 4-2: Follow the instructions below to complete Exercise 4-2. Exercise 4-1 *must* be completed before starting Exercise 4-2.

1.   Print the following reports. Your instructor may want these reports saved as PDF files and attached in an email. Refer to the Read Me box in Chapter 3, page 110, for saving reports as PDFs.

   a. Trial Balance 12/31/20XX.

   b. Journal 12/01/20XX to 12/31/20XX.

   c. Inventory Valuation Detail 12/1/20XX to 12/31/20XX.

   d. Transaction List by Vendor 12/01/20XX to 12/31/20XX.

   e. Purchases by Vendor Detail 12/01/20XX to 12/31/20XX.

   f. Transaction List by Customer 12/01/20XX to 12/31/20XX.

g. Income and Expense Graph: Dates, By Customer, Income 12/01/20XX to 12/31/20XX.

2. If necessary, close all windows. Backup to USB drive. The suggested file name is **Your Name Exercise 4-2 December.QBB**.

ANALYSIS QUESTION

Does Your Name Retailers use the periodic or perpetual system for tracking inventory and sales?

Chapter

5

Accounting Cycle and Year End

OBJECTIVES:

1. Restore data from the Exercise 4-2 backup.
2. Record a compound journal entry.
3. Write checks for expenses.
4. Make deposits.
5. Complete account reconciliation.
6. Print a trial balance (unadjusted).
7. Record and post quarterly adjusting entries in the General Journal.
8. Print adjusted trial balance and financial statements.
9. Close the fiscal year.
10. Print a Postclosing Trial Balance.
11. Make backups of Chapter 5 data.[1]

Additional textbook related resources are on the textbook website at www.mhhe.com/QBessentials2014. It includes chapter resources, including online quizzes, etc.

GETTING STARTED:

1. Start QuickBooks and open Your Name Retailers. If necessary, restore the Your Name Exercise 4-2 December backup file. This backup was made on page 174. (*Hint:* If you are using your own PC, you may not need to restore. To check that you are starting in the right place, display the 12/31/20XX trial balance. Compare it to the one on the next page).

2. To make sure you are starting in the correct place, display the 12/31/20XX (use your current year) trial balance. Compare your trial balance with the one on the next page.

---

[1]The chart in the Preface, page xii, shows the file name and size of each backup file. Refer to this chart for backing up data. Remember, you can back up to a hard drive location or external media.

The Trial Balance window showing:

Your Name Retailers Inc.
Trial Balance
As of December 31, 2014

	Dec 31, 14	
	Debit	Credit
10000 · Home State Bank	51,325.00	
11000 · Accounts Receivable	600.00	
12000 · Undeposited Funds	0.00	
12100 · Inventory Asset	940.00	
13000 · Supplies	2,700.00	
18000 · Prepaid Insurance	2,500.00	
14000 · Computer Equipment	2,400.00	
15000 · Furniture and Equipment	4,000.00	
22000 · Accounts Payable		150.00
26000 · Your Name Notes Payable		20,000.00
30000 · Common Stock		42,500.00
30200 · Dividends	200.00	
46000 · Sales		4,070.00
50000 · Cost of Goods Sold	2,035.00	
60400 · Bank Service Charges Expense	20.00	
TOTAL	66,720.00	66,720.00

3. Close the trial balance without saving.

COMPOUND TRANSACTIONS

A *compound transaction* is an entry that affects three or more accounts. The principle and interest payment on the Your Name Note Payable is an example of a compound transaction. Use QuickBooks' New General Journal Entry window to record compound transactions.

Follow these steps to record a compound journal entry.

1. From the Icon bar, select Accountant; *or* from the menu bar, select Company. Select Make General Journal Entries.

2. When the Assigning Numbers to Journal Entries screen appears, read it and click OK.

3. The Make General Journal Entries window appears. Uncheck the Adjusting Entry box— ADJUSTING ENTRY.

4. Record the following 12/31/20XX note payable payment.

   Date   *Date of Transaction*

   12/31   Pay $800 to Your Name for note payable
                               principle repayment with interest. The account
                               distribution is shown below.

Acct. No.	Account	Debit	Credit
26000	Your Name Notes Payable	542.00	
63400	Interest Expense	258.00	
10000	Home State Bank		800.00

5. Compare your Make General Journal Entries window to the one shown here.

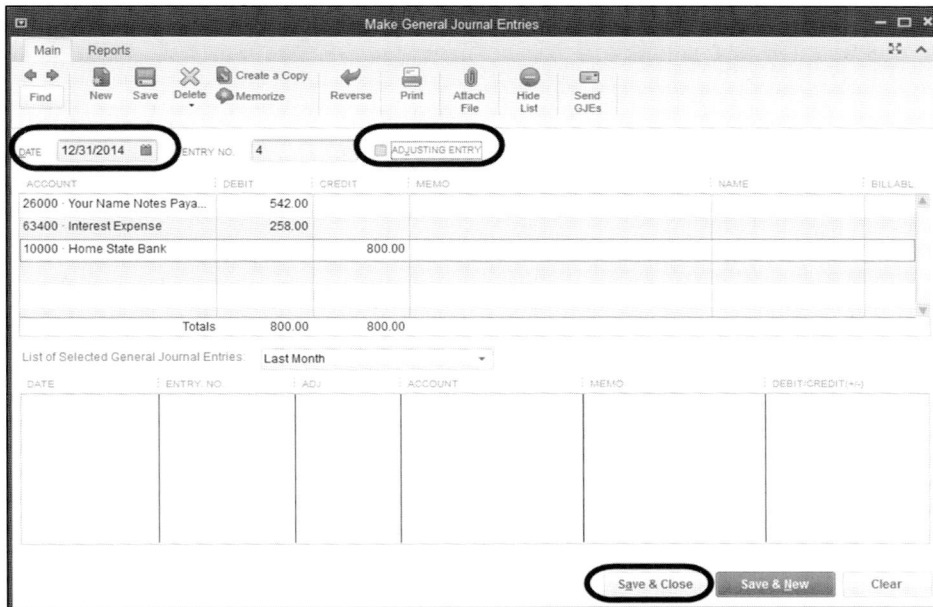

6. Click Save & Close.

WRITE CHECKS

From the Home page, use the Banking section's Write Checks icon to issue the following checks.

√ 12/31   Issue Check No. 4015 in the amount of $80 for cellular service. (*Hint:* Debit Account No. 68100, Telephone Expense; quick add the vendor, Mobile One.)

√ 12/31   Issue Check No. 4016 in the amount of $50 for Internet service. (*Hint:* Debit Account No. 61700, Computer and Internet Expenses. Quick add the vendor, ISP.)

√ 12/31   Issue Check No. 4017 in the amount of $68 for telephone service. (*Hint:* Debit Account No. 68100, Telephone Expense. Add the vendor, Everywhere Telephone Service.)

√ 12/31   Issue Check No. 4018 in the amount of $111 for Electricity/Gas. (*Hint:* Debit Account No. 68600 Utilities. Quick add the vendor, Regional Utilities.)

√ 12/31   Issue Check No. 4019 in the amount of $74 for Water/Garbage service. (*Hint:* Debit Account No. 68600 Utilities. Add the vendor, Reno Water/Garbage.)

√ 12/31   Pay $200 Dividend to sole stockholder, Your Name. Check No. 4020 payable to you. Save and close Write Checks window.

CHECK REGISTER

Click on the Check Register icon in the Banking section of the Home page to see Account No. 10000, Home State Bank activity. You can enlarge to 10000 Home State Bank window to see more transactions.

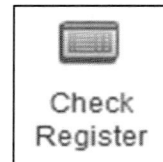

Check Register

The Account 10000 - Home State Bank check register is shown on the next page.

After comparing your Account No. 10000-Home State Bank account to the register, close.

ACCOUNT RECONCILIATION

You may want to review detailed steps for account reconciliation, pages 96-100. Using the bank statement shown on the next page, reconcile the Home State Bank account. Remember the bank service charge of $10.00.

Follow these steps to complete account reconciliation.

1. From the Banking pane of the Home page, select the Reconcile icon. All checks have cleared the bank. To reconcile, use the bank statement on the next page.

Reconcile

Statement of Account Home State Bank December 1 to December 31, 20XX Account # 923-121368			Your Name Retailers Your Address Reno, NV	
REGULAR CHECKING				
Previous Balance	11/30	51,415.00		
Deposits		1,500.00		
Checks (-)		2,973.00		
Service Charges (-)	12/31	10.00		
Ending Balance	12/31	**$49,932.00**		
DEPOSITS				
	12/31	300.00	Audio Answers	
	12/31	400.00	iPrint Design	
	12/31	800.00	Credit Card	
CHECKS				
	12/23	400.00		
	12/31	350.00		
	12/31	180.00		
	12/31	660.00		
	12/31	800.00		
	12/31	80.00	4015	
	12/31	50.00	4016	
	12/31	68.00	4017	
	12/31	111.00	4018	
	12/31	74.00	4019	
	12/31	200.00	4020	

2. Reconcile the account. Compare your Reconcile-Home State Bank screen to the one shown on the next page.

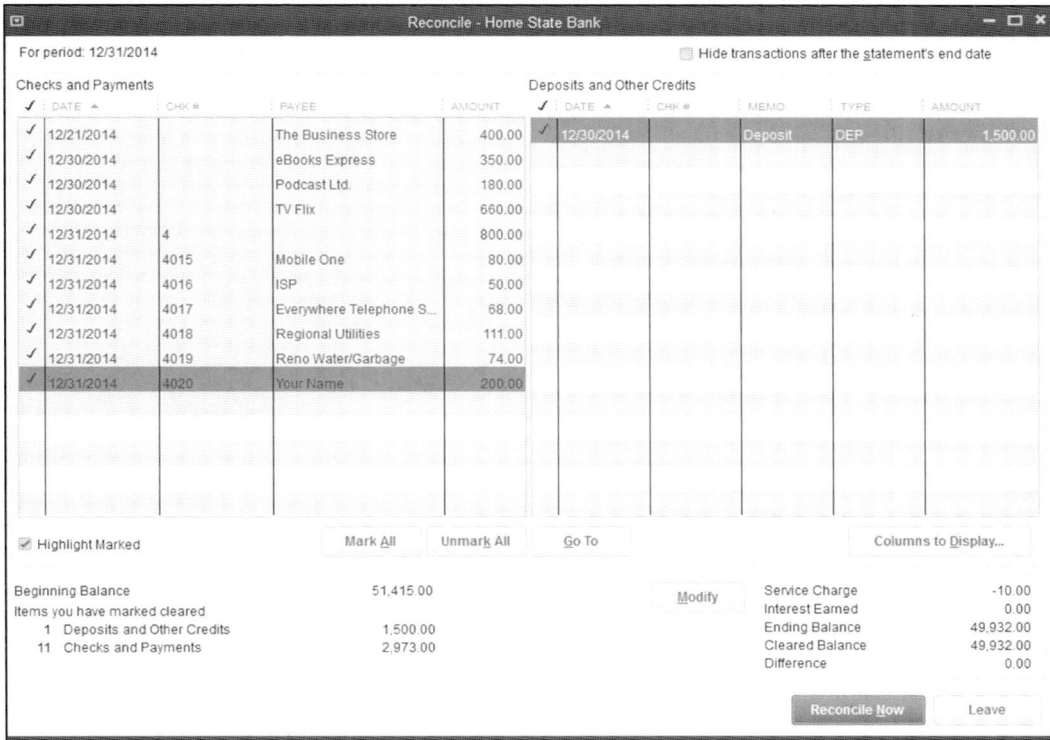

Observe that the Check Register on page 179 shows an ending balance of $49,942.00. The bank statement's ending balance shows $49,932.00. The difference is the bank service charge of $10.00. Once those fees are deducted from the check register balance, the bank statement and check register agree.

3. Make sure the Difference field shows 0.00. When satisfied, click
   Reconcile Now .

4. When the Select Reconciliation Report window displays, make sure Both is selected. Display the Reconciliation Summary report. (*Hint:* Two reports display, Reconciliation Detail and the Reconciliation Summary. Compare your Reconciliation Summary report to the one shown on the next page.

Your Name Retailers Inc.
Reconciliation Summary
10000 · Home State Bank, Period Ending 12/31/2014

	Dec 31, 14
Beginning Balance	51,415.00
▼ Cleared Transactions	
Checks and Payments - 12 items	-2,983.00
Deposits and Credits - 1 item	1,500.00
Total Cleared Transactions	-1,483.00
Cleared Balance	**49,932.00**
Register Balance as of 12/31/2014	49,932.00
Ending Balance ▶	49,932.00 ◀

5. Close the reports.

ACCOUNTING CYCLE

Chapters 3-5 in this text work together to process the tasks in the accounting cycle for October through December. The steps of the Accounting Cycle that you do in this text are shown in the table below.

QuickBooks Accounting Cycle
1. Set up a company.
2. Record transactions.
3. Post entries automatically.
4. Account Reconciliation.
5. Print the Trial Balance (unadjusted).
6. Record and post adjusting entries.
7. Print the Trial Balance (adjusted).
8. Print the financial statements: balance sheet, profit and loss, cash flow statement.
9. Close the fiscal year.
10. Interpret accounting information.

At the end of December, which is also the end of the fiscal year, you complete the remaining tasks by printing an unadjusted trial balance, recording adjusting entries, printing financial statements, and closing the fiscal year.

UNADJUSTED TRIAL BALANCE

1. Print the 12/31/20XX Trial Balance (unadjusted). Compare your unadjusted trial balance to the one shown below.

Trial Balance		
Customize Report	Share Template	Memorize Print ▼ E-mail ▼ Excel ▼ Hide Header Collapse Refresh
Dates Custom	▼ From 12/31/2014 🗓 To 12/31/2014 🗓 Sort By Default	▼

Your Name Retailers Inc.
Trial Balance
As of December 31, 2014

	Dec 31, 14	
	Debit	Credit
10000 · Home State Bank	49,932.00	
11000 · Accounts Receivable	600.00	
12000 · Undeposited Funds	0.00	
12100 · Inventory Asset	940.00	
13000 · Supplies	2,700.00	
18000 · Prepaid Insurance	2,500.00	
14000 · Computer Equipment	2,400.00	
15000 · Furniture and Equipment	4,000.00	
22000 · Accounts Payable		150.00
26000 · Your Name Notes Payable		19,458.00
30000 · Common Stock		42,500.00
30200 · Dividends	400.00	
46000 · Sales		4,070.00
50000 · Cost of Goods Sold	2,035.00	
60400 · Bank Service Charges Expense	30.00	
61700 · Computer and Internet Expenses	50.00	
63400 · Interest Expense	258.00	
68100 · Telephone Expense	148.00	
68600 · Utilities Expense	185.00	
TOTAL	66,178.00	66,178.00

2. Backup the company data through the unadjusted trial balance to your USB drive. Name your backup **Your Name Chapter 5 December UTB** in the File name field. (*Hint:* UTB is an abbreviation of unadjusted trial balance.)

3. Exit QuickBooks or continue with the next section.

END-OF-QUARTER ADJUSTING ENTRIES

It is the policy of your company to record adjusting entries at the end of the quarter to properly reflect all the quarter's business activities.

Follow these steps to record and post the adjusting entries in the journal.

1. From the Icon Bar select Accountant; *or* from the menu bar, select Company. Select Make General Journal Entries.

2. When the Assigning Numbers to Journal Entries screen appears, read it and click <kbd>OK</kbd>.

3. Make sure the box next to Adjusting Entry is checked <kbd>☑ ADJUSTING ENTRY</kbd>. When you check the Adjusting Entry box, adjusting entries are identified on QB reports. Since QB includes an Adjusted Trial Balance, make sure you have selected Adjusting Entry on the Make General Journal Entries window.

4. If necessary, type **5** in the Entry No. field. That is the first adjusting entry number.

5. Type **12/31/20XX (use your current year)** in the Date field.

6. In the Account field, select the appropriate account to debit. (See transactions 1-4 below and on pages 185-186.)

7. Type the appropriate amount in the Debit field.

8. Select the appropriate account to credit. Make sure the Credit field shows the appropriate amount.

9. Click <kbd>Save & New</kbd> to go to the next journal entry.

The following adjusting entries need to be recorded. Record and post these December 31, 20XX adjusting entries.

1. Supplies on hand are $2,400.00. (This is Journal No. 5.)

Acct. #	Account Name	Debit	Credit
64900	Supplies Expense	300.00	
13000	Supplies		300.00

Computation: Supplies $2,700.00
                     Office supplies on hand - 2,400.00
                     Adjustment $ 300.00

(*Hint:* To post your transaction, click [Save & New] after each journal entry.)

2. Adjust three months of prepaid insurance $150.00 ($50 per month x 3 months). (This is Journal No. 6.)

Acct. #	Account Name	Debit	Credit
63300	Insurance Expense	150.00	
18000	Prepaid Insurance		150.00

3. Use straight-line depreciation for your computer equipment. Your computer equipment has a five-year service life and no salvage value. (Journal No. 7.)

To depreciate computer equipment for the fourth quarter, use this calculation:

$2,400 ÷ 5 years X 3/12 months = $120.00

Acct. #	Account Name	Debit	Credit
62400	Depreciation Expense	120.00	
16000	Accumulated Depreciation-CEqmt.		120.00

Read the Tracking Fixed Assets on Journal Entries window, then click [OK].

4. Use straight-line depreciation to depreciate your furniture. The furniture has a 5-year service life and no salvage value. (Journal No. 8.)

To depreciate furniture for the fourth quarter, use this calculation:

$4,000 ÷ 5 years X 3/12 months = $200.00

Acct. #	Account Name	Debit	Credit
62400	Depreciation Expense	200.00	
17000	Accumulated Depreciation-F&E		200.00

Read the Tracking Fixed Assets on Journal Entries box, then click
OK.

5. After making the end-of-quarter adjusting entries, close the Make General Journal Entries window, then display the Adjusting Journal Entries for 12/31/20XX. (*Hint:* Report Center or Reports menu; Accountant & Taxes, Adjusting Journal Entries.) If you placed a check mark next to adjusting entries (step 3, page 184) on the Make General Journal Entries window, only adjusting entries will display.

Adjusting Journal Entries

Your Name Retailers Inc.
Adjusting Journal Entries
December 31, 2014

Date	Num	Name	Memo	Account	Debit	Credit
12/31/2014	5			64900 · Supplies Expense	300.00	
				13000 · Supplies		300.00
					300.00	300.00
12/31/2014	6			63300 · Insurance Expense	150.00	
				18000 · Prepaid Insurance		150.00
					150.00	150.00
12/31/2014	7			62400 · Depreciation Expense	120.00	
				16000 · Accumulated Depreciatio...		120.00
					120.00	120.00
12/31/2014	8			62400 · Depreciation Expense	200.00	
				17000 · Accumulated Depreciatio...		200.00
					200.00	200.00
TOTAL					770.00	770.00

If your adjusting journal entries in the Journal do *not* agree with the Adjusting Journal Entries window, edit them.

6. Close the Journal without saving.

7. Print the 12/31/20XX Adjusted Trial Balance. Compare your adjusted trial balance to the one shown.

	Adjusted Trial Balance						— □ ×
Customize Report	Share Template	Memorize	Print ▼	E-mail ▼	Excel ▼	Hide Header	Collapse	Refresh

Dates Custom ▼   From 12/31/2014 📅 To 12/31/2014 📅 Sort By Default ▼

Your Name Retailers Inc.
Adjusted Trial Balance
December 31, 2014

	Unadjusted Balance		Adjustments		Adjusted Balance	
	Debit	Credit	Debit	Credit	Debit	Credit
10000 · Home State Bank	49,932.00				49,932.00	
11000 · Accounts Receivable	600.00				600.00	
12000 · Undeposited Funds	0.00				0.00	
12100 · Inventory Asset	940.00				940.00	
13000 · Supplies	2,700.00			300.00 ▶	2,400.00 ◀	
18000 · Prepaid Insurance	2,500.00			150.00	2,350.00	
14000 · Computer Equipment	2,400.00				2,400.00	
15000 · Furniture and Equipment	4,000.00				4,000.00	
16000 · Accumulated Depreciation-CEqmt.				120.00		120.00
17000 · Accumulated Depreciation-F&E				200.00		200.00
22000 · Accounts Payable		150.00				150.00
26000 · Your Name Notes Payable		19,458.00				19,458.00
30000 · Common Stock		42,500.00				42,500.00
30200 · Dividends	400.00				400.00	
46000 · Sales		4,070.00				4,070.00
50000 · Cost of Goods Sold	2,035.00			▶	2,035.00 ◀	
60400 · Bank Service Charges Expense	30.00				30.00	
61700 · Computer and Internet Expenses	50.00				50.00	
62400 · Depreciation Expense			320.00		320.00	
63300 · Insurance Expense			150.00		150.00	
63400 · Interest Expense	258.00				258.00	
64900 · Supplies Expense			300.00		300.00	
68100 · Telephone Expense	148.00				148.00	
68600 · Utilities Expense	185.00				185.00	
TOTAL	66,178.00	66,178.00	770.00	770.00	66,498.00	66,498.00

8. Print the 10/01/20XX to 12/31/20XX Profit & Loss-Standard (income statement). Compare yours to the one shown on the next page.

9. Print the 12/31/20XX Balance Sheet-Standard. Compare yours to the one shown on the next page.

Your Name Retailers Inc.
Balance Sheet
As of December 31, 2014

	◇ Dec 31, 14 ◇
▼ ASSETS	
▼ Current Assets	
▼ Checking/Savings	
10000 · Home State Bank	▶ 49,932.00 ◀
Total Checking/Savings	49,932.00
▼ Accounts Receivable	
11000 · Accounts Receivable	600.00
Total Accounts Receivable	600.00
▼ Other Current Assets	
12100 · Inventory Asset	940.00
13000 · Supplies	2,400.00
18000 · Prepaid Insurance	2,350.00
Total Other Current Assets	5,690.00
Total Current Assets	56,222.00
▼ Fixed Assets	
14000 · Computer Equipment	2,400.00
15000 · Furniture and Equipment	4,000.00
16000 · Accumulated Depreciation-CEqmt.	-120.00
17000 · Accumulated Depreciation-F&E	-200.00
Total Fixed Assets	6,080.00
TOTAL ASSETS	62,302.00
▼ LIABILITIES & EQUITY	
▼ Liabilities	
▼ Current Liabilities	
▼ Accounts Payable	
22000 · Accounts Payable	150.00
Total Accounts Payable	150.00
Total Current Liabilities	150.00
▼ Long Term Liabilities	
26000 · Your Name Notes Payable	19,458.00
Total Long Term Liabilities	19,458.00
Total Liabilities	19,608.00
▼ Equity	
30000 · Common Stock	42,500.00
30200 · Dividends	-400.00
Net Income	594.00
Total Equity	42,694.00
TOTAL LIABILITIES & EQUITY	62,302.00

10. Print the 10/01/20XX to 12/31/20XX Statement of Cash Flows.

Your Name Retailers Inc.

Statement of Cash Flows

October through December 2014

	◇ Oct - Dec 14 ◇
▼ OPERATING ACTIVITIES	
Net Income	▶ 594.00 ◀
▼ Adjustments to reconcile Net Income	
▼ to net cash provided by operations:	
11000 · Accounts Receivable	-600.00
12100 · Inventory Asset	-940.00
13000 · Supplies	100.00
18000 · Prepaid Insurance	150.00
22000 · Accounts Payable	150.00
Net cash provided by Operating Activities	-546.00
▼ INVESTING ACTIVITIES	
14000 · Computer Equipment	-1,400.00
16000 · Accumulated Depreciation-CEqmt.	120.00
17000 · Accumulated Depreciation-F&E	200.00
Net cash provided by Investing Activities	-1,080.00
▼ FINANCING ACTIVITIES	
26000 · Your Name Notes Payable	-542.00
30000 · Common Stock	1,500.00
30200 · Dividends	-400.00
Net cash provided by Financing Activities	558.00
Net cash increase for period	-1,068.00
Cash at beginning of period	51,000.00
Cash at end of period	49,932.00

Comment

If your statement of cash flows or other financial statements *do not agree* with the textbook illustrations, drill-down to the appropriate entries. Edit the entries, then post and reprint your reports.

11. Back Up Company. The suggested file name is **Your Name Chapter 5 December Financial Statements**.

CLOSING THE FISCAL YEAR

When you close the fiscal year, all revenue and expense accounts are moved to Account No. 32000, Retained Earnings. Moving the expense and revenue accounts to retained earnings is called **closing the fiscal year**. The Dividends account must also be closed to Retained Earnings.

Follow these steps to close Dividends and close the fiscal year.

1. Journalize and post the following closing entries in the general journal (Journal Entry 9). When the Assigning Numbers to Journal Entries window appears, click [OK]. Make sure the Adjusting Entry box is unchecked—[☐ ADJUSTING ENTRY].

Make the following December 31, 20XX closing entry for dividends.

Acct. #	Account Name	Debit	Credit
32000	Retained Earnings	400.00	
30200	Dividends		400.00

2. Compare your entry to the one below.

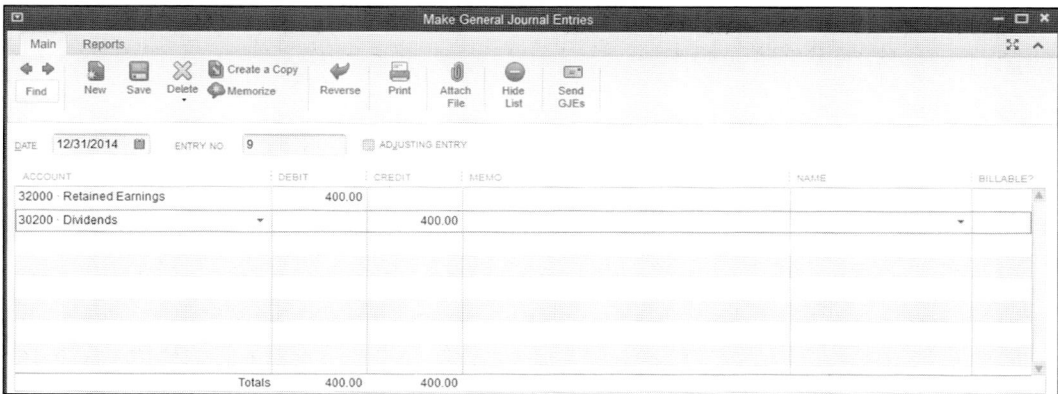

3. When satisfied, click [Save & Close].

4. When the Retained Earnings warning screen appears, read it and then click [OK].

5. From the menu bar, select Company; Set Closing Date.

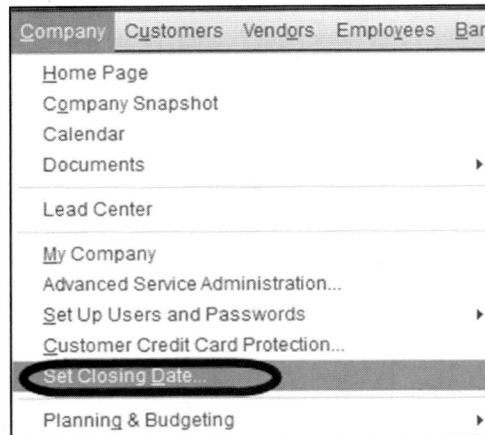

6. The Preferences window appears.

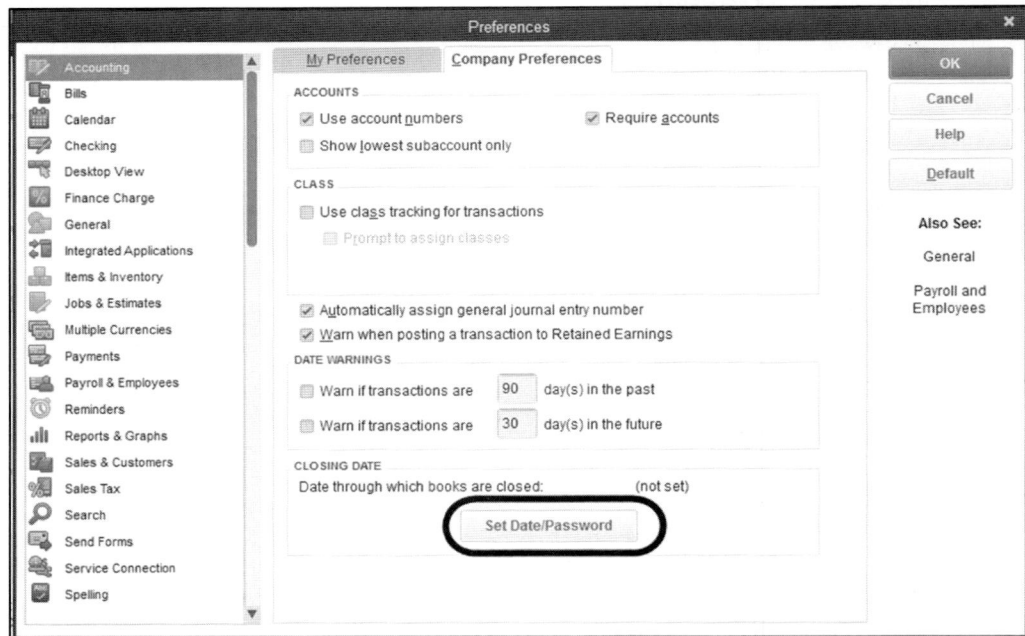

7. Click [Set Date/Password]. The Set Closing Date and Password window appears. For Closing Date, type **12/31/20XX** (use your current year). **Do not type a password!**

Set Closing Date and Password   ✕

To keep your financial data secure, QuickBooks recommends assigning all other users their own username and password, in Company > Set Up Users.

DATE

QuickBooks will display a warning, or require a password, when s~~~ or before the closing date.   More details...

☐ Exclude estimates, sales orders and pur~~~se orders from closing date restrictions

Closing Date   12/31/2014   📅

Use your current year.

PASSWORD

QuickBooks strongly recommends setting a password to protect transactions dated o~ before the closing date.

Closing Date Password   [   ]

Confirm Password   [   ]

Do not type a password.

To see changes made on or before the closing date, view the Closing Date Exception Report in Reports > Accountant & Taxes.

[OK]   [Cancel]

8. Click [OK]. When the No Password Entered window appears, read it. Then, click [No]. Click [OK] to close the Preferences window.

PRINTING THE POSTCLOSING TRIAL BALANCE

After the fiscal year is closed, a postclosing trial balance is displayed and printed. Observe that the postclosing trial balance does *not* show dividends, revenue and expense accounts.

1. Display the 01/01/20YY (use the year after your current year) trial balance. (*Hint:* From the menu bar, select Reports; Accountant & Taxes, Trial Balance.) Compare yours to the one below, when satisfied, print your postclosing trial balance.

Trial Balance report window showing:

Your Name Retailers Inc.
Trial Balance
As of January 1, 2015

	Jan 1, 15	
	Debit	Credit
10000 · Home State Bank	49,932.00	
11000 · Accounts Receivable	600.00	
12000 · Undeposited Funds	0.00	
12100 · Inventory Asset	940.00	
13000 · Supplies	2,400.00	
18000 · Prepaid Insurance	2,350.00	
14000 · Computer Equipment	2,400.00	
15000 · Furniture and Equipment	4,000.00	
16000 · Accumulated Depreciation-CEqmt.		120.00
17000 · Accumulated Depreciation-F&E		200.00
22000 · Accounts Payable		150.00
26000 · Your Name Notes Payable		19,458.00
30000 · Common Stock		42,500.00
30200 · Dividends	0.00	
32000 · Retained Earnings		194.00
TOTAL	62,622.00	62,622.00

Since the company's net income was greater than the dividends paid, Retained Earnings has a credit balance of $194.00.

2. Close the postclosing trial balance without saving.

BACKUP END-OF-YEAR DATA

1. Back up the data through year end to your USB drive. The suggested file name is **Your Name Chapter 5 EOY (Portable).QBM**. (*Hint:* EOY is an abbreviation of end of year.) Since you are going to email this file to your instructor, use the portable file format–File; Create Copy, Portable company file.

    The Save Copy or Backup window is shown on the next page. Portable company file is selected.

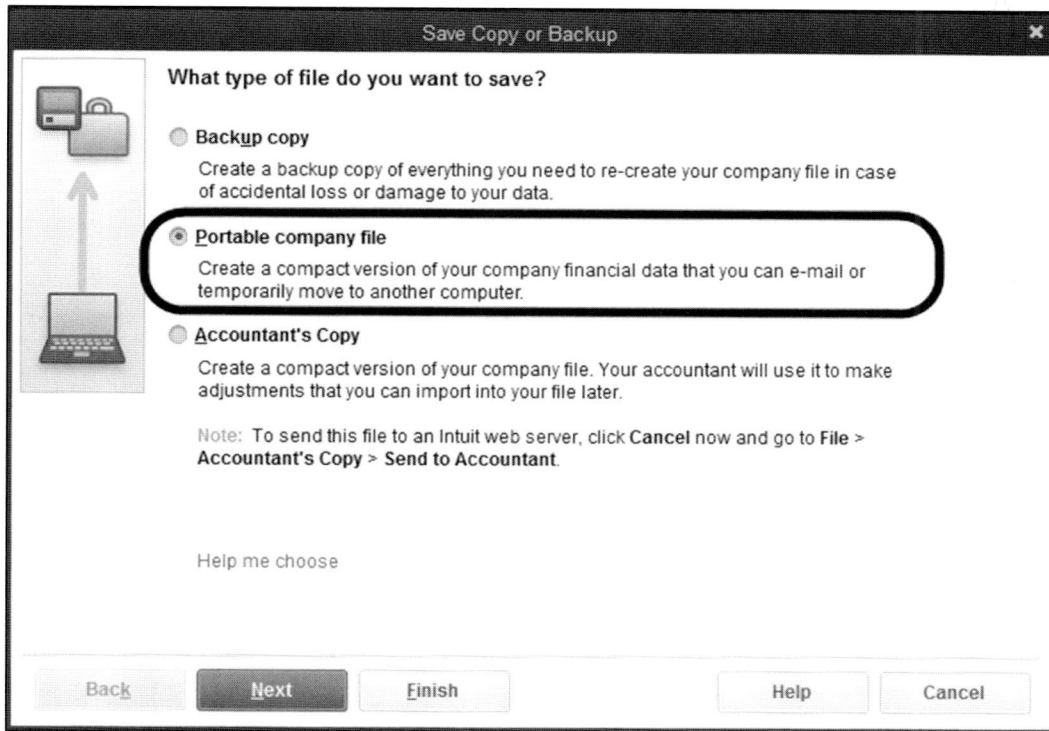

Portable company files create a compact version of your data. Files ending in a QBM extension are smaller than backups that have a .QBB file extension.

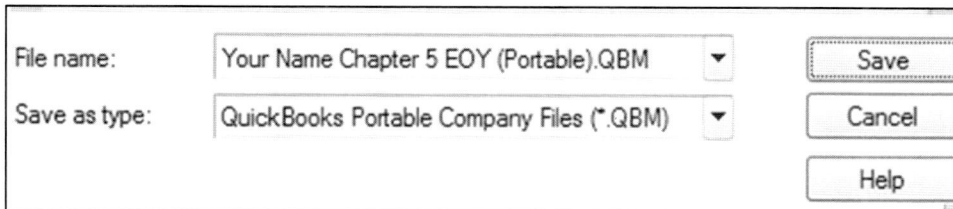

2. Exit QuickBooks or continue with the next section.

ACCOUNTANT TRANSFER

At year-end, external accountants or auditors review a company's accounting records. In this text, the external accountant is your professor. It is time to send your end-of-year portable company file via e-mail to you professor.

1. Start your e-mail program.

2. Create an e-mail message to your professor. Type **Your Name Retailers EOY** for the Subject. (Use your first and last name)

3. Attach the portable backup file **Your Name Chapter 5 EOY (Portable)** that you made on pages 194-195 to your instructor.

4. CC yourself on the message to be sure the message sends properly.

5. Send the message to your professor. You should receive a copy of it as well.

SUMMARY AND REVIEW

OBJECTIVES:

1. Restore data from the Exercise 4-2.
2. Record a compound journal entry.
3. Write checks for expenses.
4. Make deposits.
5. Complete account reconciliation.
6.   Print the trial balance (unadjusted).
7. Record and post quarterly adjusting entries in the General Journal.
8. Print adjusted trial balance and financial statements.
9. Close the fiscal year.
10. Print a Postclosing Trial Balance.
11. Make backups of Chapter 5 data.

Additional textbook related resources are on the textbook website at www.mhhe.com/QBessentials2014. It includes chapter resources, including troubleshooting tips, online quizzes, etc.

RESOURCEFUL QUICKBOOKS

Use the QuickBooks Learning Center (Help; Learning Center Tutorials) to watch the following Tracking Money Out videos. Answer these questions.

1. Expenses overview (2:54): What is the two-step process for entering and paying invoices received from vendors? Why use a two-step process to pay bills rather than write a check? List four advantages of the two-step process.

2. Building blocks of recording expenses (1:34): On the Write Checks form, when do you use the Expenses tab? When do you use the Items tab? Explain.

3. Entering and paying bills (1:41): If you use the Enter Bills window to enter an invoice, can you use Write Checks for paying the bill?

Multiple Choice questions: The Online Learning Center includes the multiple-choice questions at www.mhhe.com/QBessentials2014, select Student Edition, Chapter 5, Multiple Choice.

_____1. Compound entries affect at least how many accounts?

    a. One.
    b. Two.
    c. Three.
    d. None of the above.

_____2. Write checks icon is found in which pane on the Home page:

    a. Banking.
    b. Customers.
    c. Company.
    d. Vendors.

_____3. The Check Register displays information about:

    a. Deposits.
    b. Checks.
    c. Cash balance.
    d. All of the above.

_A_ 4. An account reconciliation is completed:

    a. When the bank statement is received.
    b. Daily.
    c. Weekly.
    d. Annually.

_C_ 5. The correct order of Accounting Cycle steps is:

    a. Record entries, Print the adjusted trial balance, Record and post adjusting entries, Close the fiscal year.
    b. Record and post adjusting entries, Account reconciliation, Print the unadjusted trial balance, Close the fiscal year.
    c. Record entries, Print the unadjusted trial balance, Record and post adjusting entries, Close the fiscal year.
    d. Record entries, Print the adjusted trial balance, Account reconciliation, Close the fiscal year.

_B_ 6. The adjusting entry for depreciation is:

    a. Debit Accumulated Depreciation account and Credit Depreciation Expense account.
    b. Debit Depreciation Expense account and Credit Accumulated Depreciation account.
    c. Debit Computer Equipment account and Credit Accumulated Depreciation account.
    d. Debit Depreciation Expense account and Credit Computer Equipment.

_D_ 7. Make General Journal Entries window is used to record:

    a. Compound entries.
    b. Adjusting entries.
    c. Closing entries.
    d. All of the above.

_C_ 8. Financial statements are prepared in the following order:

  a. Balance Sheet, Income Statement, and Statement of Cash Flow.
  b. Statement of Cash Flow, Income Statement, and Balance Sheet.
  c. Income Statement, Balance Sheet, and Statement of Cash Flow.
  d. Balance Sheet, Statement of Cash Flow, and Income Statement.

_A_ 9. Closing entries move the following account balances to Retained Earnings at the end of the fiscal year:

  a. Revenue and expense accounts.
  b. Dividend and liability accounts.
  c. Expense and asset accounts.
  d. Asset and liability accounts.

_B_ 10. Postclosing Trial Balance contains:

  a. Only statement of cash flow accounts.
  b. No revenue, expense, or dividend accounts.
  c. Only profit and loss accounts.
  d. Only stockholders' equity accounts.

Short-answer questions: To answer these questions, go online to www.mhhe.com/QBessentials2014, link to Student Edition, Chapter 5, QA Templates. The analysis question at the end of the chapter is also included.

1. Define a compound transaction.

2. What is the account distribution for the note payable payment?

3. What account is debited to pay dividends? What account is credited?

4. What account is debited to pay for cellular phone service? What account is credited?

5. What account is debited to pay for Internet service? What account is credited?

6. What account is debited to pay for water and garbage? What account is credited?

7. What is the check register and what does it show?

8. In Chapter 5 what steps of the accounting cycle did you complete?

9. Why does Your Name Retailers Inc. make adjusting journal entries?

10. What accounts never appear in a company's postclosing trial balance?

Exercise 5-1: Follow the instructions below to complete Exercise 5-1.

1. If necessary start QuickBooks and open Your Name Retailers.

2. Print the Audit Trail report for All dates. (*Hint:* Report Center; Accountant & Taxes, Audit Trail.)

👓   **Read me: Audit Trail**

When changes are made to a transaction, the Num column is shown in italics; the State column shows Latest and Prior. If the amount was changed, it is shown in boldface.

---

3. Your instructor may want you to email the Audit Trial report as a PDF attachment. To do that, display the Audit Trail report (all dates), then select File; Save as PDF. (*Hint:* There is also an E-mail button on the Audit Trial's icon bar. Select E-mail, then send the report as a

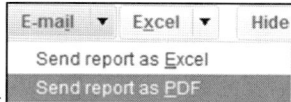

PDF– .) The suggested file name is **Chapter 5 Audit Trail.pdf**.

Exercise 5-2: Answer the questions in the space provided. Use the following abbreviations to identify reports: IS (income statement); BS (balance sheet); CFS (cash flow statement).

1. What report(s) show the net income or net loss? _IS, BS, CFS_

2. What report(s) show the cash balance? _BS, CFS_

3. What report(s) show total fixed assets? _BS_

4. What report(s) show common stock? _BS, CFS_

5. What reports(s) show cash at the beginning of the period? _CFS_

6. What report(s) show note payable accounts? _BS, CFS_

7. What report(s) show total expenses? _IS_

8. What report(s) show the gross profit? _IS_

9. What report(s) show cost of goods sold? _IS_

10. What report(s) show dividends? _BS, CFS_

ANALYSIS QUESTION:

How is the December 31, 20XX retained earnings balance computed? Show the computation.

Chapter 6

First Month of the New Year

OBJECTIVES:

1. Restore data from Your Name Chapter 5 EOY file.
2. Record one month of transactions.
3. Make bank deposit.
4. Complete account reconciliation.
5. Print a trial balance (unadjusted).
6. Record adjusting entries and print an adjusted trial balance.
7. Print financial statements.
8. Make backups of Chapter 6 data.[1]

Additional textbook related resources are on the textbook website at www.mhhe.com/QBessentials2014. It includes chapter resources, including online quizzes, etc.

GETTING STARTED:

1. Start QuickBooks an open Your Name Retailers Inc.

2. If necessary, open or restore the Your Name Chapter 5 EOY. This backup was made in the previous chapter, pages 194-195. (*Hint:* If you are using your own PC, you may not need to restore.)

3. To make sure you are starting in the correct place, display the 01/01/20YY trial balance. 20YY is the year after your current year; for example, if your current year is 2014, use 2015 for year 20YY.

   The January 1, 20YY postclosing trial balance is shown on the next page and in Chapter 5 on page 194.

---

[1]The chart in the Preface, page xii, shows the files names and size of each backup file. Refer to this chart for backing up data. Remember, you can back up to a hard drive location or external media.

Trial Balance

Your Name Retailers Inc.
Trial Balance
As of January 1, 2015

	Jan 1, 15	
	Debit	Credit
10000 · Home State Bank	49,932.00	
11000 · Accounts Receivable	600.00	
12000 · Undeposited Funds	0.00	
12100 · Inventory Asset	940.00	
13000 · Supplies	2,400.00	
18000 · Prepaid Insurance	2,350.00	
14000 · Computer Equipment	2,400.00	
15000 · Furniture and Equipment	4,000.00	
16000 · Accumulated Depreciation-CEqmt.		120.00
17000 · Accumulated Depreciation-F&E		200.00
22000 · Accounts Payable		150.00
26000 · Your Name Notes Payable		19,458.00
30000 · Common Stock		42,500.00
30200 · Dividends	0.00	
32000 · Retained Earnings		194.00
TOTAL	62,622.00	62,622.00

4.   Close the trial balance without saving.

In this chapter you will apply what you have learned so far to complete steps 2-8 in the accounting cycle for January. The steps in the accounting cycle include:

Accounting Cycle
1.   Set up a company.
2.   Record transactions.
3.   Post entries.
4.   Account Reconciliation.
5.   Print the Trial Balance (unadjusted).
6.   Record and post adjusting entries.
7.   Print the Trial Balance (adjusted).
8.   Print the financial statements: Balance Sheet, Profit and Loss, Cash Flow Statement.
9.   Close the fiscal year.
10.   Interpret accounting information.

RECORD FIRST MONTH OF NEW FISCAL YEAR TRANSACTIONS

Record the following transactions from your Check Register for the month of January 20YY. (*Hint:* 20YY is the year after your current year. If your current year is 2014, use 2015 for year 20YY).

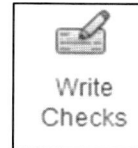

Write
Checks

Check Number	Date	Description of Transaction	Payment	Deposit	Balance
					49,932.00
4021	1/3	The Business Store (Acct.15000, Furniture and Equipment) for computer furniture[2]	500.00		49,432.00
4022	1/4	The Office Supply Store (Acct. No. 13000, Supplies)	100.00		49,332.00

Record the following vendor and customer transactions for the month of January.

Read Me: Enter Bills window

When entering invoices on the Enter Bills window, use the Ref. No. field for the invoice number. This changes the procedure from earlier chapters. The Memo field is blank.

Bill

VENDOR	Podcast Ltd.	▼	DATE	01/05/2015
ADDRESS	Podcast Ltd. Howie Hansen 1341 Barrington Road Los Gatos, CA 90046 USA		REF. NO.	Inv. 201PS
			AMOUNT DUE	450.00
			BILL DUE	02/04/2015
TERMS	Net 30 ▼ DISCOUNT DATE			
MEMO				

---

[2]If a Set Check Reminder window appears, read it. Then click <OK> to close.

Date	Description of Transaction
1/05	Enter bill (Invoice No. 201PS) for items received from Podcast Ltd. for the purchase of 30 audio files, $15 each, for a total of $450. (*Reminder:* Type **Inv. 201PS** in the Ref. No. field.)
1/05	Enter bill (Invoice No. 150eB) for items received from eBooks Express for the purchase of 32 PDF files, $25 each, for a total of $800. (*Reminder:* Type **Inv. 150eb** in the Ref. No. field.)
1/05	Invoice No. 400TV received from TV Flix for the purchase of 30 video files, $30 each, for a total of $900.
1/10	Returned two PDF files to eBooks Express Credit Memo No. CM3, $50.
1/15	Create invoice to sell 10 eBooks (PDF files) on account to iPrint Design for a total credit sale of $500, Invoice # 9.
1/15	Create invoice to sell 30 Podcasts (audio files) on account to Audio Answers for a total credit sale of $900, Invoice # 10.
1/15	Sold 16 TV Programs (video files) on account to Video Solutions for a total credit sale of $960, Invoice # 11.
1/17	Audio Answers returned 2 Podcasts (audio files), $60, Credit No. 12. Apply to 1/15 invoice.
1/18	Create sales receipt (Sale No. 3) for credit card sales for 10 eBooks for $500; 1 Podcasts for $30; and 12 TV Programs for $720; for total credit card sales of $1,250.
1/20	Received a $600 check from Video Solutions in payment of 12/24 credit sale less return.
1/20	Your Name Retailers Inc. pays all outstanding December and January vendor bills less any returns for a total of $2,250. (*Hint:* eBooks Express $50 credit)

1/21	Enter bill to purchase computer furniture on account from The Business Store, Invoice BOS80, for a total of $800, terms Net 30 days. (Account No. 15000 Furniture and Equipment)
1/23	Received a check in full payment of Audio Answers' account less return, $840.
1/24	Received a check in full payment of iPrint Design's account, $500.
1/24	Received a check in full payment of Video Solution's account, $960.
1/25	Enter bill (Invoice No. 175eB) received from eBooks Express for the purchase of 8 PDF files, $25 each, for a total of $200.
1/25	Invoice No. 425TV received from TV Flix for the purchase of 11 video files, $30 each, for a total of $330.
1/25	Invoice No. 230PS received from Podcast Ltd. for the purchase of 6 audio files, $15 each, for a total of $90.
1/26	Returned two audio files to Podcast Ltd., CM4, $30.
1/27	Create invoice to sell 16 eBooks (PDF files) on account to iPrint Design for a total credit sale of $800, Invoice # 13.
1/27	Sold 5 Podcasts (audio files) on account to Audio Answers for a total credit sale of $150 Invoice # 14.
1/27	Sold 6 TV Programs (video files) on account to Video Solutions for a total credit sale of $360, Invoice # 15.
1/27	Enter sales receipt for credit card sales. Sold 2 eBooks for $100; 1 Podcasts for $30; and 6 TV Programs for $360; for total credit card sales of $490, Sale No. 4.
1/28	Video Solutions returned 1 TV Programs (video files), Credit No. 16. Apply $60 credit to 1/27 invoice.

1/29   Received a check in full payment of Audio Answers' account, $150.

1/29   Received a check in full payment of iPrint Design's account, $800.

1/29   Your Name Retailers Inc. pays all outstanding vendor bills less any returns for a total of $1,390. (*Hint:* Podcast Ltd. $30 credit.)

Record the following compound entry for the month of January: (*Hint:* Company; Make General Journal Entries)

1/30   Pay the note payable in the amount of $800.00. The account distribution is:

Acct. No.	Account	Debit	Credit
26000	Your Name Note Payable	555.00	
63400	Interest Expense	245.00	
10000	Home State Bank		800.00

Write checks for these additional January transactions.

1/30   Issue Check No. 4031 to Mobile One in the amount of $80 for cellular service. (Account No. 68100 Telephone Expense)

1/30   Issue Check No. 4032 to ISP in the amount of $50 for Internet service. (Account No. 61700 Computer and Internet Expense)

1/30   Issue Check No. 4033 to Everywhere Telephone Service in the amount of $68 for telephone service. (Account No. 68100 Telephone Expense)

1/30   Issue Check No. 4034 to Reno Water/Garbage in the amount of $111 for Electricity/Gas. (Account No. 68600 Utilities Expense.)

1/30   Issue Check No. 4035 to Reno Water/Garbage for $74 for Water/Garbage service. (Account No. 68600 Utilities Expense).

1/30   View the Check Register. Select Check 4034, then click
[Edit Transaction]. The Write Checks window appears for the
disbursement. Check No. 4034 should be written to
Regional Utilities, not Reno Water/Garbage. Write the check
correctly to Regional Utilities to pay $111 electricity bill.
(*Hint:* Use Payee pulldown menu.) Close the Write Checks
window and the Check Register.

MAKE DEPOSIT

1/30   Record 8 deposits in the amount of $5,590. This includes
payments received from customers and credit card sales.

CHECK REGISTER

Display the check register to see Account No. 10000, Home State Bank
activity for January. Compare to one shown on page 210. If necessary,

select the check that needs to be changed, then select [Edit Transaction] to
go to the Write Checks window.

The Home State Bank Check Register is shown on the next page.

DATE	NUMBER	PAYEE		PAYMENT	✔	DEPOSIT	BALANCE
	TYPE	ACCOUNT	MEMO				
01/03/2015	4021	The Business Store		500.00			49,432.00
	CHK	15000 · Furniture and Equipment	22000				
01/04/2015	4022	The Office Supply Store		100.00			49,332.00
	CHK	13000 · Supplies	22000				
01/20/2015	To Print	eBooks Express		750.00			48,582.00
	BILLPMT	22000 · Accounts Payable	22000				
01/20/2015	To Print	Podcast Ltd.		600.00			47,982.00
	BILLPMT	22000 · Accounts Payable	22000				
01/20/2015	To Print	TV Flix		900.00			47,082.00
	BILLPMT	22000 · Accounts Payable	22000				
01/29/2015	To Print	eBooks Express		200.00			46,882.00
	BILLPMT	22000 · Accounts Payable	22000				
01/29/2015	To Print	Podcast Ltd.		60.00			46,822.00
	BILLPMT	22000 · Accounts Payable	22000				
01/29/2015	To Print	The Business Store		800.00			46,022.00
	BILLPMT	22000 · Accounts Payable	22000				
01/29/2015	To Print	TV Flix		330.00			45,692.00
	BILLPMT	22000 · Accounts Payable	22000				
01/30/2015						5,590.00	51,282.00
	DEP	-split-	Deposit				
01/30/2015	4031	Mobile One		80.00			51,202.00
	CHK	68100 · Telephone Expense					
01/30/2015	4032	ISP		50.00			51,152.00
	CHK	61700 · Computer and Internet Expense					
01/30/2015	4033	Everywhere Telephone Service		68.00			51,084.00
	CHK	68100 · Telephone Expense					
01/30/2015	4034	Regional Utilities		111.00			50,973.00
	CHK	68600 · Utilities Expense					
01/30/2015	4035	Reno Water/Garbage		74.00			50,899.00
	CHK	68600 · Utilities Expense					
01/30/2015	10			800.00			50,099.00
	GENJRN	26000 · Your Name Notes Payable [split]					

ENDING BALANCE **50,099.00**

Backup. The suggested file name is **Your Name Chapter 6 January Check Register.QBB**. (If a screen appears that says number of backup copies has been exceeded, click No, don't delete.)

ACCOUNT RECONCILIATION

Use the January bank statement on the next page to reconcile the Home State Bank account. Check numbers are shown on the following bank statement. Depending on whether you recorded a check number for each vendor payment, check numbers may or may not be included on the Reconcile window.

Statement of Account Home State Bank January 1 to January 31, 20YY		Account #923-121379	Your Name Retailers Inc. Your Address Reno, NV	
REGULAR CHECKING				
Previous Balance	12/31	49,932.00		
Deposits		5,590.00		
Checks (-)		5,423.00		
Service Charges (-)	1/31	10.00		
Ending Balance	1/31	**$50,089.00**		
DEPOSITS				
	1/18	1,250.00	Credit Card	
	1/27	490.00	Credit Card	
	1/30	600.00	Video Solutions	
	1/30	840.00	Audio Answers	
	1/30	500.00	iPrint Design	
	1/30	960.00	Video Solutions	
	1/30	150.00	Audio Answers	
	1/30	800.00	iPrint Design	
CHECKS				
	1/4	500.00	4021	
	1/4	100.00	4022	
	1/22	750.00	4023	
	1/22	600.00	4024	
	1/22	900.00	4025	
	1/30	800.00	4026	
	1/30	200.00	4027	
	1/30	60.00	4028	
	1/30	330.00	4029	
	1/31	800.00	4030	
	1/31	80.00	4031	
	1/31	50.00	4032	
	1/31	68.00	4033	
	1/31	111.00	4034	
	1/31	74.00	4035	

Once the $10 Service Charge is deducted from the account register balance, the bank statement and account register agree.

Check Register Balance:	$50,099.00
Bank Service Charge:	10.00
Bank Statement Balance:	$50,089.00

1. Prepare the account reconciliation for January.

Hint: Your Reconcile window may not show all of the check numbers. That is okay.

2. Compare your Reconciliation Summary report to the one shown on the next page.

Reconciliation Summary

Your Name Retailers Inc.
Reconciliation Summary
10000 · Home State Bank, Period Ending 01/31/2015

	Jan 31, 15
Beginning Balance	49,932.00
Cleared Transactions	
Checks and Payments - 16 items	-5,433.00
Deposits and Credits - 1 item	5,590.00
Total Cleared Transactions	157.00
Cleared Balance	50,089.00
Register Balance as of 01/31/2015	50,089.00
Ending Balance	50,089.00

UNADJUSTED TRIAL BALANCE

1. Print the 1/31/20YY Trial Balance (unadjusted). Compare your unadjusted trial balance to the one shown below.

Your Name Retailers Inc.
Trial Balance
As of January 31, 2015

	Debit	Credit
10000 · Home State Bank	50,089.00	
11000 · Accounts Receivable	300.00	
12000 · Undeposited Funds	0.00	
12100 · Inventory Asset	985.00	
13000 · Supplies	2,500.00	
18000 · Prepaid Insurance	2,350.00	
14000 · Computer Equipment	2,400.00	
15000 · Furniture and Equipment	5,300.00	
16000 · Accumulated Depreciation-CEqmt.		120.00
17000 · Accumulated Depreciation-F&E		200.00
22000 · Accounts Payable	0.00	
26000 · Your Name Notes Payable		18,903.00
30000 · Common Stock		42,500.00
30200 · Dividends	0.00	
32000 · Retained Earnings		194.00
46000 · Sales		5,290.00
50000 · Cost of Goods Sold	2,645.00	
60400 · Bank Service Charges Expense	10.00	
61700 · Computer and Internet Expenses	50.00	
63400 · Interest Expense	245.00	
68100 · Telephone Expense	148.00	
68600 · Utilities Expense	185.00	
TOTAL	67,207.00	67,207.00

2. Backup. The suggested file name is **Your Name Chapter 6 UTB.QBB**.

END-OF-MONTH ADJUSTING ENTRIES

Your Name Retailers Inc. changed their adjusting entry policy for the new fiscal year. The new policy is to record adjusting entries at the end of each month to properly reflect all the month's business activities. Make the following adjusting entries for the month of January on 01/31/20YY. (*Hint:* On the Make General Journal Entries window, put check mark next to Adjusting Entry—[☑ ADJUSTING ENTRY].)

1. Supplies on hand are $2,300.00. (This is Entry No. 11.)

Acct. #	Account Name	Debit	Credit
64900	Supplies Expense	200.00	
13000	Supplies		200.00

Computation: Supplies $2,500.00
                Office supplies on hand   - 2,300.00
                Adjustment $ 200.00

2. Adjust one month of prepaid insurance ($50/month). (Entry No. 12.)

Acct. #	Account Name	Debit	Credit
63300	Insurance Expense	50.00	
18000	Prepaid Insurance		50.00

3. Use straight-line depreciation for your computer equipment. Your computer equipment has a five-year service life and no salvage value. (Entry No. 13.)

To depreciate computer equipment for the month, use this calculation: $2,400 ÷ 5 years X 1/12 months = $40.00

Acct. #	Account Name	Debit	Credit
62400	Depreciation Expense	40.00	
16000	Accumulated Depreciation-CEqmt.		40.00

4. Use straight-line depreciation to depreciate furniture. The furniture has a 5-year service life and no salvage value. (Entry No. 14.) To depreciate furniture for the month, use this calculation: $4,000 ÷ 5 years X 1/12 month = $67.00

Acct. #	Account Name	Debit	Credit
62400	Depreciation Expense	67.00	
17000	Accumulated Depreciation-F&E		67.00

5. You purchased new furniture during the month. Use straight-line depreciation to depreciate your furniture. The furniture has a 5-year service life and a $100 salvage value.

   Use the following adjusting entry. (Entry No. 15.) The computation is: ($500 + $800 -$100)÷ 5 years X 1/12 month = $20.00

Acct. #	Account Name	Debit	Credit
62400	Depreciation Expense	20.00	
17000	Accumulated Depreciation-F&E		20.00

6. After journalizing and posting the adjusting entries, close the Make General Journal Entries window, then display or print the Adjusting Journal Entries as of 01/31/20YY.

Comment: If your unadjusted and adjusted trial balances *do not agree* with the textbook illustration, drill-down to the appropriate entries. Edit the entries, then reprint your reports.

Adjusting Journal Entries

Customize Report | Share Template | Memorize | Print | E-mail | Excel | Hide Header | Expand | Refresh

Dates Custom From 01/31/2015 To 01/31/2015 Sort By Default

Your Name Retailers Inc.
Adjusting Journal Entries
January 31, 2015

Date	Num	Name	Memo	Account	Debit	Credit
01/31/2015	11			64900 · Supplies Expense	200.00	
				13000 · Supplies		200.00
					200.00	200.00
01/31/2015	12			63300 · Insurance Expense	50.00	
				18000 · Prepaid Insurance		50.00
					50.00	50.00
01/31/2015	13			62400 · Depreciation Expense	40.00	
				16000 · Accumulated Depreciation-CEqmt.		40.00
					40.00	40.00
01/31/2015	14			62400 · Depreciation Expense	67.00	
				17000 · Accumulated Depreciation-F&E		67.00
					67.00	67.00
01/31/2015	15			62400 · Depreciation Expense	20.00	
				17000 · Accumulated Depreciation-F&E		20.00
					20.00	20.00
TOTAL					377.00	377.00

ADJUSTED TRIAL BALANCE

1. Print the 1/31/20YY Adjusted Trial Balance.

Adjusted Trial Balance

Customize Report | Share Template | Memorize | Print | E-mail | Excel | Hide Header | Collapse | Refresh

Dates Custom From 01/31/2015 To 01/31/2015 Sort By Default

Your Name Retailers Inc.
Adjusted Trial Balance
January 31, 2015

	Unadjusted Balance		Adjustments		Adjusted Balance	
	Debit	Credit	Debit	Credit	Debit	Credit
10000 · Home State Bank	50,089.00				50,089.00	
11000 · Accounts Receivable	300.00				300.00	
12000 · Undeposited Funds	0.00				0.00	
12100 · Inventory Asset	985.00				985.00	
13000 · Supplies	2,500.00			200.00	2,300.00	
18000 · Prepaid Insurance	2,350.00			50.00	2,300.00	
14000 · Computer Equipment	2,400.00				2,400.00	
15000 · Furniture and Equipment	5,300.00				5,300.00	
16000 · Accumulated Depreciation-CEqmt.		120.00		40.00		160.00
17000 · Accumulated Depreciation-F&E		200.00		87.00		287.00
22000 · Accounts Payable	0.00				0.00	
26000 · Your Name Notes Payable		18,903.00				18,903.00
30000 · Common Stock		42,500.00				42,500.00
30200 · Dividends	0.00				0.00	
32000 · Retained Earnings		194.00				194.00
46000 · Sales		5,290.00				5,290.00
50000 · Cost of Goods Sold	2,645.00				2,645.00	
60400 · Bank Service Charges Expense	10.00				10.00	
61700 · Computer and Internet Expenses	50.00				50.00	
62400 · Depreciation Expense			127.00		127.00	
63300 · Insurance Expense			50.00		50.00	
63400 · Interest Expense	245.00				245.00	
64900 · Supplies Expense			200.00		200.00	
68100 · Telephone Expense	148.00				148.00	
68600 · Utilities Expense	185.00				185.00	
TOTAL	67,207.00	67,207.00	377.00	377.00	67,334.00	67,334.00

2. Close reports, then backup. The suggested file name is **Your Name Chapter 6 January Financial Statements.QBB**.

3. Exit QuickBooks or continue with the next section.

SUMMARY AND REVIEW

OBJECTIVES:

1. Restore data from Your Name Chapter 5 EOY.
2. Record one month of transactions.
3. Make bank deposit.
4. Complete account reconciliation.
5. Print a trial balance (unadjusted).
6. Record adjusting entries and print an adjusted trial balance.
7. Print financial statements.
8. Make backups of Chapter 6 data.

Additional textbook related resources are on the textbook website at www.mhhe.com/QBessentials2014. It includes chapter resources, including troubleshooting tips, online quizzes, narrated PowerPoints, etc.

RESOURCEFUL QUICKBOOKS

1. Click on Help menu, select Year-End Guide.

   What are the three task areas that must be addressed at year-end? List them.

2. From the Year-End Guide page, link to Print financial reports. Answer these questions.

   a. What does the Trial Balance report tell you? (Click More. . .)

   b. What does the Profit & Loss Standard report tell you?

   c. What does the Balance Sheet Standard report tell you?

Multiple Choice Questions: The Online Learning Center includes the multiple-choice questions at www.mhhe.com/QBessentials2014, select Student Edition, Chapter 6, Multiple Choice.

_C_ 1. The January 1, 20YY Trial Balance contains:

    a. The same accounts as the 12/31/20XX post closing trial balance.
    b. No revenue, expense, or dividend accounts.
    c. Both of the above.
    d. None of the above.

_C_ 2. In Chapter 6, you enter transactions for:

    a. The first month of the new fiscal year.
    b. January.
    c. Both of the above.
    d. None of the above.

_B_ 3. In Chapter 6, you complete which steps in the Accounting Cycle?

    a. Steps 1.-9.
    b. Steps 2.-8.
    c. Steps 3.-7.
    d. All the steps.

_D_ 4. In Chapter 6, all the following Banking section icons are used _except_:

    a. Reconcile.
    b. Check register.
    c. Write checks.
    d. Enter bills.

_B_ 5. In Chapter 6, all the following Customers section icons are used _except_:

    a. Create invoices.
    b. Estimates.
    c. Create sales receipts.
    d. Receive payments.

_____A_6. In Chapter 6, the following Vendors section icon was used:

    a. Pay bills.
    b. Purchase Orders.
    c. Enter bills against inventory.
    d. Write bills.

_____D_7. In Chapter 6, the Company section icon was used:

    a. Chart of accounts.
    b. Items and services.
    c. Both of the above.
    d. None of the above.

_____C_8. The Year-End Guide checklist includes all of the following *except*:

    a. Reconcile all bank and credit card accounts.
    b. Print financial reports.
    c. Back up company file access.
    d. Access to the QuickBooks Knowledge Base.

_____A_9. The work flow for invoicing is:

    a. Create invoice, Receive payment, Record deposit.
    b. Create sales receipt, record deposit.
    c. Enter bill, Pay bill.
    d. Receive invoice, Pay bill.

_____D_10. The QuickBooks menu bar Help selection includes:

    a. Ask Intuit.
    b. Support.
    c. Year-end guide.
    d. All of the above.

Short-answer and True/make true questions: To answer these questions, go online to<u>www.mhhe.com/QBessentials2014</u>, link to Student Edition, Chapter 6, QA Templates. The analysis question at the end of the chapter is also included.

1. Your Name Retailers Inc. fiscal year begins on January 1.

2. Step 4 of the accounting cycle is reconciling the bank statement.

3. The check register's balance does *not* show the bank service charge.

4. Your check register and bank statement are used as source documents for recording entries.

5. In this chapter, Your Name Retailers Inc. makes adjusting journal entries on a quarterly basis.

6. In this chapter, accounting records are completed for January 1 - March 31, 20YY.

7. Your Name Retailers Inc. makes closing journal entries on a monthly basis.

8. For the period of January 1 to January 31, 20YY, Your Name Retailers Inc. net income (loss) is $_____.

9. At the end of the month, Your Name Retailers Inc. total assets are $_____.

10. At the end of the month, Your Name Retailers Inc. total liabilities are $_____.

11. At the end of the month, Your Name Retailers Inc. had generated cash flow from/for operating activities of $_____.

12. At the end of the month, Your Name Retailers Inc. had generated cash flow from/for financing activities of $_____.

Exercise 6-1: Follow the instructions below to complete Exercise 6-1.

1. If necessary, start QB and open Your Name Retailers Inc.

2. If necessary, restore the Your Name Chapter 6 January Financial Statements file. This backup was made on page 217.

3. Back up the file as a portable company file. (*Hint:* File; Create Copy, Portable Company File.) The suggested file name is **Your Name Exercise 6-1 (Portable).QBM**.

4. Print the 01/01/20YY to 01/31/20YY Journal.

5. Print the 01/31/20YY trial balance.

6. Print the financial statements:

    a. Profit & Loss-Standard from 01/01/20YY to 01/31/20YY).

    b. Balance Sheet-Standard as of 01/31/20YY.

    c. Statement of Cash Flows from 01/01/20YY to 01/31/20YY

7. Print the Audit Trail for all dates.

Read Me: Save reports as PDF Files

Your instructor may want you to email reports as PDF attachments. To do that, follow these steps:

1. Display the report.
2. Select Print; Save as PDF. *Or,* select E-mail; Send reports as PDF.
3. The suggested file name is **Exercise 6-1 Journal.pdf**, etc.

You need Adobe Reader to save as PDF files. If download the free Adobe Reader, www.adobe.com.

Exercise 6-2:

Send an e-mail to your professor and attach a copy of Your Name Exercise 6-1 (Portable).QBM file. (*Hint:* Follow the Accountant Transfer steps 1-5 in Chapter 5.)

ANALYSIS QUESTION:

Why did Your Name Retailers Inc. generate more cash from operating activities than net income for January?

Project 1

Your Name Hardware Store

In Project 1, you complete the business processes for Your Name Hardware Store, a merchandising business. Your Name Hardware Store sells shovels, wagons, and wheel barrows. It is organized as a corporation. The purpose of Project 1 is to review what you have learned about merchandising businesses and use their typical source documents.

Source documents that generate transaction analysis for accounts payable, inventory, accounts receivable, and cash are included in this project. You will also complete account reconciliation. At the end of Project 1, a checklist is shown listing the printed reports that should be completed. The step-by-step instructions also remind you to print reports and backup at regular intervals.

GETTING STARTED

Follow these steps to open Your Name Hardware Store:

Step 1:   Start QuickBooks 2014. From the menu bar, select File; Close Company.

Step 2:   The No Company Open window appears. Restore the backup file, Your Name Hardware Store.QBB. You created this company and backed it up in Exercises 1-1 and 1-2 on page   24. If the Your Name Hardware Store.QBB backup file does <u>not</u> exist, complete Exercises 1-1 and 1-2 on page 24.

When Save Company File as window appears, rename the company file Your Name Project 1 Begin.qbw.

File name:	Your Name Project 1 Begin.qbw	▾	Save
Save as type:	QuickBooks Files (*.QBW)	▾	Cancel
			Help

Step 3: Confirm company information. Select [My Company]. The My Company window shows information about Your Name Hardware Store. (*Hint:* Your first and last name should be shown before Hardware Store.)

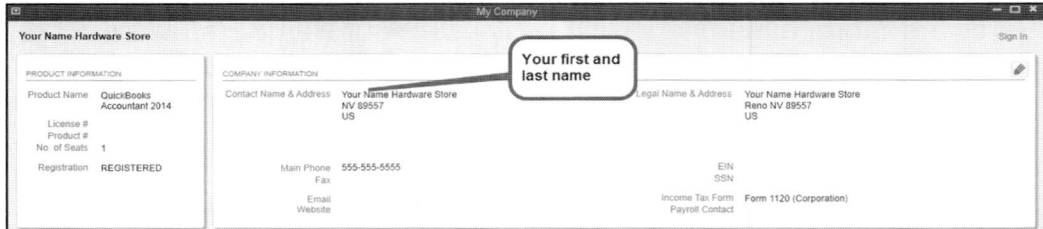

Step 4: If needed, edit the company name by selecting [pencil icon]. When satisfied that company information is correct, close the My Company window.

COMPANY PREFERENCES

Step 5: From the menu bar, select Edit; Preferences. Click on Company Preferences tab and select Accounting.

Step 6: Click on the box next to Use account numbers. Make sure boxes next to Date warnings are unchecked.

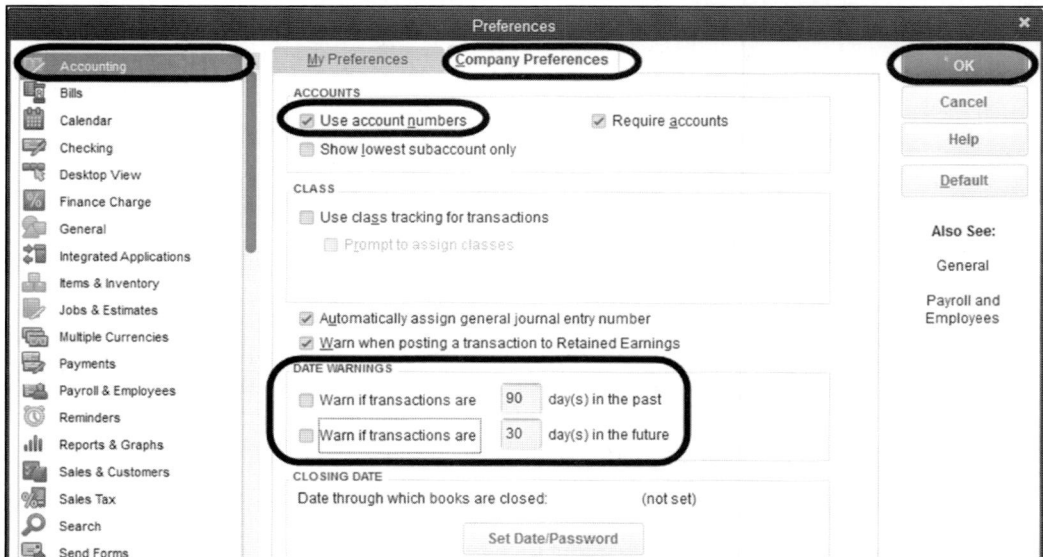

Click [OK] to save selections.

Step 7: From the menu bar, select Edit; Preferences. Click on the My Preferences tab and select Checking. Put check marks next to Open the Write Check Form with…account, Open the Pay Bills form with…account, and the Open the make deposits form with…account. For each of these selections, choose Home State Bank account.

SELECT DEFAULT ACCOUNTS TO USE

☑ Open the Write Checks   form with   Home State Bank   ▼   account

☑ Open the Pay Bills   form with   Home State Bank   ▼   account

☐ Open the Pay Sales Tax   form with   ▼   account

☑ Open the Make Deposits   form with   Home State Bank   ▼   account

Click [OK] to save selections.

Step 8: From the menu bar, select Edit; Preferences. Click on My Preferences tab and select Send Forms. Uncheck box next to Auto-check the Email Later checkbox if customer's Preferred Delivery Method is e-mail. In the e-mail using area, select Web Mail.

☐ Auto-check the "Email Later" checkbox if customer's Preferred Delivery Method is e-mail.

SEND E-MAIL USING:

◉ Web Mail

◯ Outlook

To save preferences, click [OK]. When the Warning window says that QuickBooks must close all its open windows to change this preference, click [OK].

Step 9:   From the menu bar, select Edit; Preferences, Items & Inventory, Company Preferences tab. Put a check mark next to Inventory and purchase orders are active.

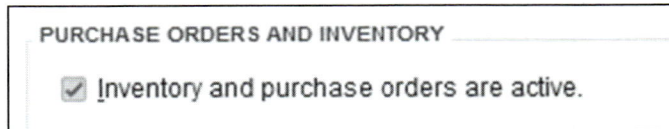

> PURCHASE ORDERS AND INVENTORY
>
> ☑ Inventory and purchase orders are active.

To save preferences, click [OK]. To see the Home page, click [🏠 Home].

CHART OF ACCOUNTS

Step 10:   Delete the following accounts:

48300 Sales Discounts
51800 Merchant Account Fees
80000 Ask My Accountant

Step 11:   Edit the following accounts and delete what currently displays as the Description. (*Hint:* Add account number 10000 to Home State Bank.)

Account	New Name	Type	Tax Line Mapping
10000 Home State Bank	Home State Bank	Bank	**B/S-Assets: Cash**
Security Deposits Asset	**Prepaid Insurance**	**Other Current Asset**	**B/S-Assets: Other Current Assets**
Capital Stock	**Paid in Capital**	**Equity**	**B/S-Liabs/Eq.: Paid in or Capital Surplus**
Dividends Paid	**Dividends**	**Equity**	**Unassigned**
Opening Balance Equity	**Common Stock**	**Equity**	**B/S-Liabs/Eq.: Capital Stock - Common Stock**
Utilities	**Utilities Expense**	**Expense**	**Other Deductions: Utilities**

Step 12: Add Account No. 26000.

New Account	Description	Type	Income Tax Line
Your Name Notes Payable	None	**Long Term Liability**	**B/S-Liabs/Eq.: Loans from stockholders**

Step 13: Make a backup to your USB drive. Use **Your Name Hardware Store Chart of Accounts (Portable).QBM.**   (*Hint:* Backups in Project 1 are portable files: File; Create Copy, Portable company file.)

Step 14: You purchased Your Name Hardware Store in December of last year. (*Hint:* Use 12/31/last year to enter opening balances.) Use this Balance Sheet to record the beginning balances. Then display the chart of accounts.

Your Name Hardware Store Balance Sheet January 1, 20XX (Your current year)		
ASSETS		
Current Assets		
Home State Bank	$ 82,000.00	✓
Prepaid Insurance	2,900.00	
Total Current Assets		$84,900.00
Fixed Assets		
Furniture and Equipment	6,000.00	✓
Total Fixed Assets		6,000.00
Total Assets		$90,900.00
LIABILITIES AND STOCKHOLDERS' EQUITY		
Your Name Notes Payable	9,500.00	
Total Liabilities		$9,500.00
Common Stock		81,400.00
Total Liabilities and Equity		$90,900.00

NAME		TYPE	BALANCE TOTAL	ATTACH
◊ 10000 · Home State Bank		Bank	82,000.00	
◊ 18700 · Prepaid Insurance		Other Current Asset	2,900.00	
◊ 15000 · Furniture and Equipment		Fixed Asset	6,000.00	
◊ 17000 · Accumulated Depreciation		Fixed Asset	0.00	
◊ 24000 · Payroll Liabilities		Other Current Liability	0.00	
◊ 26000 · Your Name Notes Payable		Long Term Liability	9,500.00	
◊ 30000 · Common Stock		Equity	81,400.00	
◊ 30100 · Paid in Capital		Equity	0.00	
◊ 30200 · Dividends		Equity	0.00	
◊ 32000 · Retained Earnings		Equity		
◊ 46000 · Merchandise Sales		Income		
◊ 60000 · Advertising and Promotion		Expense		
◊ 60200 · Automobile Expense		Expense		
◊ 60400 · Bank Service Charges		Expense		
◊ 61700 · Computer and Internet Expenses		Expense		
◊ 62400 · Depreciation Expense		Expense		
◊ 63300 · Insurance Expense		Expense		
◊ 63400 · Interest Expense		Expense		
◊ 63500 · Janitorial Expense		Expense		
◊ 64300 · Meals and Entertainment		Expense		
◊ 64900 · Office Supplies		Expense		
◊ 66000 · Payroll Expenses		Expense		
◊ 66700 · Professional Fees		Expense		
◊ 67100 · Rent Expense		Expense		
◊ 67200 · Repairs and Maintenance		Expense		
◊ 68100 · Telephone Expense		Expense		
◊ 68500 · Uniforms		Expense		
◊ 68600 · Utilities Expense		Expense		

Account ▼   Activities ▼   Reports ▼   Attach   ☐ Include inactive

BACKUP

Step 15: Make a backup to your USB drive. Use **Your Name Hardware Store Beginning Balances (Portable).QBM**. (*Hint:* You may want to display the 12/31 balance sheet and compare to the one shown on the previous page.)

VENDORS

Step 16: Go to the Vendor Center and add the following vendors.

Vendor name:	**AAA Shovels**
Opening Balance.	**0.00**
As of:	**1/1/current year**
Company Name:	**AAA Shovels**

Full Name:	**Tim Newton**
Address:	**3000 First Avenue**
	Santa Cruz, CA 90036
Work Phone:	**310-555-2243**
Fax:	**310-555-2245**
Main Email:	**tim@aaa.biz**
Website:	**www.aaashovels.biz**

Payment Settings:

Account No.	**20000**
Payment Terms:	**Net 30**
Credit Limit:	**15,000.00**

Additional Info:

Vendor Type:	**Suppliers**

Vendor name:	**BBB Wheel barrows**
Opening Balance:	**0.00**
As of:	**1/1/current year**
Company Name:	**BBB Wheel barrows**
Full Name:	**Baker Bayou**
Address:	**46011 Mesquite Street**
	El Paso, TX 76315
Work Phone:	**915-555-3000**
Fax:	**915-555-3100**
Main Email:	**Baker@BBB.com**
Website:	**www.BBBwheel.com**

Payment Settings:

Account No.	**20000**
Payment Terms:	**Net 30**
Credit Limit:	**15,000.00**

Additional Info:

Vendor Type:	**Suppliers**

Vendor name:	**CCC Wagons**
Opening Balance:	**0.00**
As of:	**1/1/current year**
Company Name:	**CCC Wagons**
Full Name:	**Caitlin Conner**

Address:	**2301 Dirt Road**
	Dugout, AZ 86003
Work Phone:	**928-555-2288**
Fax:	**928-555-2299**
Main Email:	**Caitlin@CCC.net**
Website:	**www.CCCwagons.net**

Payment Settings:

Account No.	**20000**
Payment Terms:	**Net 30**
Credit Limit:	**15,000.00**

Additional Info:

Vendor Type:	**Suppliers**

INVENTORY ITEMS

Step 17:   Enter the following inventory parts:

Item Name/Number:	**Shovels**
Purchase Description:	**Shovels**
Purchase Cost:	**15.00**
COGS Account:	50000, Cost of Goods Sold
Preferred Vendor:	**AAA Shovels**
Sales Description:	Shovels
Sales Price:	**30.00**
Income Account:	**46000, Merchandise Sales**
Asset Account:	12100, Inventory Asset
On Hand:	0.00
Total Value:	0.00
As of:	01/01/20XX

Item Name/Number:	**Wheel barrows**
Purchase Description:	**Wheel barrows**
Purchase Cost:	**75.00**
COGS Account:	50000, Cost of Goods Sold
Preferred Vendor:	BBB Wheel barrows
Sales Description:	Wheel barrows
Sales Price:	**100.00**
Income Account:	46000, Merchandise Sales
Asset Account:	12100, Inventory Asset

On Hand:	0.00
Total Value:	0.00
As of:	01/01/20XX

Item Name/Number:	**Wagons**
Purchase Description:	**Wagons**
Purchase Cost:	**20.00**
COGS Account:	Cost of Goods Sold
Preferred Vendor:	CCC Wagons
Sales Description:	Wagons
Sales Price:	**50.00**
Income Account:	46000, Merchandise Sales
Asset Account:	12100, Inventory Asset
On Hand:	0.00
Total Value:	0.00
As of:	01/01/20XX

CUSTOMERS

Step 18: Go to the Customer Center and add the following retail Customers:

Customer Name:	**Dawn Bright**
Opening Balance:	**0.00**
As of:	**1/1/20XX**
Full Name:	**Dawn Bright**
Address:	**1800 W. Peoria Avenue**
	Reno, NV 92731
Main Phone:	**503-555-8630**
Main Email:	**db@myemail.com**

Payment Settings:

Account No.:	**DB1**
Payment Terms:	**Net 30**
Preferred Payment Method:	**Check**
Credit Limit:	**10,000.00**

Additional Info:

Customer Type:	**Retail**

Customer Name:	**Roy Lars**
Opening Balance:	**0.00**
As of:	**1/2/20XX**
Full Name:	**Roy Lars**
Address:	**603 Nature Drive**
	Reno, NV 97401
Main Phone:	**541-555-7845**
Main E-mail:	**roy@mail.biz**

Payment Settings:

Account No.:	**RL2**
Payment Terms:	**Net 30**
Preferred Payment Method:	**Check**
Credit Limit:	**10,000.00**

Additional Info:

Customer Type:	**Retail**

Customer Name:	**Shar Watsonville**
Opening Balance:	**0.00**
As of:	**1/1/20XX**
Full Name:	**Shar Watsonville**
Address:	**3455 West 20th Avenue**
	Reno, NV 97402
Main Phone:	**541-555-9233**
Main E-mail:	**sharon@email.com**

Payment Settings:

Account No.:	**SW3**
Payment Terms:	**Net 30**
Preferred Payment Method:	**Check**
Credit Limit:	**10,000.00**

Additional Info:

Customer Type:	**Retail**

Customer Name:	**Credit Card Sales**
Opening Balance:	**0.00**
As of:	**1/1/20XX**
Additional Info; Type:	**Retail**

BACKUP

Step 19: Make a backup to your USB drive. Use **Your Name Hardware Store Vendors Inventory Customers (Portable).QBM** as the filename.

TRANSACTIONS FROM SOURCE DOCUMENT ANALYSIS

Step 20: After analyzing the source documents, record the appropriate transactions. All transactions occur during January of your current year.

AAA SHOVELS
INVOICE

BILL TO	Your Name Hardware Store Your address Reno, NV 89557	SHIP TO	Your Name Hardware Store Your address Reno, NV 89557	Invoice # 74A	
				Invoice Date January 6	
				Customer ID	

DATE	YOUR ORDER #	OUR ORDER #	SALES REP.	F.O.B.	SHIP VIA	TERMS	TAX ID

QTY	ITEM	UNITS	DESCRIPTION	DISCOUNT %	TAXABLE	UNIT PRICE	TOTAL
25			shovels			15.00	375.00
						Subtotal	375.00
						Tax	
						Shipping	
						Miscellaneous	
						BALANCE DUE	375.00

CCC WAGONS
INVOICE

BILL TO	Your Name Hardware Store You're address Reno, NV 89557	SHIP TO	Your Name Hardware Store Your address Reno, NV 89557	Invoice # 801
				Invoice Date January 6
				Customer ID

DATE	YOUR ORDER #	OUR ORDER #	SALES REP.	F.O.B.	SHIP VIA	TERMS	TAX ID

QTY	ITEM	UNITS	DESCRIPTION	DISCOUNT %	TAXABLE	UNIT PRICE	TOTAL
30			Wagons			20.00	600.00
						Subtotal	600.00
						Tax	
						Shipping	
						Miscellaneous	
						BALANCE DUE	600.00

BBB
WHEEL BARROWS
INVOICE

BILL TO	Your Name Hardware Store Your address Reno, NV 89557	SHIP TO	Your Name Hardware Store Your address Reno, NV 89557	Invoice # ER555
				Invoice Date January 6
				Customer ID

DATE	YOUR ORDER #	OUR ORDER #	SALES REP.	F.O.B.	SHIP VIA	TERMS	TAX ID

QTY	ITEM	UNITS	DESCRIPTION	DISCOUNT %	TAXABLE	UNIT PRICE	TOTAL
32			Wheel barrows			75.00	2,400.00
						Subtotal	2,400.00
						Tax	
						Shipping	
						Miscellaneous	
						BALANCE DUE	2,400.00

Your Name Hardware Store   SALES RECEIPT

Your Address
Reno, NV 89557   Your phone number

SOLD TO:
Credit card sales

| | | SALES NUMBER | 1 |
| | | SALES DATE | January 10 |

SHIPPED TO:

QUANTITY	DESCRIPTION	UNIT PRICE	AMOUNT
4	Shovels		120.00
5	Wheel barrows		500.00
8	Wagons		400.00
		SUBTOTAL	1,020.00
		TAX	
		FREIGHT	
			$1,020.00

DIRECT ALL INQUIRIES TO:
Your Name   Your Name Hardware Store
Your phone number   Your Address
email: your email   Reno, NV 89557

THANK YOU FOR YOUR BUSINESS!

Your Name Hardware Store   SALES RECEIPT

Your Address
Reno, NV 89557   Your phone number

SOLD TO:
Credit card sales

| | | SALES NUMBER | 2 |
| | | SALES DATE | January 12 |

SHIPPED TO:

QUANTITY	DESCRIPTION	UNIT PRICE	AMOUNT
3	Shovels		90.00
4	Wheel barrows		400.00
5	Wagons		250.00
		SUBTOTAL	740.00
		TAX	
		FREIGHT	
			$740.00

DIRECT ALL INQUIRIES TO:
Your Name   Your Name Hardware Store
Your phone number   Your Address
email: your email   Reno, NV 89557

THANK YOU FOR YOUR BUSINESS!

Your Name Hardware Store   INVOICE

Your Address
Reno, NV 89557   Your phone number

SOLD TO:
Dawn Bright
1800 W. Peoria Avenue
Reno, NV 92731

INVOICE NUMBER | 1
INVOICE DATE | January 12

SHIPPED TO:
Same

QUANTITY	DESCRIPTION	UNIT PRICE	AMOUNT
1	Shovel		30.00
		SUBTOTAL	30.00
		TAX	
		FREIGHT	

PAY THIS AMOUNT: $30.00

DIRECT ALL INQUIRIES TO:
Your Name
Your phone number
email: your email

MAKE ALL CHECKS PAYABLE TO:
Your Name Hardware Store
Attn: Accounts Receivable
Your Address
Reno, NV 89557

THANK YOU FOR YOUR BUSINESS!

Your Name Hardware Store   SALES RECEIPT

Your Address
Reno, NV 89557   Your phone number

SOLD TO:
Credit card sales

SALES NUMBER | 3
SALES DATE | January 17

SHIPPED TO:

QUANTITY	DESCRIPTION	UNIT PRICE	AMOUNT
2	Shovels		60.00
7	Wheel barrows		700.00
3	Wagons		150.00
		SUBTOTAL	910.00
		TAX	
		FREIGHT	

$910.00

DIRECT ALL INQUIRIES TO:
Your Name
Your phone number
email: your email

Your Name Hardware Store
Your Address
Reno, NV 89557

THANK YOU FOR YOUR BUSINESS!

Memo

Date: 1/20 current year

Re: Vendor Payments

Your Name Hardware Store pays all outstanding vendor bills for a total of $3,375.00. (*Hint*: The required payment method is Check from Home State Bank; assign check numbers 1-3 automatically.) Refer to the remittances that follow.

AAA Shovels:	$375.00
BBB Wheel barrows	2,400.00
CCC Wagons	600.00
Total	$3,375.00

Note: On the Pay Bills window, select Assign check number. In the Check No. field, type **1, 2, 3**.

REMITTANCE

Invoice #	74A
Customer ID	Your Name Hardware Store
Date	January 20
Amount Enclosed	375.00

AAA Shovels
3000 First Avenue
Santa Cruz, CA
90036

PHONE (310)5552243
FAX (310)555-2245
E-MAIL tim@aaa.biz

REMITTANCE

Invoice #	ER555
Customer ID	Your Name Hardware Store
Date	January 20
Amount Enclosed	2,400.00

BBB Wheel barrows
46011 Mesquite St.
El Paso, TX 76315

PHONE (915)555-3000
FAX (915)555-3100
E-MAIL Baker@BBB.com

REMITTANCE

Invoice #	801
Customer ID	Your Name Hardware Store
Date	January 20
Amount Enclosed	600.00

CCC Wagons 2301 Dirt Road Dugout, AZ 86003	PHONE (928)555-2288 FAX (928)555-2299 E-MAIL Caitlin@CCC.net

Your Name Hardware Store   SALES RECEIPT

Your Address
Reno, NV 89557   Your phone number

SOLD TO:
Credit card sales

SALES NUMBER | 4
SALES DATE | January 21

SHIPPED TO:

QUANTITY	DESCRIPTION	UNIT PRICE	AMOUNT
6	Shovels		180.00
8	Wheel barrows		800.00
9	Wagons		450.00
		SUBTOTAL	1,430.00
		TAX	
		FREIGHT	
			$1,430.00

DIRECT ALL INQUIRIES TO:
Your Name   Your Name Hardware Store
Your phone number   Your Address
email: your email   Reno, NV 89557

THANK YOU FOR YOUR BUSINESS!

Memo

Date: 1/21 current year

Re: Rent

Write Check No. 4 to vendor, Stevens Rentals, for $1,350 in payment of rent. (*Hint:* Add vendor as needed; uncheck To be printed. Account: Rent Expense.)

Your Name Hardware Store   INVOICE

Your Address
Reno, NV 89557   Your phone number

SOLD TO:
Shar Watsonville   INVOICE NUMBER | 2
3455 West 20th Avenue   INVOICE DATE | January 22
Reno, NV 97402

SHIPPED TO:
Same

QUANTITY	DESCRIPTION	UNIT PRICE	AMOUNT
1	Wagon		50.00
		SUBTOTAL	50.00
		TAX	
		FREIGHT	

PAY THIS AMOUNT $50.00

DIRECT ALL INQUIRIES TO: **MAKE ALL CHECKS PAYABLE TO:**
Your Name   Your Name Hardware Store
Your phone number   Attn: Accounts Receivable
email: your email   Your Address
                                       Reno, NV 89557

THANK YOU FOR YOUR BUSINESS!

AAA SHOVELS
INVOICE

BILL TO	Your Name Hardware Store Your address Reno, NV 89557	SHIP TO	Your Name Hardware Store Your address Reno, NV 89557

Invoice # 88A

Invoice Date   January 24

Customer ID

DATE	YOUR ORDER #	OUR ORDER #	SALES REP.	F.O.B.	SHIP VIA	TERMS	TAX ID

QTY	ITEM	UNITS	DESCRIPTION	DISCOUNT %	TAXABLE	UNIT PRICE	TOTAL
15			shovels			15.00	225.00
						Subtotal	225.00
						Tax	
						Shipping	
						Miscellaneous	
						BALANCE DUE	225.00

CCC WAGONS
INVOICE

BILL TO	Your Name Hardware Store Your address Reno, NV 89557	SHIP TO	Your Name Hardware Store Your address Reno, NV 89557	Invoice # 962
				Invoice Date January 24
				Customer ID

DATE	YOUR ORDER #	OUR ORDER #	SALES REP.	F.O.B.	SHIP VIA	TERMS	TAX ID

QTY	ITEM	UNITS	DESCRIPTION	DISCOUNT %	TAXABLE	UNIT PRICE	TOTAL
18			Wagons			20.00	360.00
						Subtotal	360.00
						Tax	
						Shipping	
						Miscellaneous	
						BALANCE DUE	360.00

BBB
WHEEL BARROWS
INVOICE

BILL TO	Your Name Hardware Store Your address Reno, NV 89557	SHIP TO	Your Name Hardware Store Your address Reno, NV 89557	Invoice # ER702
				Invoice Date January 24
				Customer ID

DATE	YOUR ORDER #	OUR ORDER #	SALES REP.	F.O.B.	SHIP VIA	TERMS	TAX ID

QTY	ITEM	UNITS	DESCRIPTION	DISCOUNT %	TAXABLE	UNIT PRICE	TOTAL
20			Wheel barrows			75.00	1,500.00
						Subtotal	1,500.00
						Tax	
						Shipping	
						Miscellaneous	
						BALANCE DUE	1,500.00

Your Name Hardware Store   SALES RECEIPT

Your Address
Reno, NV 89557   Your phone number

SOLD TO:
Credit card sales   SALES NUMBER   5
                                                         SALES DATE   January 26

SHIPPED TO:

QUANTITY	DESCRIPTION	UNIT PRICE	AMOUNT
6	Shovels		180.00
6	Wheel barrows		600.00
6	Wagons		300.00
		SUBTOTAL	1,080.00
		TAX	
		FREIGHT	
			$1,080.00

DIRECT ALL INQUIRIES TO:
Your Name   Your Name Hardware Store
Your phone number   Your Address
email: your email   Reno, NV 89557

THANK YOU FOR YOUR BUSINESS!

**Your Name
Hardware Store**

Memo

Date: 1/27 current year

Re: Your Name Notes Payable

Write Check No. 5 to Your Name (*HINT:* Add New, Other) for $420.80 in payment of Your Name Notes Payable. Use the following Expenses distribution:

Account	Debit	Credit
Your Name Notes Payable	340.00	
Interest Expense	80.80	
Home State Bank		420.80

Your Name Hardware Store

Memo

Date: 1/27 current year

Re: Utilities

Write Check No. 6 to Rainer Utilities for $225.65 in payment of electricity and gas expenses. (*Hint:* Add new vendor, Account Utilities Expense.)

Your Name Hardware Store   SALES RECEIPT

Your Address
Reno, NV 89557   Your phone number

SOLD TO:
Credit card sales   SALES NUMBER   6
                                                         SALES DATE   January 29

SHIPPED TO:

QUANTITY	DESCRIPTION	UNIT PRICE	AMOUNT
4	Shovels		120.00
5	Wheel barrows		500.00
8	Wagons		400.00
		SUBTOTAL	1,020.00
		TAX	
		FREIGHT	
			$1,020.00

DIRECT ALL INQUIRIES TO:
Your Name   Your Name Hardware Store
Your phone number   Your Address
email: your email   Reno, NV 89557

THANK YOU FOR YOUR BUSINESS!

Your Name Hardware Store

Memo

Date: 1/30 current year

Re: Customer payments

Received checks in full payment of customer accounts:

1.   Received a check in full payment of Dawn Bright's account, $30.

2.   Received a check in full payment of Shar Watsonville's account, $50.

Your Name Hardware Store

Memo

Date: 1/30 current year

Re: Credit Card Receipts

Record deposit to Home State Bank in the amount of $6,280 ($6,200 from credit card sales; $30 and $50 from customer sales.)

Home State Bank
Your Name Hardware Store
Your Address
Reno, NV 89557
Your phone number

Date: January 30

Checks:	Check Number	Amount
1	Credit cards	$ 6,200.00
2	D. Bright	$ 30.00
3	S. Watsonville	$ 50.00
4		
5		
6		
7		
8		
9		
10		
11		
12		
13		
14		
15		
16		
17		
18		
19		
20		
	Totals:	$ 6,280.00

List of Deposits:

Coin:	Totals:
Quarters	$ -
Dimes	$ -
Nickles	$ -
Pennies	$ -
Total:	$ -

Cash:	Totals:
$1	$ -
$5	$ -
$10	$ -
$20	$ -
$50	$ -
$100	$ -
Total:	$ -
Total Cash:	$ -

Total Deposit: $ 6,280.00

Below is a list of the transactions recorded during January:

					Your Name Hardware Store				
3:12 PM					Transaction List by Date				
11/06/13					January 2014				
Type	Date	Num	Adj	Name	Memo	Account	Clr	Split	Debit	Credit
Jan 14										
Bill	01/06/2014	Inv. 74A		AAA Shovels		20000 · Accounts Payable		12100 · Inventory Asset		375.00
Bill	01/06/2014	Inv. 801		CCC Wagons		20000 · Accounts Payable		12100 · Inventory Asset		600.00
Bill	01/06/2014	Inv. ER555		BBB Wheel barrows		20000 · Accounts Payable		12100 · Inventory Asset		2,400.00
Sales Receipt	01/10/2014	1		Credit Card Sales		12000 · Undeposited Funds	✓	-SPLIT-	1,020.00	
Sales Receipt	01/12/2014	2		Credit Card Sales		12000 · Undeposited Funds	✓	-SPLIT-	740.00	
Invoice	01/12/2014	1		Dawn Bright		11000 · Accounts Receivable		46000 · Merchandise Sales	30.00	
Sales Receipt	01/17/2014	3		Credit Card Sales		12000 · Undeposited Funds	✓	-SPLIT-	910.00	
Bill Pmt -Check	01/20/2014	1		AAA Shovels	20000	10000 · Home State Bank		20000 · Accounts Payable		375.00
Bill Pmt -Check	01/20/2014	2		BBB Wheel barrows	20000	10000 · Home State Bank		20000 · Accounts Payable		2,400.00
Bill Pmt -Check	01/20/2014	3		CCC Wagons	20000	10000 · Home State Bank		20000 · Accounts Payable		600.00
Sales Receipt	01/21/2014	4		Credit Card Sales		12000 · Undeposited Funds	✓	-SPLIT-	1,430.00	
Check	01/21/2014	4		Stevens Rentals		10000 · Home State Bank		67100 · Rent Expense		1,350.00
Invoice	01/22/2014	2		Shar Watsonville		11000 · Accounts Receivable		46000 · Merchandise Sales	50.00	
Bill	01/24/2014	Inv. 88A		AAA Shovels		20000 · Accounts Payable		12100 · Inventory Asset		225.00
Bill	01/24/2014	Inv. 962		CCC Wagons		20000 · Accounts Payable		12100 · Inventory Asset		360.00
Bill	01/24/2014	Inv. ER702		BBB Wheel barrows		20000 · Accounts Payable		12100 · Inventory Asset		1,500.00
Sales Receipt	01/26/2014	5		Credit Card Sales		12000 · Undeposited Funds	✓	-SPLIT-	1,080.00	
Check	01/27/2014	5		Your Name		10000 · Home State Bank		-SPLIT-		420.80
Check	01/27/2014	6		Rainer Utilities		10000 · Home State Bank		68600 · Utilities Expense		225.65
Sales Receipt	01/29/2014	6		Credit Card Sales		12000 · Undeposited Funds	✓	-SPLIT-	1,020.00	
Payment	01/30/2014			Dawn Bright		12000 · Undeposited Funds	✓	11000 · Accounts Receivable	30.00	
Payment	01/30/2014			Shar Watsonville		12000 · Undeposited Funds	✓	11000 · Accounts Receivable	50.00	
Deposit	01/30/2014				Deposit	10000 · Home State Bank		-SPLIT-	6,280.00	
Jan 14										

BACKUP

Step 21: Back up to your USB drive. The suggested filename is **Your Name Hardware Store January (Portable).QBM**.

ACCOUNT RECONCILIATION

Step 22: Complete account reconciliation for Account No. 10000, Home State Bank on 01/31/20XX. Use the bank statement shown here. (*Hint:* Remember to enter the $25.00 for Bank Service Charges.)

Statement of Account Home State Bank January 1 to January 31 Account No. 937522			Your Name Hardware Store Your Address Reno, NV	
REGULAR CHECKING				
Previous Balance	12/31	$82,000.00		
Deposits		6,280.00		
Checks (-)		5,371.45		
Service Charges (-)	1/31	25.00		
Ending Balance	1/31	**$82,883.55**		
DEPOSITS				
	1/30	30.00	Dawn Bright	
	1/30	50.00	Shar Watsonville	
		6,200.00	Credit Card	
CHECKS				
	1/20	375.00	1	
	1/20	2,400.00	2	
	1/20	600.00	3	
	1/21	1,350.00	4	
	1/27	420.80	5	
	1/28	225.65	6	

REPORTS

Step 23: Print the Summary Reconciliation report.

Step 24: Print the journal (all dates).

Step 25: Print the trial balance (01/31/20XX).

Step 26: Print the vendor balance detail, customer balance detail, and inventory stock status by item.

Step 27: Print the income and expense graph by account and expenses (01/01/20XX to 01/31/20XX).

Step 28: Print the January financial statements: Profit & Loss-Standard, Balance Sheet-Standard, and Statement of Cash Flow.

Step 29: Print the audit trail (all dates).

BACKUP AND E-MAIL

Step 30: Make a backup of Project 1, Your Name Hardware Store to your USB drive. Use **Your Name Hardware Store Complete (Portable).QBM** as the file name.

Step 31: Send an e-mail message to your professor and to yourself with the Your Name Hardware Store Complete (Portable) file attached. Type **Your Name Hardware Store Complete** in the Subject line of the e-mail.

If PDF files are the preferred format for saving reports, email those to your instructor.

Step 32: Receive the Your Name Hardware Store Complete e-mail with the correct company file attached. Print it.

Step 33: Turn in completed Check Your Progress: Project 1 and required printouts to your professor.

Student Name_____**Date**_____

CHECK YOUR PROGRESS: PROJECT 1, Your Name Hardware Store

1. What are the total debit and credit balances on the Trial Balance?   *98,925.00*

2. What are the total assets on January 31?   *93,428.55*

3. What is the balance in the Home State Bank account on January 31?   *82,883.55*

4. How much is total income on January 31?   *6,280.00*

5. How much net income (net loss) is reported on January 31?   *783.55*

6. What is the balance in the Inventory-Shovels account on January 31?   *225.00*

7. What is the balance in the Inventory-Wheel barrows account on January 31?   *1,500.00*

8. What is the balance in the Inventory-Wagons account on January 31?   *360.00*

9. During January sales per week for shovels were?   *5.9*

10. What is the balance in the Common Stock account on January 31?   *81,400*

11. What is the total cost of goods sold on January 31?   *3,815*

12. Were any Accounts Payable incurred during the month of January? (Circle your answer.)   (YES)   NO

Project

2

Student-Designed Merchandising Business

You have learned how to complete the accounting cycle for merchandising businesses. Project 2 gives you a chance to create a merchandising business of your own.

You select retail as the business type, edit your business's Chart of Accounts, create beginning balances and transactions, and complete QuickBooks' computer accounting cycle. Project 2 also gives you an opportunity to review the software features learned so far.

Before you begin, you should design your business. You will need the following:

1. Company information that includes business name, address, and telephone number.

2. Select retail as the business type.

3. A Chart of Accounts

4. A beginning Balance Sheet for your business.

5. One month's transactions for your business. These transactions must include accounts receivable, accounts payable, inventory, sales, and dividends. You should have a minimum of 25 transactions; a maximum of 35 transactions. These transactions should result in a net income.

6. Complete another month of transactions that result in a net loss.

A suggested checklist of printouts is shown on the next page.

PROJECT 2 **CHECKLIST OF PRINTOUTS** *Ask your professor how these should be turned in…*	
	Chart of Accounts
	Check Register
	Vendor List
	Item List
	Customer List
	Reconciliation-Summary and Detail
	Journal
	Trial Balance
	Profit & Loss-Standard
	Balance Sheet-Standard
	Statement of Cash Flows
	Audit Trail

Appendix A

Review of Accounting Principles

Appendix A is a review of basic accounting principles and procedures. Standard accounting procedures are based on the double-entry system. This means that each business transaction is expressed with one or more debits and one or more credits in a journal entry and then posted to the ledger. The debits in each transaction must equal the credits.

The double-entry accounting system is based on the following premise: each account has two sides—a debit (left) side and credit (right) side. This is stated in the *accounting equation* as:

Assets = Liabilities + Equities

Assets are the organization's resources that have a future or potential value. Asset accounts include: Cash, Marketable Securities, Accounts Receivable, Supplies, Prepaids, Inventory, Investments, Equipment, Land, Buildings, etc.

Liabilities are the organization's responsibilities to others. Liability accounts include: Accounts Payable, Notes Payable, Unearned Rent, etc.

Equities are the difference between the organization's assets and liabilities. Equity accounts for organizations that are sole proprietorships or partnerships include: Capital and Withdrawals. Equity accounts for organizations that are corporations include contributed capital accounts like Common Stock which represent external ownership and Retained Earnings which represent internal ownership interests. Temporary equity-related accounts known as revenue and expense accounts recognize an organization's income producing activities and the related costs consumed or expired during the period.

Since assets are on the left side of the accounting equation, the left side of the account increases. This is the usual balance, too; assets increase on the left side and have a debit balance. Liabilities and Equities accounts are on the right side of the equation. Therefore, they increase on the right side and normally carry credit balances.

Another way to show the accounting equation and double-entry is illustrated below.

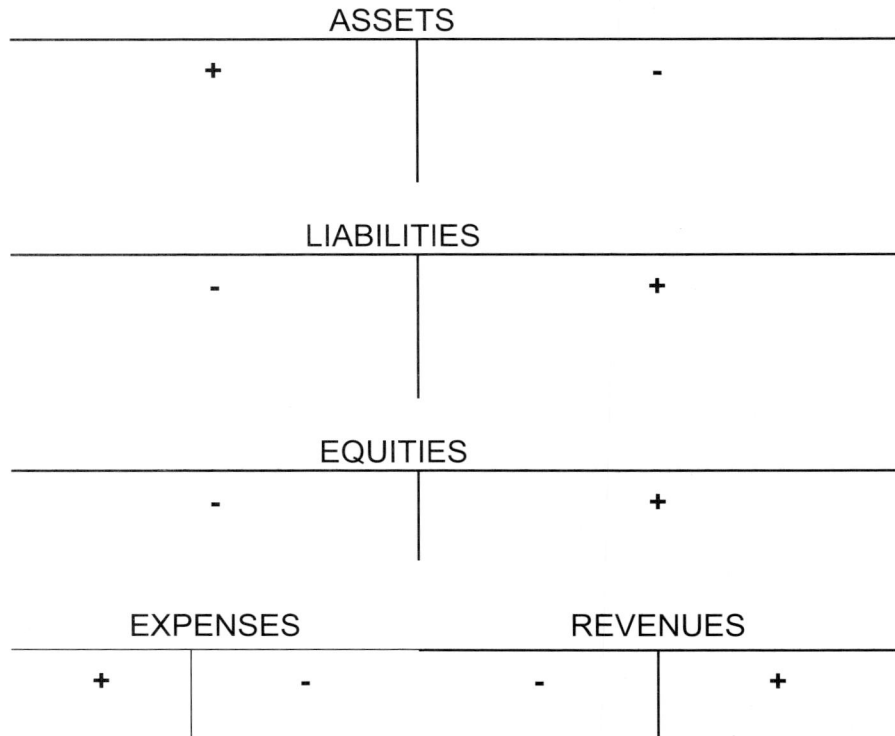

ASSETS
+	-

LIABILITIES
-	+

EQUITIES
-	+

EXPENSES		REVENUES	
+	-	-	+

Each element of the accounting equation, Assets, Liabilities, and Equities, behaves similarly to their placement in the equation. Assets have debit balances; Liabilities have credit balances; Equities have credit balances; Expenses have debit balances because they decrease equity; and Revenues have credit balances because they increase equity.

In computerized accounting it is important to number each account according to a system. This is called the Chart of Accounts. The Chart of Accounts is a listing of all the general ledger accounts. The QuickBooks chart of accounts shows the account number and name, Type (this classifies the accounts for financial statements) and Balance total. To view the chart of accounts: go to the QuickBooks Home page Company pane and click on the Chart of Accounts icon. The Your Name Retailers Inc. chart of account is shown on the next page as an example of a typical merchandising business' chart of accounts.

NAME ▲	TYPE	BALANCE TOTAL	ATTACH
10000 · Home State Bank	Bank	51,000.00	
13000 · Supplies	Other Current Asset	2,500.00	
14000 · Computer Equipment	Fixed Asset	1,000.00	
15000 · Furniture and Equipment	Fixed Asset	4,000.00	
16000 · Accumulated Depreciation-CEqmt.	Fixed Asset	0.00	
17000 · Accumulated Depreciation-F&E	Fixed Asset	0.00	
18000 · Prepaid Insurance	Other Current Asset	2,500.00	
22000 · Accounts Payable	Accounts Payable	0.00	
24000 · Payroll Liabilities	Other Current Liability	0.00	
26000 · Your Name Notes Payable	Long Term Liability	20,000.00	
30000 · Common Stock	Equity	41,000.00	
30100 · Paid in Capital	Equity	0.00	
30200 · Dividends	Equity	0.00	
32000 · Retained Earnings	Equity		
46000 · Sales	Income		
51800 · Freight In	Cost of Goods Sold		
60000 · Advertising and Promotion Exp.	Expense		
60200 · Automobile Expense	Expense		
60400 · Bank Service Charges Expense	Expense		
61700 · Computer and Internet Expenses	Expense		
62400 · Depreciation Expense	Expense		
63300 · Insurance Expense	Expense		
63400 · Interest Expense	Expense		
64900 · Supplies Expense	Expense		
66000 · Payroll Expenses	Expense		
67100 · Rent Expense	Expense		
67200 · Repairs and Maintenance Expense	Expense		
68100 · Telephone Expense	Expense		
68600 · Utilities Expense	Expense		

Account ▼   Activities ▼   Reports ▼   Attach   ☑ Include inactive

Report information in the form of financial statements is important to accounting. The Balance Sheet reports the financial position of the business on a specific date. It shows that assets are equal to liabilities plus equities—the accounting equation. The Profit & Loss shows the difference between revenue and expenses for a specified period of time (month, quarter, or year). The Income Statement is another name for Profit & Loss. QuickBooks tracks revenue and expense data for an entire year. At the end of the year when all revenue and expense accounts are closed, the resulting net income or loss is moved into the equity account, Retained Earnings. The Statement of Cash Flows reports the operating, financial, and investing activities for the period. It shows the sources of cash coming into the business and the destination of the cash going out.

The most important task you have is accurately recording transactions into the appropriate accounts. QuickBooks helps you by organizing the software into Home, Vendors, Customers, Employees Company,

Banking, and Report Centers. By selecting the appropriate Center and/or icon, you can record transactions into the right place using easy-to-complete forms. Once transactions are entered, QuickBooks keeps this information in a database. Then the data can be accessed and viewed as journal entries or transaction listings, account or ledger activities, reports, or analysis.

One of the most important tasks is deciding how to enter transactions. Recording and categorizing business transactions will determine how QuickBooks uses that information. For instance, observe that the chart of accounts shows Account 10000 – Home State Bank-Cash, classified as a Bank Type; Account No. 11000 Accounts Receivable is Accounts Receivable. The Type column classifies the account for the financial statements—Asset, Liability, and Equity accounts go on the Balance Sheet; Income, Cost of Goods Sold, and Expense accounts go on the Profit & Loss Statement.

As you work with QuickBooks, you see how the accounts, recording of transactions, and reports work together to provide your business with the information necessary for making informed decisions.

Another important aspect of accounting is determining whether the basis for recording transactions is cash or accrual. In the cash basis method, revenues and expenses are recognized when cash changes hands. In other words, when the customer pays for their purchase, the transaction is recorded. When the resource or expense is paid for by the business, the transaction is recorded.

In the accrual method of accounting, revenues and expenses are recognized when they occur. In other words, if the company purchases inventory on April 1, the transaction is recorded on April 1. If inventory is sold on account on April 15, the transaction is recorded on April 15 *not* when cash is received from customers. Accrual basis accounting is seen as more accurate because assets, liabilities, revenues, and expenses are recorded when they actually happen.

The chart on the next page summarizes Appendix A, Review of Accounting Principles.

ACCOUNTING EQUATION:	Assets =	Liabilities +	Owners Equities +	Revenues –	Expenses
Definition:	Something that has future or potential value "Resources"	Responsibilities to others "Payables" "Unearned"	Internal and External ownership	Recognition of value creation	Expired, used, or consumed costs or resources
Debit Rules: DR	Increase	Decrease	Decrease	Decrease	Increase
Credit Rules:CR	Decrease	Increase	Increase	Increase	Decrease
Account Types and Examples	**Current Assets:** Cash, Marketable Securities, Accounts Receivable, Inventory, Prepaids **Plant Assets:** Land, Buildings, Equipment, Accumulated Depreciation **Noncurrent Assets:** Investments, Intangibles	**Current Liabilities:** Accounts Payable, Unearned Revenue, Advances from Customer **Noncurrent or Long-term Liabilities:** Bonds Payable, Notes Payables, Mortgage Payable	**Sole Proprietor:** (both internal and external) Name, Capital; Name, Withdrawals **Partnership:** (both internal and external) Partner A, Capital; Partner A, Withdrawals, etc. **Corporation:** External: Common Stock, Preferred Stock, Paid-in Capital Internal: Retained Earnings, Dividends	**Operating Revenue:** Sales, Fees Earned, Rent Income, Contract Revenue **Other Revenue:** Interest Income	**Product/Services Expenses:** Cost of Goods Sold, Cost of Sales **Operating Expenses:** Selling Expenses, Administrative Expense, General Expense, Salary Expense, Rent Expense, Depreciation Expense, Insurance Expense **Other Expenses:** Interest Expense

T-Account Rules

	Assets		Liabilities		Owners Equities		Revenues		Expenses	
	Acquire resources	Consume resources	Pay bills Recognize earnings	Buy on credit Receive cash or other assets before earning it	Internal: Net Loss External: Owners reduce ownership thru withdrawals or dividends	Internal: Net Income External: Investment made by owners in company	Sales returns Sales discount given	Sales Earned Income	Resources consumed expired or used	
	increase	*decrease*	*decrease*	*increase*	*decrease*	*increase*	*decrease*	*increase*	*Increase*	*decrease*

Basic Financial Statements:

Income Statement
Revenue−Expense=Net Income (NI) or
Net Loss (NL)
(Prepare first)

Statement of Equity
Beginning* + NI (or −NL) - (Dividends or Withdrawals) = Ending*
*for Sole Proprietors and Partnerships use "Capital" and Withdrawals
for Corporations use "Retained Earnings" and Dividends
(Prepare second)

Balance Sheet
Assets=Liabilities + Equities
(Prepare third)

Statement of Cash Flows
Operating+/-Investing+/-Financing+Beginning Cash=Ending Cash
(Prepare last)

McGraw-Hill Education, *Computer Accounting Essentials with QuickBooks 2014, 7e*

Appendix B

Troubleshooting and QuickBooks Tips

Appendix B, Troubleshooting and QuickBooks Tips, includes the following.

QUICKBOOKS FOR THE MAC

To learn about Windows operating system compatibility with the Mac, go online to http://www.apple.com/findouthow/mac/#windowsmac. Every new Mac lets you install and run Windows at native speeds, using a built-in utility called Boot Camp.

Setup is simple and safe for your Mac files. After you've completed the installation, you can boot up your Mac using either OS X or Windows. Or if you want to run Windows and Mac applications at the same time — without rebooting — you can install Windows using VMware Fusion (http://www.vmware.com/products/fusion/overview.html) or Parallels software (http://www.parallels.com/products/desktop/).

The 140-day software CD included with the textbook is compatible (Windows 8, 7, and Vista).

INSTALLATION AND REGISTRATION

There is one CD included with the text, QuickBooks 2014 Student Trial Edition software. This is a 140-day single user copy of the software. Follow these steps to install software and register the software.

1. Close all programs and disable anti-virus software.
2. Insert the QuickBooks 2014 Student Trial Edition CD in your CD drive.
3. Follow the screen prompts to install the software.
4. Use the License and Product number located on the QuickBooks software CD envelope.
5. You can use the software for 30 days without registering. There are three ways to register.

   a. Register the software during installation.

   b. From the menu bar select, Help; Register QuickBooks. (If Register QuickBooks is not shown on the Help menu, QuickBooks has been registered.)

   c. Register QuickBooks by calling 888-246-8848; outside US, 520-901-3220.)

SOFTWARE REGISTRATION

If <u>Register QuickBooks</u> is shown on the Help menu, you have <u>not registered</u> your copy of QuickBooks. When QuickBooks is open, you can verify that your copy of QuickBooks is registered by pressing the <F2> function key. The Product Information window appears and displays either REGISTERED or UNREGISTERED based on the registration status. Once the software included with the textbook is registered, you have access for 140 days.

QUICKBOOKS FOR THE CLASSROOM

For software installation in the school's computer lab or classroom, please refer to the Intuit Education Program at http://accountants.intuit.com/intuit-education-program or email education@intuit.com, (866) 570-3843. Prices for classroom site licenses are shown below.

- 10 computers, $300.00*
- 25 computers, $460.00
- 50 computers, $690.00
   *Pricing is subject to change.

These site licenses do not allow Multi-User Access. Multi-user mode means more than one person (up to five) work with a single company data file at the same time. QuickBooks site licenses do not have this feature.

DEFAULT FILE LOCATIONS

Company Files

The default location for company files with qbw extensions is:

Windows 7, 8 and Vista: C:\Users\Public\Public Documents\Intuit\ QuickBooks\Company Files

Recommended Backup Routine: .QBB and .QBM Extensions

Back up your company file at the end of each classroom session or each day to a network drive; external hard drive; removable storage device such as a CD, USB flash drive, or to a remote site over the Internet. Do not store backups on your computer's hard drive where you store your working data—if your computer's hard disk fails, you may lose your backup files as well as your working data.

Set Default Location for Backups

When you first use the backup feature, you need to enter the default location where you want to store your backups. You can set or change this default using these instructions.

1.   Go to the File menu and click Create Copy or Create Backup to Save Copy or Backup.
2.   Click Backup Copy, click <Next>, and then click the Options button.
3.   Click Browse to find the location where you want to store your backups. The directory you choose remains your default until you change it.

Backups can be made to external media, a hard drive location, or network drive location. The textbook recommends a USB flash drive.

SET UP FOLDERS FOR DATA MANAGEMENT

You may want to organize QuickBooks' file types in separate folders. QuickBooks' file types include portable backup files (.QBM extensions) and company files (.QBW extensions).

How Do I Show File Extensions?

To show files extensions, follow these steps.

1.   Right-click on the <Start> button; left-click Explore. (The selection in Windows 7 is Open Windows Explorer.)
2.   Click on the Organize down-arrow. Select Folder and Search Options. Click on the View tab.
3.   Uncheck Hide extensions for known file types.

> ☐ Hide extensions for known file types

4.   Click <OK> to close the Folder Options window.
5.   Close Windows Explorer.

QuickBooks Company Files Folder

You may want to set up a folder for QuickBooks' company files. QuickBooks' company files end in the extension .QBW.

Before restoring files, set up a folder labeled QuickBooks Company Files_QBW.

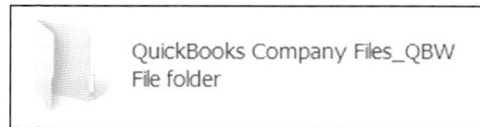

QuickBooks Company Files_QBW
File folder

When you restore files in QuickBooks, a Save Company File as window appears. In the Save in field, select the QuickBooks Company Files_QBW folder.

By saving the company files to its own folder, you store the company files (.QBW files) in a different location than the backed up files (.QBM or .QBB extensions).

When a company is opened in QuickBooks, the following file extensions are associated with that company file:
1.   .QBW: QuickBooks working file or company file
2.   .DSN: Database source name
3.   .ND: network data file
4.   .TLG: transaction logs

Your Name QB Backups Folder

After completing work, you are instructed to save the backed up files to a separate folder labeled Your Name QB Backups [use your first and last name].

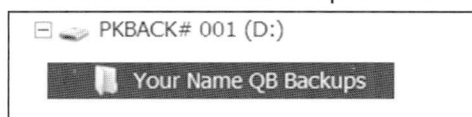

PKBACK# 001 (D:)

Your Name QB Backups

If all the chapters, projects, and practice sets are completed in *Computer Accounting Essentials with QuickBooks 2014, 7e,* 35 files are backed up.

File	Type	Size
sample_product-based business (Portable).QBM	QuickBooks Portable Company File	2,029 KB
Your Name Accounting Beginning Balances (Portable).QBM	QuickBooks Portable Company File	374 KB
Your Name Accounting Chart of Accounts (Portable).QBM	QuickBooks Portable Company File	373 KB
Your Name Accounting December (Portable).QBM	QuickBooks Portable Company File	380 KB
Your Name Accounting EOY (Portable).QBM	QuickBooks Portable Company File	482 KB
Your Name Accounting Financial Statements (Portable).QBM	QuickBooks Portable Company File	471 KB
Your Name Accounting UTB (Portable).QBM	QuickBooks Portable Company File	470 KB
Your Name Chapter 2 End (Portable).QBM	QuickBooks Portable Company File	2,034 KB
Your Name Chapter 3 October 1.QBB	QuickBooks Company Backup File	6,644 KB
Your Name Chapter 3 October Check Register.QBB	QuickBooks Company Backup File	6,752 KB
Your Name Chapter 3 October End.QBB	QuickBooks Company Backup File	6,864 KB
Your Name Chapter 4 End.QBB	QuickBooks Company Backup File	7,496 KB
Your Name Chapter 4 November.QBB	QuickBooks Company Backup File	7,488 KB
Your Name Chapter 4 Vendors and Inventory.QBB	QuickBooks Company Backup File	7,484 KB
Your Name Chapter 4 Vendors.QBB	QuickBooks Company Backup File	7,488 KB
Your Name Chapter 5 December Financial Statements.QBB	QuickBooks Company Backup File	7,524 KB
Your Name Chapter 5 December UTB.QBB	QuickBooks Company Backup File	7,528 KB
Your Name Chapter 5 EOY (Portable).QBM	QuickBooks Portable Company File	680 KB
Your Name Chapter 6 January Check Register.QBB	QuickBooks Company Backup File	7,568 KB
Your Name Chapter 6 January Financial Statements.QBB	QuickBooks Company Backup File	7,664 KB
Your Name Chapter 6 UTB.QBB	QuickBooks Company Backup File	7,632 KB
Your Name Exercise 4-2 December.QBB	QuickBooks Company Backup File	7,508 KB
Your Name Exercise 6-1 (Portable).QBM	QuickBooks Portable Company File	779 KB
Your Name Hardware Store (Backup Oct 16,2013 02 04 PM).QBB	QuickBooks Company Backup File	6,488 KB
Your Name Hardware Store Beginning Balances (Portable).QBM	QuickBooks Portable Company File	373 KB
Your Name Hardware Store Chart of Accounts (Portable).QBM	QuickBooks Portable Company File	373 KB
Your Name Hardware Store Complete (Portable).QBM	QuickBooks Portable Company File	490 KB
Your Name Hardware Store January (Portable).QBM	QuickBooks Portable Company File	437 KB
Your Name Hardware Store Vendors Inventory Customers.QBM	QuickBooks Portable Company File	382 KB
Your Name Retailers Inc. (Backup Oct 15,2013 03 26 PM).QBB	QuickBooks Company Backup File	6,548 KB
Your Name sample_service-based business (Portable).QBM	QuickBooks Portable Company File	1,356 KB
Your Name Sports End (Portable).QBM	QuickBooks Portable Company File	473 KB
Your Name Sports January (Portable).QBM	QuickBooks Portable Company File	388 KB
Your Name Sports Starting Balance Sheet (Portable).QBM	QuickBooks Portable Company File	350 KB
Your Name Sports Vend Inv Cust (Portable).QBM	QuickBooks Portable Company File	378 KB

Types of Backup Files

QuickBooks includes three types of backup files:

1. Backup copy (.QBB extensions)
2. Portable company file (.QBM extensions)
3. Accountant's copy (.QBX or .QBA extensions)

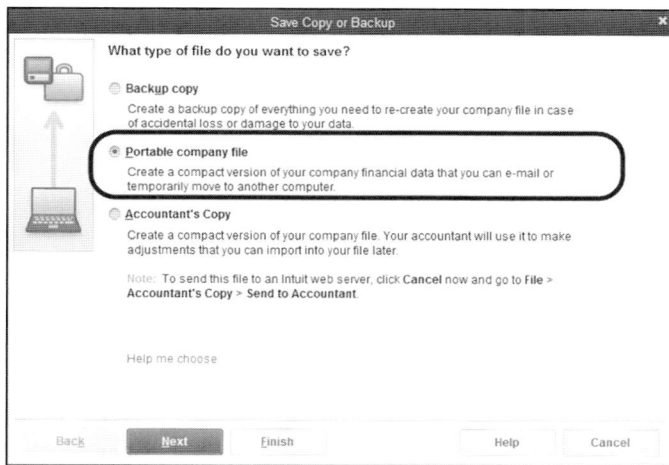

In *Computer Accounting Essentials with QuickBooks 2014, 7e*, the methods shown for backing up are the Portable company file (.QBM) selection or the Backup copy (.QBB) file. Portable company files are smaller than Backup copy files. For emailing a file, portable company files (.QBM) are recommended.

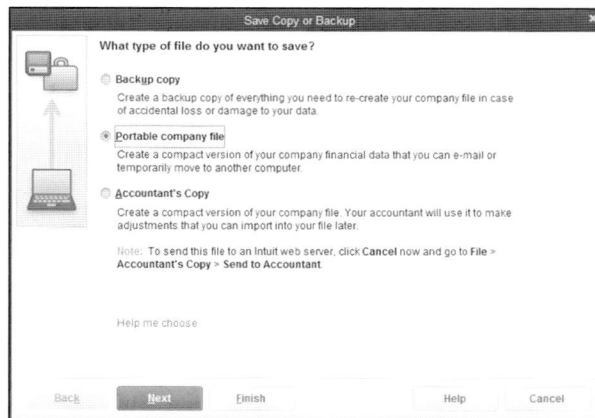

Backup Location No Longer Available

QuickBooks saves the location where files are backed up. If you decide to use another backup location, this Warning window will appear.

Click OK, then select the location where you want to back up. Type the file name, then save.

Restore Previous Local Backup

If you want to restore a file previously backed up with the company that is currently open, use the File; Restore Previous Local Backup selection. The most recent file backed up is shown first on the list of backup files.

TROUBLESHOOTING BACKUP AND RESTORE: USING USB DRIVES

USB drives use different file systems. To see your USB drive's file system, right-click on the drive letter, left-click Properties, then select the General tab. Some USB drives are more reliable than others. If you are experiencing difficulty using a USB drive when either restoring from or backing up to it, use your Desktop instead. In other words, backup to your desktop first, then copy the file to a USB drive. Do the same thing in reverse when you want to restore a file. Copy the file from the USB drive to your desktop, then restore the file from your desktop instead of from a USB drive.

Create Copy or Backup: Portable Company Files

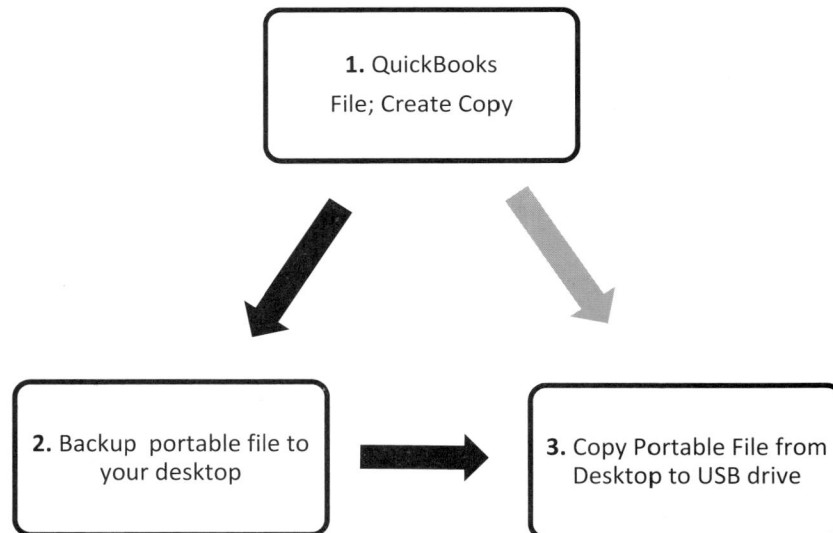

```
        ┌─────────────────────┐
        │  1. QuickBooks      │
        │  File; Create Copy  │
        └─────────────────────┘
         ↙                  ↘
┌──────────────────────┐   ┌──────────────────────┐
│ 2. Backup portable   │ → │ 3. Copy Portable File│
│ file to your desktop │   │ from Desktop to USB  │
│                      │   │ drive                │
└──────────────────────┘   └──────────────────────┘
```

Restore a file

1. If the portable file resides on a USB drive, copy the file from the USB drive to your desktop.

2. Start QuickBooks. Open or restore the file from your desktop instead of the USB drive.

QBW File Already Exists

When restoring a file, if a screen prompts "[File name]…qbw already exists. Do you want to replace it?"

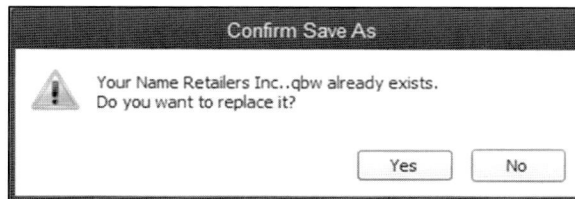

Click [No]. In the File name field, change the name slightly; for example, add your initials.

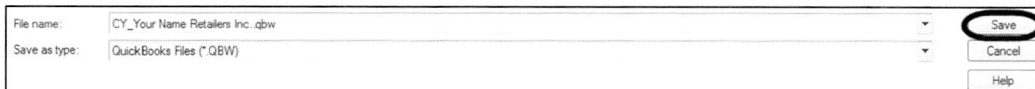

Now that you changed the file name, you can click [Save] to continue restoring your file. (*Hint:* Your Name Retailers Inc. is used in this example. Your file name may differ.)

You could also delete the files associated with the company. Then, restore the file without changing its name.

QuickBooks Login Password

When opening a QB company, if a QuickBooks Login window appears, click [**OK**] to continue. (*Hint:* You do not need to type a password if a password has <u>not</u> been set up.)

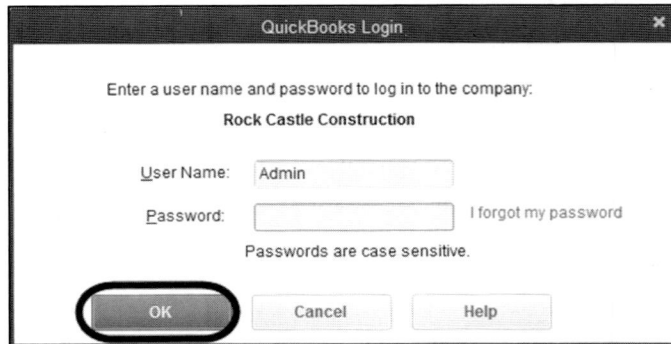

Or, if you set up a password, type it. In Chapter 2, the authors suggest that you do <u>not</u> type a password to avoid the need for typing one when restoring or opening company files.

USE EXCEL WITH QUICKBOOKS

Your instructor may want you to email QuickBooks assignments completed in *Computer Accounting Essentials with QuickBooks 2014.* QuickBooks includes a way to export reports to Excel.
Follow these steps to export a QuickBooks report to Excel.

1. Display the report for the appropriate date.
2. You have two choices: E-mail, then select Send report as Excel; *or,* select the Excel button. In these steps you click Excel ▼ , Create New Worksheet. The Send Report to Excel window appears. Accept the default, in new workbook. The selection for in an existing workbook allows you to add worksheets to an existing file.

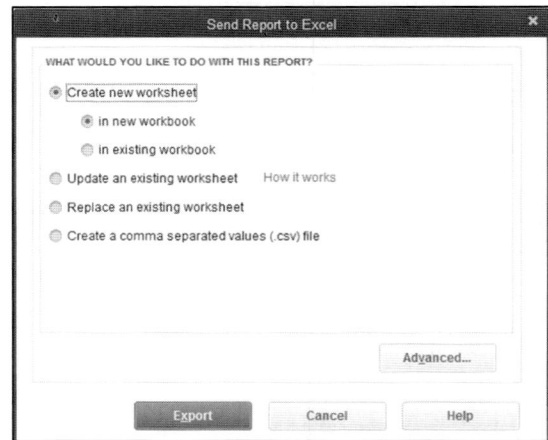

3. Click Export .
4. Excel opens. Save the workbook.

5.   Close the QuickBooks report.

E-MAIL REPORT AS A PDF FILE

You can email reports as PDF files.

When you send a report as a PDF file, the report is attached to an email message. If you do not have Acrobat Reader, you can download it for free from www.adobe.com.

1.   Display the report you want to email as a PDF file.
2.   Click E-mail, Send report as PDF.

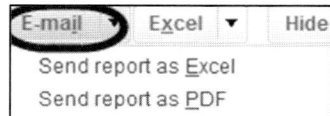

3.   If an Email Security window appears, read the information. Then put a check mark in the Do not display this message in the future box. Click <OK>.
4.   If a Choose Your Email Method window appears, select

. The Preferences window appears. If using Outlook, select it. (If Web Mail is selected and that is how you are sending email, do not change it.)
5.   Your email account opens. The report is an attached PDF file. Type the recipient's email address and send. Go to the File menu, and then click Save as PDF.

You can also display the report, select Print, then save as PDF file. Then, email an attachment.

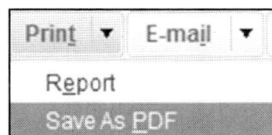

PRINTING AND FILTERING REPORTS

There are numerous ways to print or display reports. For example, you can filter reports for the type of transaction.

After completing an Exercise, let's say you want to look at the vendor bills paid. In this example, Project 1, Your Name Hardware Store is used.

1. From the Reports menu or Report Center, select Accountants & Taxes, Journal. In the From field, type the appropriate from and to dates.

2. Select Customize Report. The Modify Report: Journal window appears. Select the Filters tab.

3. In the Filter list, select Transaction Type. In the Transaction Type field, select Bill Payment.

4. Click <OK>. The Journal appears with the vendor payments, Bill Pmt-Check, shown.

5. Click <OK>. The Journal appears showing vendor payments only. The Journal window is shown below.

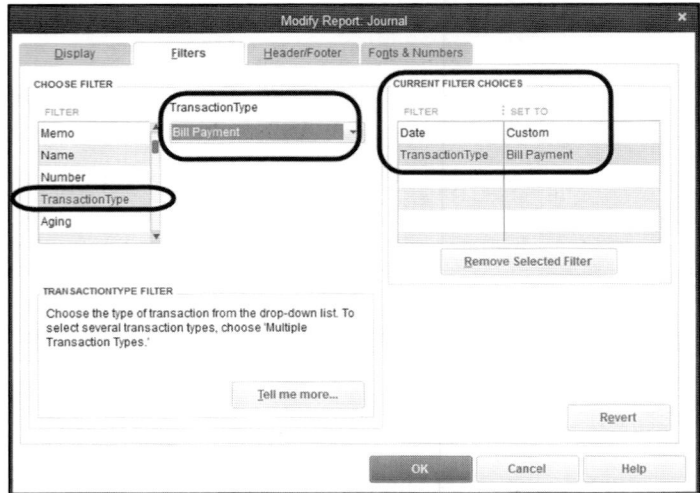

ADD SHORTCUTS TO THE ICON BAR

1. From the menu bar, select View; Customize Icon Bar. Click

   [Add...]. You can also delete shortcuts that you do not want to appear on the Icon Bar.

2. The Add Icon Bar Item window appears. Select an item to add. Observe the Label and Description field identifies the item. You can also customize the label and description. Click [OK].

3. The Customize Icon Bar window appears. To reorder the icons, drag an icon's diamond up or down to the position you want.

ICON BAR LOCATION

The Icon Bar can be located on the top, left, or it can be hidden. To change the location of the Icon Bar, from the menu bar, select View. The Left Icon Bar is selected. Other selections include Top Icon Bar or Hide Icon Bar.

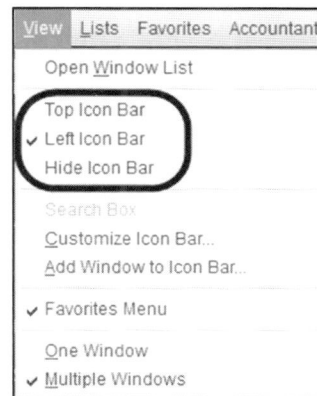

UNINSTALL QUICKBOOKS AND REMOVE ALL QUICKBOOKS FILES AND FOLDERS

It is sometimes necessary to uninstall QuickBooks, rename installation files left behind, and then reinstall QuickBooks. This may be required when a QuickBooks function is damaged or when simply reinstalling QuickBooks does not correct an issue. This process is called a **Clean Install** or **Clean Uninstall**.

Note: Be sure to have your QuickBooks download file or your installation CD and installation license available before uninstalling QuickBooks. Read the instructions on this website to determine which uninstall method you prefer http://support.quickbooks.intuit.com/support/Articles/HOW12212.

TOGGLE QUICKBOOKS TO ANOTHER EDITION

The student trial version software, included with the textbook, can be used on one computer for 140 days.

Before following these steps, check with your instructor for his or her preference. The software site license purchased by the school and the 140-day CD included with the textbook are the same software version.

1. From the menu bar, select File; Toggle to Another Edition. The Select QuickBooks Industry-Specific Edition window appears. Select QuickBooks Pro.

2. Click [Next >] and the version of QuickBooks changes to the Pro.

QUICKBOOKS RELEASES

The screen images that appear in the textbook were done with QuickBooks Accountant 2014. If you are using your own laptop or PC, the author suggests updating the software. When you compare screen images with the textbook, you may notice some differences. For example, if you are using QuickBooks 2014 at school and the computer lab is not updating the software, this could result in some differences in screen images, or if you are not updating to the new release on your laptop or PC.

Periodically, updates to QuickBooks software are available for download (by way of the quickbooks.com website) or internally through your software. These updates improve program functionality and fix known issues with the software. Read this online support site information, http://support.quickbooks.intuit.com/support/Articles/HOW12418 .

UPDATE QUICKBOOKS

During restore, there are two types of prompts to update files.

1. Update Company window.
2. Security Warning window.

Update Company During Restore

If an Update Company window appears during restore, click <Yes>. An Update Company window appears.

A Working window appears.

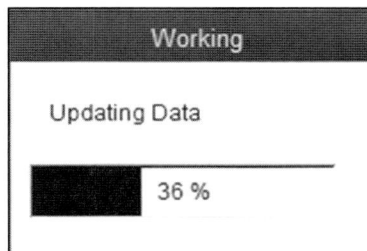

When the data is restored successfully window appears, select <OK>.

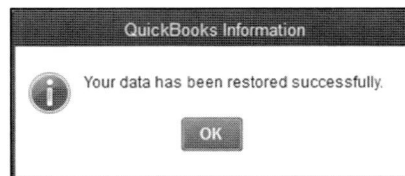

Update Company and Security Warning During Restore

QuickBooks updates automatically. If an Update Company window appears during restore, click <Yes>. An Update Company window appears.

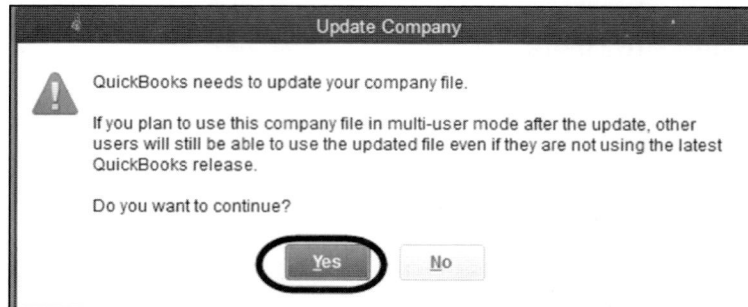

If a Security Warning window appears, Click <Yes>.

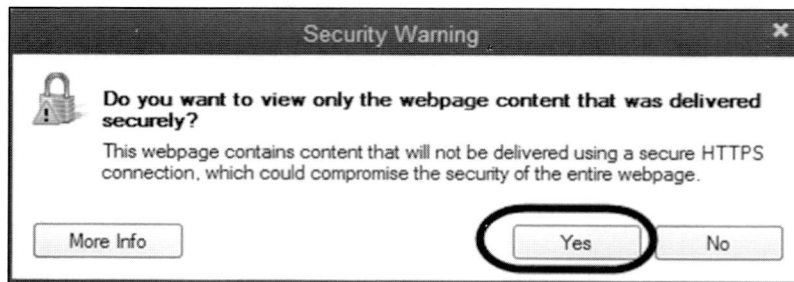

You can press the function key <F2> to see the QuickBooks release being used.

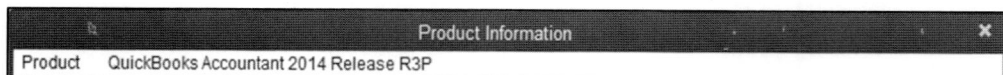

Your release number may differ. If some of your screen images look different when compared to the illustrations in the textbook, you or the computer lab may not have updated QuickBooks. For more information, refer to page 270, QuickBooks Releases.

QUICKBOOKS SUPPORT FROM INTUIT

QuickBooks support is available from Intuit, the publisher of QuickBooks software, at http://support.quickbooks.intuit.com/support.
From the support website, you can:

- Get install help.
- Get downloads & updates
- Go to new user resource center.
- Type search words or error message number.

HELP WINDOWS

Use the <F1> function key for Help from any QuickBooks window. When you press <F1>, a Have a Question window appears. In the example below, <F1> was selected from the Home page.

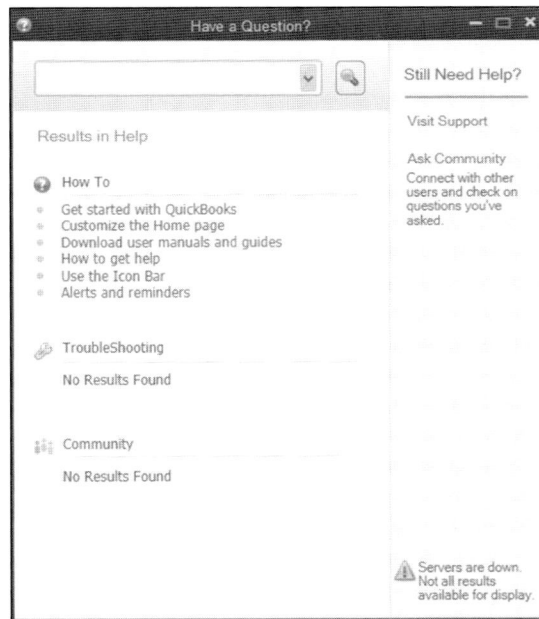

You can search help, type a word in the Search field, Visit Support, or Ask Community. when the Chart of Accounts is selected, then <F1>, context-sensitive help appears.

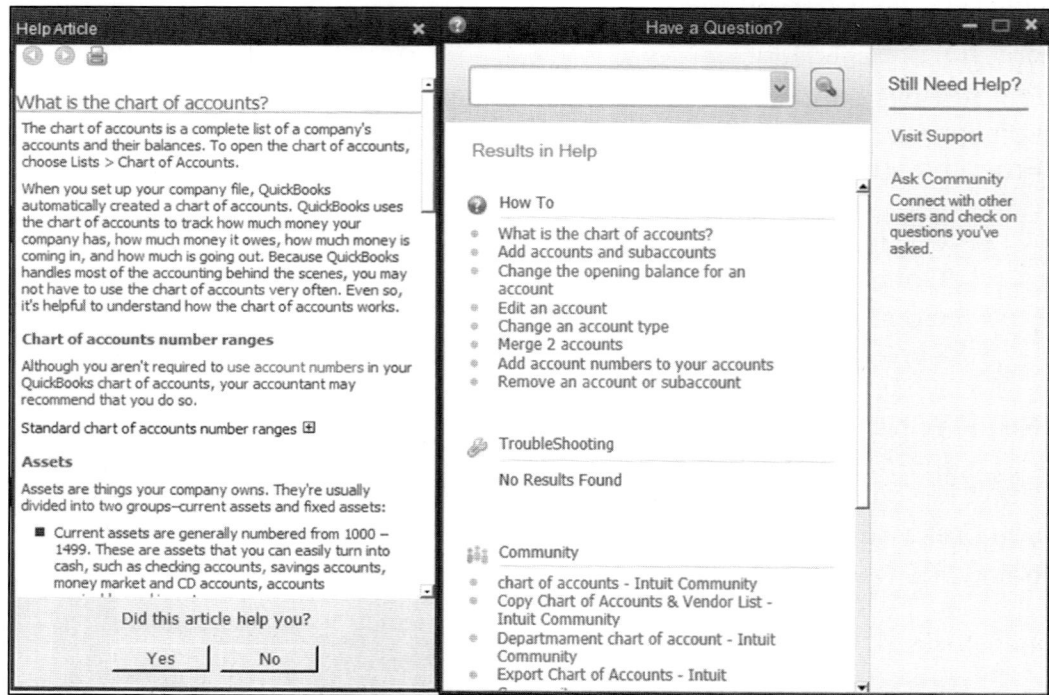

Appendix C

Glossary

Appendix C lists a glossary of terms used in *Computer Accounting Essentials with QuickBooks 2014, 7th Edition*. Appendix C is also included on the textbook website at www.mhhe.com/QBessentials2014.

accounting equation
The accounting equation is stated as assets = liabilities + equities. (p. 251)

accounts payable
A group of accounts that show the amounts owed to vendors or credits for goods, supplies, or services purchased on account. (p. 114)

accounts payable ledger
On the accounts payable ledger, vendors and payable details are shown. The vendor balance detail report shows all the transactions related to each vendor. The totals shown in the Balance column are the company's unpaid balances. (p. 128)

accounts payable transactions
Purchases on account from vendors. (p. 114)

accounts receivable
Group of accounts that show the amounts customers owe for services or products sold on credit. (p. 139)

accounts receivable ledger	Customers and receivables accounts which are grouped together. The customer balance detail report shows all transactions related to customers, grouped by customer and job. The totals in the Balance column are the unpaid balances for each customer and job. (p. 145)
accounts receivable transactions	Credit transactions from customers. (p. 139)
account reconciliation	As you write checks, withdraw money, make deposits, and incur bank charges, each of these transactions is recorded in QuickBooks and then matched with the bank's records. This matching process is called reconciliation. (p. 96)
assets	The organization's resources that have future or potential value. (p. 251)
backing up	Saving your data to a hard drive, network drive, or external media. Backing up insures that you can start where you left off the last time you used QB 2014. (p. 15)
balance sheet	Lists the types and amounts of assets, liabilities, and equity as of a specific date. (p. 81)
bill	A request for payment or products and services. Also called invoice. (p. 128)

chart of accounts	List of all the accounts in the company's general ledger. (p. 75)
closing the fiscal year	Moving expense and revenue accounts to retained earnings. (p. 191)
compound transaction	An entry that affects three or more accounts. (p. 176)
credit sales	Refers to sales made to customers that will be paid for later. (p. 145)
customer invoice	Request for payment to a customer for products or services sold. (p. 139)
desktop	Also called the Home page. (p. 38)
equities	The difference between the company's assets and liabilities. (p. 251)
external media	Backing up to a drive other than the computer's hard drive or network drive. (p. 15)
general journal entries	The general journal shows the debits and credits of transactions and can be used to record any type of transaction. In this text, you use the general journal to record adjusting and closing entries. (p. 176)
graphical user interface (GUI)	The general look of a program is called its graphical user interface. (p. 36)

home page	Displays information about the company. The QB Home page includes areas for vendors, customers, employees, company, banking and their accompanying workflow processes. The Home page is also called the desktop. (p. 38)
income statement	An income statement is where a business reports its revenues and expenses and determines its net income or loss for a period. QuickBooks refers to the income statements as the Profit & Loss. (p. 188)
icon bar	The icon bar contains shortcuts to the tasks and reports you use the most. You can place the Icon Bar to the left of the QB desktop, above it, or hide it. The Icon Bar can also be customized. (p. 37)
inventory items	A product that is purchased for sale and is tracked in the Inventory account on the balance sheet. (p. 119)
invoice	A request for payment or products and services. Also called bill. (p. 128)
liabilities	Liabilities are the company's responsibilities to others. Liability accounts include accounts payable, notes payable, unearned rent, etc. (p. 251)
menu bar	Contains menus for File, Edit, View, Lists, Company, Customers, Vendors, Employees, Banking, Reports, Window and Help. (p. 42)

preferences	By setting preferences, you can customize QuickBooks to suit the needs of your business and personal style of working. Preferences allow you to configure the way in which some functions and keys work in QuickBooks. (p. 73)
profit & loss	This report is also known as an income statement. It summarizes income and expenses for the month, so you can tell whether you're operating at a profit or a loss. The report shows subtotals for each income or expense account in your chart of accounts. The last line shows your net income (or loss) for the month. (p. 188)
resourceful QuickBooks	On the QB menu bar, select Help, Learning Center Tutorials to watch the following types of videos: New to QB, Tracking Money In, Tracking Money Out, Reports, etc. (pp. 21, 65, 106, 167, 197, 217)
restore	Previously backed up data can be restored or retrieved from the File menu's Restore Previous Local Backup selection. Files can also be restored from the No Company Open window; select the Open or restore an existing company. (p. 15)
statement of financial position	Lists the types and amounts of assets, liabilities, and equity as of a specific date. Also called the balance sheet. (p. 81)

taskbar	In Windows 7/Vista/XP, the Start button and taskbar are located at the bottom of the screen. (p. 38)
title bar	Contains company name and the program name. (p. 37)
trial balance	This report shows the balance of each account in debit and credit format. Use the trial balance report to see account balances before recording adjusting journal entries. (p. 102)
USB drive	USB is an abbreviation of Universal Serial Bus. USB drives are known as flash drives, pen drives, etc. USBs are used as storage media. (p. vii)
vendors	A person or company from which the company buys products or services. (p. 114)

Index